IN SELWAY SHADOWS:
LAST FLIGHT OF 148Z

RICHARD H. HOLM, JR.

Other titles by R.H. Holm, Jr.:

Points of Prominence: Fire Lookouts of the Payette National Forest

Bound for the Backcountry: A History of Idaho's Remote Airstrips

Bound for the Backcountry II: A History of Airstrips in the Wallowas, Hells Canyon, and the Lower Salmon River

Idaho's Wilderness Visionary: Harry Shellworth

To purchase copies of *In Selway Shadows: Last Flight of 148Z* contact author at: boundforthebackcounty@gmail.com

Published by Cold Mountain Press, McCall, ID

Front cover photograph: N148Z on the Forest Service ramp in Missoula, Montana, 1978. Wayne Williams photograph.

Rear cover photograph: View of the Selway River canyon from Bear Wallow Lookout with rays of sun cast upon Pinchot Point, 1978. Gary Miller photograph.

Cover and interior design by TeaBerryCreative.com

ISBN: Print 979-8-218-60108-9
         eBook 979-8-218-60109-6

First Edition
Printed in the United States of America

To the pilots and passengers aboard
N148Z and their families

TABLE OF CONTENTS

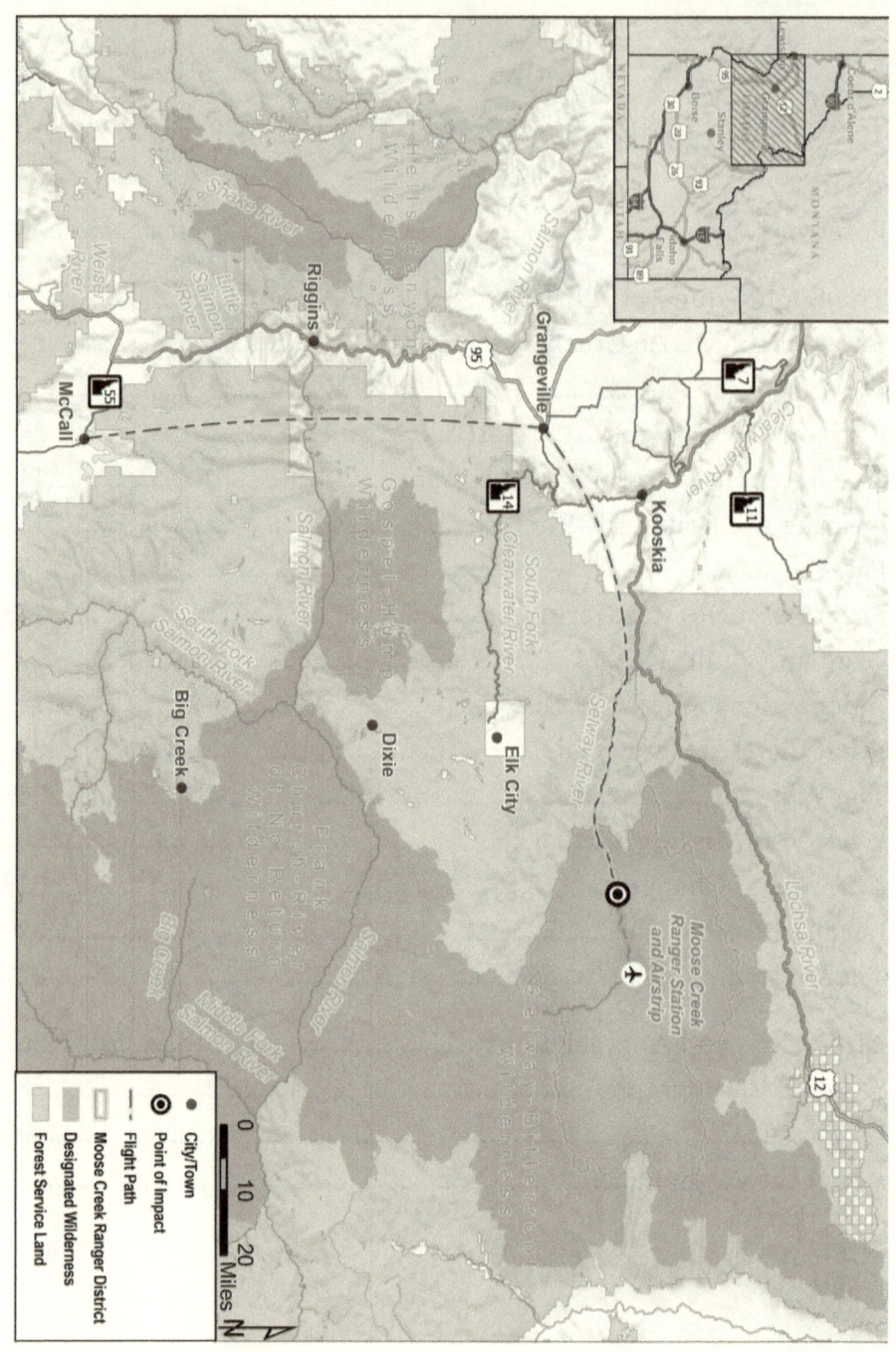

JUNE 11, 1979 FLIGHT OF 148Z. *(Jacob Bonessi)*

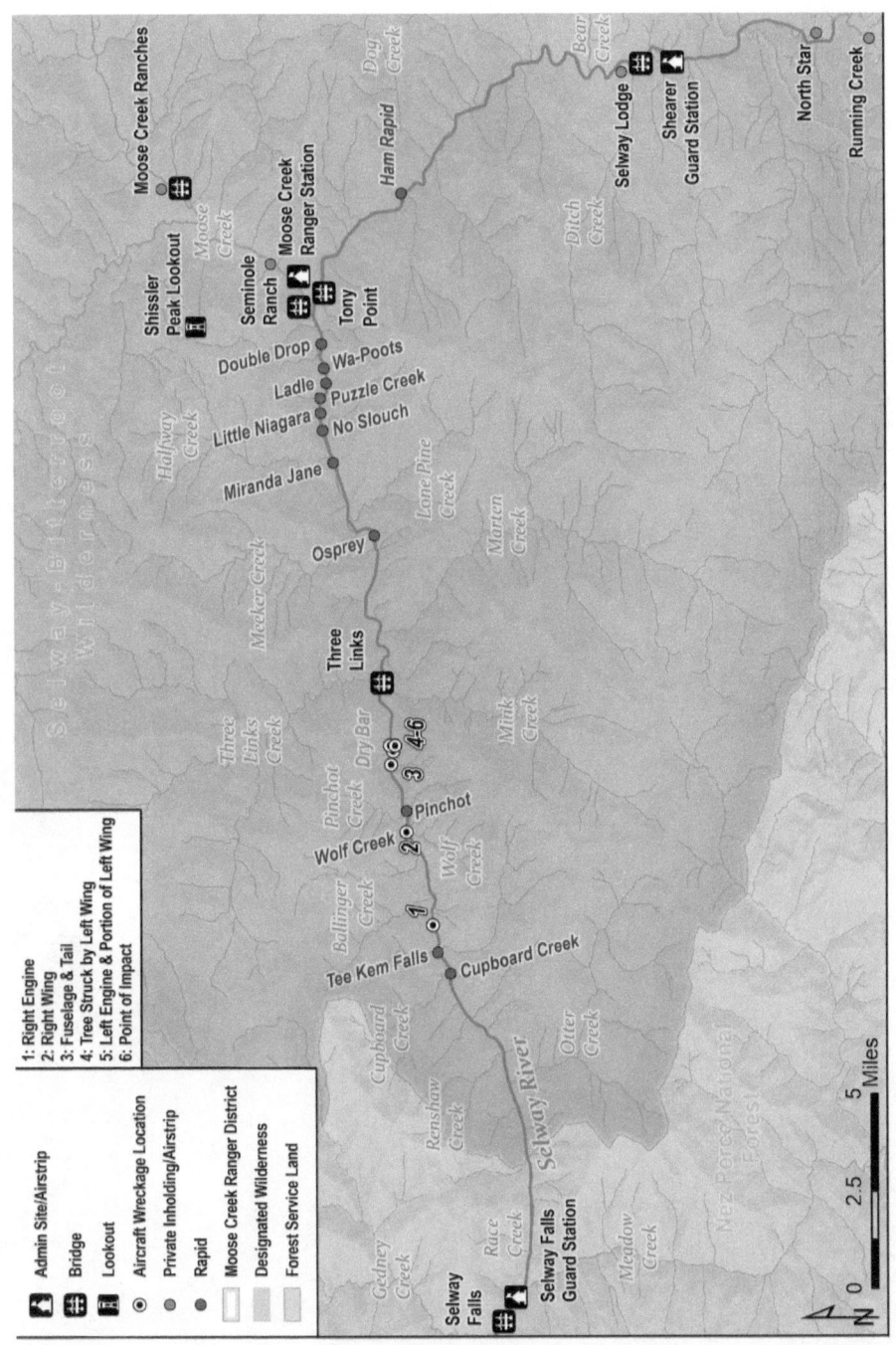

SELWAY RIVER CORRIDOR AND POINTS OF INTEREST. *(Jacob Bonessi)*

1

FOREWORD

The mountains of Idaho, poems of geology stretching beyond
any boundaries and seemingly even beyond the world...The
[Bitterroot] divide—ascending in triangles to the sky and
descending in ovals and circles. It was triangles going up and ovals
coming down, and on the divide it was springtime in August.
—NORMAN MACLEAN, "USFS 1919"

On the morning of June 11, 1979 an astonishing, courageous, astounding, heroic, and tragic event occurred in the Idaho backcountry along the Selway River ten miles below the Moose Creek Ranger Station. Tragic because the airplane crash killed ten people and was preventable, astonishing because there were survivors, courageous because one of the survivors swam the river and hiked miles with and without trails for help, heroic because countless strangers, friends, and coworkers within hours of the overdue aircraft quickly formed search, rescue, and recovery efforts; astounding because there were multiple eyewitnesses on the ground—including a photographer.

1

The plane was a United States Forest Service (USFS) Douglas DC-3 (148Z) dispatched from McCall, Idaho, to carry nearly a dozen employees from Grangeville, Idaho, to the remote Moose Creek Ranger Station located in the heart of the 1.3-million acre Selway-Bitterroot Wilderness at the confluence of the Selway River and Moose Creek.

• • •

As an avid collector of Idaho backcountry history, I came across this story while writing the book *Bound for the Backcountry*, a historical look at remote airstrips in central Idaho. The story was part of Idaho aviation lore. Although commonplace among longtime local aviators, pilots still spoke of it with awe and respect. Pilot mentors of mine, who either knew Whitey Hachmeister or John Slingerland (pilots of 148Z), or both, occasionally brought it up as a teachable example while addressing emergency flight situations in the backcountry. Each time I heard the story it entailed some sidebar memory about an unforgettable photograph of an engine falling off the airplane printed in newspapers across the nation.

Intrigued by the description of the snapshot, I called several regional newspapers for a copy from their files for use in my book. None could be located. I even tracked down the photographer by telephone; he told me he never kept a copy, and the negative(s) were the property of *The Spokesman-Review* newspaper in Spokane, Washington. Another dead end. Research at the time did not yet include extensive online archives and databases. Libraries with knowledgeable librarians reigned. Even newspaper archives required a trip to the nearest major library housing microfiche for states' media. I knew the photograph appeared in *The Spokesman-Review* and, conveniently, I was wintering in Seattle, Washington, while my future wife finished graduate studies. For a person bent on historical research, a trip to a university library is a cherished occasion. Intent on discovering the elusive image, I picked my way through the narrow streets surrounding the University of Washington and found public parking. The walk to the library was lined with cherry trees in full bloom; a glorious early April day. Guided by a campus kiosk map, I strolled up Grant Lane to the academic walls of the stately gothic-style Suzzallo Library and stopped at the information desk, where I was directed to the proper floor. Minutes later, I found row upon row of grey metal cabinets stacked with drawers neatly filled with individual labeled cardboard boxes of microfiche reels. Viewing machines connected to coin-operated printers stood alongside.

Conditioned to such research methods, I promptly located the box with the June 1979 *Spokesman-Review* papers, unboxed the reel, and spooled it to the empty pick up wheel. I manually spun to June 12, 1979 and there it was…even in somewhat fuzzy black and white pixilation it was more vivid than expected. I could see why nearly 40 years later people still talked about it. I stared at the backlit screen, entranced. I then began reading the related news article and slowly spun through the succeeding days of headlines, articles, and pictures. Along the way, I squared up the print view guides on the screen, pressed print, and fed the printers from a roll of coins. I left the library with a thick folder of photocopies and dense emotions. The pink euphoria of the cherry trees had dulled. Part of me was elated that I had finally found the much talked-about photograph, yet I was melancholy. Little did I know that I would spend years of my life trying to unravel the whole story and the lives it touched. I did not make the connection that day, but later a memory from my early twenties surfaced where I, too, had flown on a Region 4 DC-3

(142Z) outfitted with side-mounted seats from McCall to a wilderness destination (Chamberlain Basin) and back in July 2007 as a USFS volunteer. The experience, combined with further research and flying 148Z's final route several times as a pilot in command of my own aircraft, added perspective. Consequently, when I look at the photograph now, the sense of tragedy is heightened, particularly by my having learned the stories of all aboard, meeting some of their families, some of their friends, and having realized some of their unfulfilled aspirations.

· · ·

The Selway-Bitterroot Mountains are within the northern granitic composite mass known as the Idaho Batholith covering 15,400 square miles in central Idaho. The Bitterroot Divide is distinctive and generates the zig-zagging section of the Idaho and Montana state boundaries, and its physical presence dominates the surrounding landscape. The silhouette of the mountain range is comprised of impressive peaks—Trapper Peak, El Capitan, Como Peaks, and Mount Jerusalem, some reaching skyward at over 10,000 feet MSL (Mean Sea Level). These glaciated mountains are fringed to the west by the impressive Selway Crags jutting upwards at 7,000 to 8,200 feet MSL. Formed by extensive glaciation, the high country is dotted with cirque lakes and classic U-shaped valleys. From all of these mountain summits the terrain plunges downward in thick swirls of green trees. The overwhelming lushness of the ecosystems is a product of a unique micro area of the Pacific Maritime climate. The snowpack of this massive and remote region of mountains drains primarily into the Lochsa and Selway rivers, which in turn through a number of other waterways, flows into the mighty Columbia River and out to the Pacific Ocean.

For people who lived in the region at the time of the Selway River DC-3 crash, it was engrained in their memories. It is like asking someone where they were when Mount St. Helens erupted. Neuroscience research suggests the human brain forms far more indelible memories when under the influence of intense emotion—a reason why these vivid recollections remain so clear decades later.

The 1979 DC-3 accident occurred on the Moose Creek Ranger District within the Nez Perce National Forest (NF) and in the Northern Region (Region 1) of the USFS headquartered in Missoula, Montana. The USFS manages public lands across the United States and is divided into nine regions. Each region is further split into individual national forests which are segmented into ranger districts. Region 1 encompasses northern Idaho, Montana, and North Dakota. The Agency as a whole has long used aircraft as a vital tool, particularly for the purposes of access to manage remote resources and for wildland fire management. While certainly few and far between, aircraft and fire-related tragedies have occurred from the beginning. One of the most significant tragedies endured by the Agency was in Region 1 on the Helena NF northeast of Helena, Montana, on August 5, 1949, when 15 smokejumpers parachuted from a Douglas DC-3 (NC24320) to fight the Mann Gulch Fire on the north slopes of the Missouri River. After the smokejumpers landed, unexpected high winds caused a massive blowup, killing 13 firefighters, 12 of whom were smokejumpers. Author Norman Maclean wrote an exhaustive account of this tragedy in his book, *Young Men and Fire*, posthumously published in 1992.

More specific to aviation and the Moose Creek Ranger District was the tragic August 4, 1959 accident of a Ford Tri-Motor (N8419) at the Moose Creek Ranger Station. The aircraft crashed while trying to negotiate unanticipated winds on landing, and it claimed the lives of the Nez Perce NF supervisor and two smokejumpers. Two years later, to the day, another tragedy was avoided when 20 smokejumpers were trapped by a wildfire on Higgins Ridge, located approximately 7 miles northeast of the Moose Creek Ranger Station. Tragedy was sidestepped owing to the heroism of Rod Snider, the pilot who lifted them to safety with a Bell 47B-3 (N8409E) helicopter despite multiple near-fatal flights. Like Mann Gulch, this event too has been well documented. The Montana Public Broadcasting Service produced a documentary in 2023 titled *Higgins Ridge*.

Surprisingly, until now, the deadliest USFS-related aircraft accident has gone undocumented for more than 40 years, other than newspaper articles and a 1979 investigation report. Bound within and articulated in comprehensive detail is the tragic story of the ill-fated June 11, 1979 flight of DC-3 148Z. Like two major tributaries comprised of smaller streams before they converge to form a major river, there are many distinct stories before they merge as one. The aircraft, its pilots, and the Program in which it operated (Region 4 [Intermountain] based in Ogden, Utah) form one of the stories. The other relates to the civilians aboard the aircraft, Moose Creek employees, first responders, rescuers, and recovery crews all directly or indirectly associated with Region 1. While the regions share a geographic boundary line at the Salmon River and are under the same agency umbrella of the USFS, from management and operation perspectives the two rarely interact. This history pulls from an extensive gathering of primary and secondary documents and is told through the eyes of the survivors, rescuers, friends and families of victims, eyewitnesses, investigators, Moose Creek District employees, and former Region 4 aviation employees. But the story is more than just about a Douglas DC-3, its crew, and its passengers: it is also about the heroism of people who helped and about one of the more unique, isolated ranger districts ever.

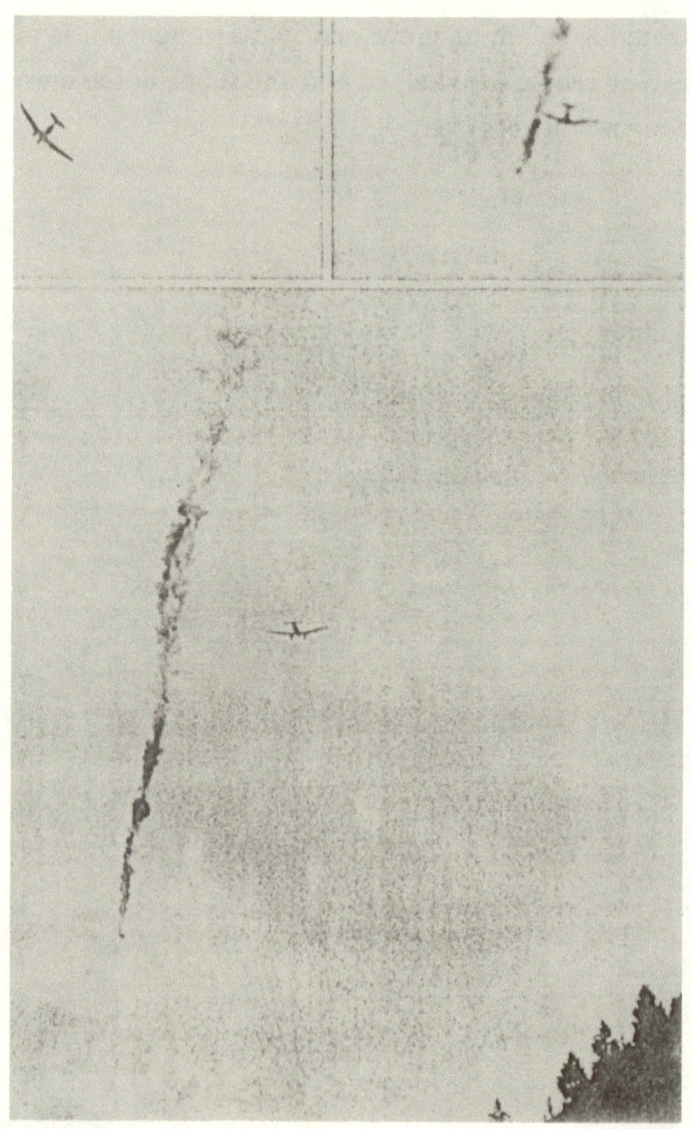

FRAMES FROM BACKPACKER HAL BLEGEN'S CAMERA
SHOWING 148Z'S MOMENTS BEFORE CRASHING INTO
THE SELWAY RIVER. (*H. Blegen/ USFS Collection*)

THE CONFLUENCE OF MOOSE CREEK AND SELWAY RIVER LOOKING
UPSTREAM, 1958. MOOSE CREEK RANGER STATION ADMINISTRATIVE
SITE AND AIRFIELDS (CENTER RIGHT). *(Hughes Collection)*

2

THE FLIGHT—JUNE 11, 1979

The emergencies you train for almost never happen.
It's the one you can't train for that kills you.
—ERNEST K. GANN, *FATE IS THE HUNTER*

District Ranger Art Seamans awoke at the Moose Creek Ranger Station on the morning of June 11, 1979 to the chorus of birds and chatter of squirrels. Sun lit the canvas sides of the large wall tent that he and his wife Joyce called home for the summer. His two young daughters, Cindy and Nancy, slept in an adjacent wall tent. Both temporary quarters were features located among the cluster of log buildings comprising the historic ranger station. Joyce busied herself in their kitchen at the front of the tent preparing breakfast. The two chatted about the day ahead. Art donned his two-tone green and tan government uniform. Shirt buttoned, he clipped his brass badge on his chest pocket shaped with the Agency's shield. Of stout build, standing nearly six feet tall, Art filled his uniform. After running a comb through his wavy brown hair, he slid on his wrist watch. Ready for the day, Art sat at the picnic-style table flanked with wooden benches, enjoyed a cup of coffee, and ate his breakfast.

• • •

For Art, the Moose Creek District ranger, late spring was a time to gear up for the season ahead in the backcountry. Months of planning were already behind him. He had hired his seasonal employees and volunteers, organized fulltime staff, prepped the administrative facility, and selected the fire lookouts to staff. By early June it was time to execute his plans. The kickoff to the summer season for ranger districts across the Idaho backcountry was "Guard School," where employees learned or brushed-up on fire training, traditional tool use, trail maintenance techniques, wilderness ethics, and general duties.

Art's Resource Assistant Don Easthouse and Fire Management Officer (FMO) Larry Keown were two of several employees in charge of helping Art organize the training and school. Larry oversaw fire operations on the District, as well as recreation and law enforcement. Art decided that one of the USFS DC-3s would be needed to transport some of the attendees and their gear. Earlier Guard Schools hosted 40–60 people, including guest speakers. Region 1 of the USFS, however, did not own a DC-3 for its smokejumper operations, and instead relied on a contract with a third-party vendor. The contract over the years changed, and in 1978 and 1979 Region 1 used Aero-Dyne Aviation based in Renton, Washington. In addition to the contracted DC-3s, the Region had other jump ships—principally leased de Havilland Twin Otters. However, through interagency connections, Region 4's fleet of four DC-3/C-47s configured as jump ships could be used for other official USFS missions. Considering the number of people on the manifest list along with the gear, it was more cost-efficient, time-efficient, and logistically more streamlined than the second alternative of using the local fixed-wing operator, who would have to make at least a half-dozen flights, using single-engine Cessna 206s. Instead, the DC-3 could do it all in two flights. The decision for Art and his management team was easy: request a Region 4 DC-3 as had been done for three years.[1]

By June 6, Art and Don had Dick Thompson, a Nez Perce NF dispatcher; called the Region 4 base on the Payette NF in McCall to determine the availability of one of its DC-3s. Unfortunately, only one of the four DC-3/C-47s was expected to be on the flight line during the second week of June, and it had already been reserved by the Big Creek Ranger District on the Payette NF to fly personnel and gear to the Chamberlain Guard Station for its Guard School. A dispatcher contacted Ed Allen, the FMO of the Big Creek Ranger District. He told dispatch that Moose Creek could have the plane, and they would make a few flights with a local contractor in smaller aircraft instead. With the airplane secured, Art estimated up to 20 people for the flight manifest, including himself and his family. Once the personnel were flown to Moose Creek, he also arranged for the plane to fly a second cargo-only trip from Grangeville with the summer supplies, which included personal gear, food, lumber, and horse grain. The second flight would also be available for any last-minute stragglers who wanted to attend.

On Friday June 8, Art called local pilot Thomas "Frank" Hill, who owned Grangeville Air Service, a 135 Air Taxi business at the Grangeville (Idaho County) Airport, to confirm that he would haul out

---

1   Region 4 C-47 (N146Z) was used for the Moose Creek Guard School flights in June 1976 and on June 16, 1977, and on June 12, 1978.

some trash, as well as employees, the morning before Guard School. Frank then mentioned to Art that if he needed a ride or any additional gear brought in, the Cessna 206 to Moose Creek would be empty. Art discussed it with his family and they decided to go in early. Joyce was particularly pleased, since it afforded her more time to bake a cake for the welcoming party on Monday.

Frank was a widely respected backcountry pilot who practiced agricultural flying and flight instruction. He was slight, calm, and iconic. He dressed casually: collared shirt, jacket, and blue jeans, wore a ball cap over his graying hair, and shaded his eyes with wire-rimmed glasses. Usually he smoked while he flew, and in the absence of ashtrays, he rolled the bottom of one pant leg to tap ash. He and his wife Joanne lived in a house at the Grangeville Airport, where they raised their kids and served as the airport managers. One of the mainstays for the Hills' business was the fixed-wing contract with the Nez Perce NF, where the company did weekly flying tied to the operations at Moose Creek. Frank and his seasonal pilots were integrated into the activities at Moose Creek and in many ways became part of each other's families.

• • •

Today was the official kickoff to the summer season. Excited and slightly jittery, Art excused himself from the kitchen table, thanked Joyce for the meal, and headed to his office. As he sauntered along smiling, he thought how fortunate he was to be working in such a place with equally fantastic people. The air was fragrant with pine-resin and the scent of fresh mowed grass from the station's landing field. The tall ponderosa pines with their silvery needles reflected the sunshine; majestic western red cedars with massive gray trunks cast long shadows on the grass. Art saw some of his employees milling about the station, completing last-minute tasks in preparation for the arriving DC-3.

The office, a short walk from the wall tents, was in a log building constructed in the 1920s. The ranger's office occupied one side of the main floor and the other was the primary kitchen, commonly referred to as the cookhouse. Art twisted the metal knob on the rear door. As he whistled his way through the entry, the door chafed a little, then the screen door thumped behind him and the damp, yet dusty smell of the ever-curing wood hung in the air. Art left the exterior door open to enjoy the cool mountain air before the heat of the day set in. The room had changed little over the last half century. It was a step back in time. Shafts of golden sunlight pierced the multi-paned windows hung in wood sashes. Old maps wafered the walls, and in one corner a set of oak filing cabinets. Art's wooden desk fit an accompanying oak bent chair. His desktop was neatly organized with a typewriter, paper notepads, writing implements, a gas-powered Coleman lantern. No electricity.

The floors creaked as he made his way to his desk—a reminder that the heavily trafficked floors had carried the weight of all the rangers before him. Like many of the original, now famous rangers in the Agency, Art had graduated from Yale University with a degree in forestry. It was his fifth season as the district ranger—his dream job. Moose Creek was one of the last places where a ranger managed from the field and from the back of a horse. At his desk he began writing out his welcoming speech to new and old employees, as well as those attending from adjoining ranger districts, other forests, and those there to speak or offer training. He knew many of the people; many he did not, others were new hires he had only visited with on the phone. Of upmost importance to Art was a good first impression, impressing upon them how much he loved Moose Creek. The multiday Guard School was hard work, but it was also a time to enjoy good food together, socialize, and generally get to know each other or become reacquainted. While the Selway-Bitterroot Wilderness is a spectacular place, what made Moose Creek special were the people, and Art could never stress that enough.

Engrossed in desk duties in the hours leading up to the arrival of the DC-3, Art lost track of time. At 1008 hours he was interrupted by Warren Miller, a longtime Moose Creek employee who was on radio dispatch duties in an adjacent room, "Art, we have a situation." Warren then informed him that Grangeville dispatcher Ollie Goldammer had just called to see if DC-3 148Z had arrived. At 1022 hours, Grangeville radioed Moose Creek, noting that the plane was 55 minutes overdue. Warren and Art then made several attempts to contact the DC-3 with no response. At 1028 hours Art gave orders to send out a search aircraft from Grangeville. Ollie responded, "Already taken care of...we have aircraft in the air."

• • •

Among the first employees to arrive Monday, June 11 at the Grangeville Airport about the same time as 148Z, was 17-year-old Bryant Stringham from the nearby community of Cottonwood. Thin, with sandy blond hair, a boyish face, Bryant's outward appearance was that of an all-American high school student. For his age, however, he was anything but typical. He had just finished his junior year of high school, where he played football. When not in school, he spent his time outside, working on his Boy Scout projects, and was active in the local Church of Latter-day Saints

(LDS). His parents, Bud and Joyce, had instilled a work ethic, in him and his three younger sisters from the time they learned to walk. Bud and Joyce owned and operated their own beauty salon and barbershop, and in 1979 Bud was training for a supplementary job to become a full-time, state-certified meat inspector. Bryant was the youngest person working on the Moose Creek District in 1979, but he had proved a hard worker the previous season for Art as an assistant station guard. Tasks included tending to the stock, painting, fencing, cutting firewood, and delivering mail to fire lookout stations. He got the job through family friend Ken Hatcher, who worked for the USFS in Grangeville as a radio technician. Art and he were friends, and Ken had recommended Bryant for the job. It was a good fit. His parents introduced him to outdoor recreation; they often took family camping trips on the lower Selway River to hunt, fish, and hike.

Bryant was familiar with the USFS's DC-3s, having first ridden to Moose Creek as a passenger on one the year before. Unlike the year before, where he was relegated to the rear of the plane, he was determined this time to sit farther forward, as close to the cockpit as possible, for a better view out the front windows, and able to watch the pilots, so he arrived early at the airport.

• • •

Pilot Marvin "Whitey" Hachmeister and co-pilot John B. Slingerland flew DC-3 148Z to Grangeville and arrived on time. They were met by John "Mike" Uszuko, a Grangeville smokejumper, who was wearing the hat of loadmaster at the jumper loft. He was in charge of helping the pilots weigh cargo and fill out and file the necessary weight and balance paperwork for the corresponding flight. Since he had worked on the District off and on for several years and begun his career as a Region 1 smokejumper in 1974, Uszuko was familiar with both Moose Creek and the DC-3.

• • •

As a pilot, Whitey had an excellent reputation. Although not outspoken, and known as a gruff character with a nonchalant demeanor, Whitey was liked by everyone who worked with him. His small figure and white hair added to his intrepid persona, having served in the US Navy during World War II as a merchant seaman and a combat air crewman before transferring to the Air Force in 1948. He then fought in the Korean Conflict, flying B-26 bombers. Returning stateside, he was honorably discharged with the rank of major, eventually in 1967 flying for the USFS. Whitey was an experienced aviator holding an Air Transport Pilot (ATP) rating, a Certified Flight Instructor (CFI) rating, and was an aviation mechanic holding an Airframe and Powerplant (A&P) certificate. He had over 12,000 hours in fixed-wing aircraft and had experience in several large complex planes such as DC-4s and Convairs (CV-240, CV-340, and CV-440). By 1972, he exclusively flew Douglas DC-3/C-47 on assignments throughout the Intermountain Region in the summers, with a preference for missions based from McCall. At this point, he and his wife Leona moved from Layton, Utah, to a home in west Boise, Idaho, and enjoyed family life with their five daughters. When not at home or in the cockpit, Whitey enjoyed the outdoors: riding his motorcycle, flying his Cessna 172, fishing, hunting. In fact, he was such an avid bird hunter that he and his two German shorthairs were featured in the November 1969 *Field & Stream* magazine where the author of the article described him as "Summertime Forest Service pilot, full-time sportsman, and the dog's owner."

To gear up for the 1979 flying season, Region 4 pilots crewing the Agency's DC-3/C-47s met in Boise for two days of pilot recurrent training, beginning on Monday, June 4. On Wednesday, Whitey and seasonal employee John Slingerland, as co-pilot, flew DC-3 148Z forty-five minutes north to McCall. The plane had recently been released from maintenance and was assigned to the McCall Smokejumper Base for preseason training.

• • •

McCall sits at 5,013 feet MSL at the north end of a long glaciated valley edged in by granite, timbered-covered mountains rising off the valley floor another 3,000–4,000 feet. To the west are rolling, forested hills that drop into open western ranching scenery. The community itself is scattered about the south shores of Payette Lake, once home to a large sawmill operation, which, combined with the rich natural resources of the area, fueled the local economy. By 1979, with a population of less than 2,000, the mill had closed and the town was in a transition to tourism.

To the north and east lie several million acres of unpopulated national forest managed by the USFS. As a part of the Idaho Batholith, these wildlands contain some of the more remote terrain in the Lower-48 states, and in the late 1970s the Idaho Primitive Area, founded in 1931, was awaiting federal wilderness status for what would become, in 1980, the 2.3 million-acre River of No Return Wilderness. The latter, along with the 360-degrees of surrounding frontcountry, makes the central part of the state impassible by motor vehicle, and it has been coined collectively "the Idaho backcountry." This difficult-to-access region spawned the development of more than 100 designated aircraft landing fields, the highest concentration found anywhere in the nation. These runways provide relatively quick entry to places otherwise inaccessible except by days of ground travel. The phenomena of these uncommon landing strips attracts recreational users and backcountry aviation enthusiasts from around the world. The USFS was responsible for the development of many of the backcountry airfields in order to better manage the remote lands. Consequently, McCall, on the periphery of the remote area, became an aviation headquarters for the general public. By 1979, the Payette NF (as part of Region 4) occupied a designated paved ramp at the northwest corner of the city airport. The Region stored, fueled, and loaded its fleet of aircraft while on assignment in the area. The ramp was unsecured and was easily entered from Mission Street, which extended north about one mile to the smokejumper base and other USFS administrative facilities.

• • •

On June 6 at 0625 hours, Whitey and John landed 148Z and taxied to the USFS ramp in McCall. They then flew two back-to-back local training drops for the smokejumpers—the first at 0655 hours with a flight time of 25 minutes and the second at 0750 hours with a flight time of 20 minutes. By 0805 hours the missions were completed. Whitey and John were scheduled to fly more training jump missions in McCall with 148Z, but low clouds and relentless rain grounded them the following day. On Friday June 8, a small window of flyable weather opened in the valley and they flew two loads of jumpers on local training drops with flight times of less than 30 minutes each at 0835 hours and 0941 hours. The plane was not scheduled to fly again until Monday June 11, depending on weather.

John was based in McCall and stayed to prepare for Monday's flight to Moose Creek, but Whitey wanted to return to Boise to spend the weekend with his wife. A USFS flight was headed to Boise on Saturday, and another one was returning through McCall on Sunday, so Whitey tagged along. On Sunday, Whitey attended church with Leona at the Shepherd of the Valley Lutheran Church, a mile and half north of their home. After church, Whitey enjoyed the afternoon working in his yard and entertaining fellow USFS pilot Rudy Hartman and his wife on his back patio. Around 1700 hours, Whitey's mother and Leona drove him to the airport for his flight to McCall in preparation for Monday's mission to Grangeville and Moose Creek. Whitey hopped a flight in an Agency plane piloted by boss and friend Chris Hayne, who was then flying on to Salmon, Idaho. After landing around 1900 hours, Whitey drove to Golden's Trailer Court on S. 3rd Street in downtown McCall, where he kept a camp trailer to live in whenever based in McCall during the summer.

Like Whitey, John had a reputation as a seasoned aviator. John had five grown kids from his first marriage to Candace. In 1970 with his second wife, Delores "Dee," he moved to McCall from California. The two became active members in the community, especially with youth winter-skiing groups, which they often hosted at their home on Brundage Drive. John grew up in Chicago, Illinois, the youngest of three children. In early 1941, he enlisted in the Naval Cadet program and was commissioned as a second lieutenant in the Marine Corps the following year. During World War II, he flew a variety of airplanes as a carrier pilot in the South Pacific. John was then assigned to a Marine base at El Toro, California, where he taught fighter plane tactics, and in 1945 earned the rank of major. He also flew in the Korean Conflict from 1951 to 1953. During his tour in Korea, John was wounded and subsequently retired in 1953 on disability as a lieutenant colonel. The injury resulted in the amputation of his lower left leg and for the rest of his life he had a prosthetic leg. John left military service highly decorated: Distinguished Flying Cross, the Navy Marine Corps Medal, the Air Medal with four stars, the United National Service Medal, the Asiatic Pacific Medal with three stars, the American Theatre Medal, and the World War II Victory Medal. In spite of his injuries, he was able to obtain a medical certificate for flying and had a successful commercial aviation career as a pilot at Flying Tiger Freight Service based in San Francisco, California, and later at Fremont Sky Sailing in Fremont, California. Over the course of his career he flew more than 10,000 hours in a number of impressive aircraft: sailplanes, bi-planes, Twin Beeches, Boeing B-17s, R4Ds, C-46s, T-6s, Grumman Wildcats, Hellcats, Tigercats, and several Navy jets such as the McDonnell Phantom, Grumman Panther, and the McDonnell Banshee.

When he arrived in McCall, he took up seasonal flying for Johnson Flying Service, mainly operating Cessna 180s, 182s, 185s, and 206s, until in 1978 he started with the USFS. With shaggy streaked white hair and sideburns, John was rather relaxed for someone with such a sparkling military career. Steve Riggers, a nephew of John's, said, "I've never met a finer human being than John Slingerland. He was highly respected in his community and an inspiration to many." Steve noted that his uncle was an excellent swimmer; and when John and Dee moved to McCall, he was captivated by downhill skiing and started taking lessons from Corey Engen at Brundage Mountain Ski Area. At the time, Corey was an internationally recognized skier and had been the captain of the 1948 US Olympic ski-jumping team. "Corey really took an interest in my uncle and helped him learn the sport. It was truly inspiring to see John ski…a man with a prosthetic overcoming such barriers and obstacles. He became such a good skier you would never guess he had any limitations."

On the day of the June 8 flights with Whitey in 148Z, John received troubling news: a very close pilot friend of his, Dennis Conner, had been killed in a Fairchild C-119 while making a retardant run on a fire in the Los Padres NF. He spent the succeeding days mourning the loss. For distraction, he launched his prized 14-foot aluminum outboard fishing boat, dubbed "The Klondike," on Payette Lake and spent most of the day fishing.

On Sunday, John and his wife met with Rudy Hartman and his wife, ate breakfast, and drove around McCall to look at lots suitable for building a new house. When the Hartmans left for Boise in the afternoon, John again went fishing on the lake to sort his thoughts and grieve. As he trolled along in his 15-horse-powered outboard boat, he doubtlessly reflected on all of the acquaintances and friends who had died during his nearly 40 years of flying, and how certain deaths upset him more than others. He mulled the painful loss of his son Bruce, who had died five years earlier in a hang-glider accident. And, the equally sorrowful death of his older brother, Chester, an experienced fighter pilot who was shot down in 1945 over Germany in a P-47 Thunderbolt while on his fifty-fourth combat mission. He also no doubt relived his own close calls. But like any pilot who has flown in central Idaho, he likely gazed up at the granite skyline highlighted by Jughandle Mountain, Nick Peak, Lick Creek Summit, Crestline Ridge, and the divide to the north into the expansive Salmon River country, thinking of all the times he sailed over each apex of terrain on the horizon. Before the end of that long June day, John returned home for dinner and told Dee he was feeling better about life and ready to fly the next day.

On Monday June 11, John and Whitey met with Rudy at the Pancake House, a popular breakfast spot for coffee and a bite to eat. They laughed about this and that and discussed the great qualities and characteristics of the DC-3/C-47 versus the other aircraft in the USFS fleet. The three concluded they were all very fortunate to be primarily assigned to the tried-and-true "Doug" as it was called. After breakfast, the group drove to the USFS ramp at the airport. Whitey and John began preflighting the airplane in a systematic and thorough manner, ending with John dipping the wing tanks for a final fuel check. The two loaded into the Doug and ran the final pre-start check list. The big sleek aircraft, with its art deco lines and orange stripe running down the beltline of the fuselage, glistened in the morning sun against the backdrop of the Lick Creek Range to the east. They cranked up the right engine. Rudy, who was watching from the ramp, noted the right engine took double the typical blade rotations during the start, but it ran normal thereafter. The left engine then started and cranked off as usual.

Rudy observed the pilots taxi out, run-up the engines, and pull onto Runway 16. As Whitey pushed the throttle levers to full power, the sound of the plane's big radials reverberated through the cool morning air heard for miles. The DC-3 picked up speed gradually, the tail lifted, and then as the wings generated more lift, the main tires departed the runway, the landing gear retracted, and gracefully the plane began a wide arching turn to the north.

The pilots steered the plane on a direct line from McCall to Grangeville, which encompasses a variety of mountainous topography. Climbing out over the blue waters of Payette Lake, Whitey and John hit the top of the climb west of Secesh Summit and leveled off while easing the controls into the cruise settings. Undoubtedly, as they crossed the main Salmon River, the two pointed out remote runways and ranches along the river's corridor and picked out familiar features as they made their way north—Hat Point Lookout, Buffalo Hump, Slate Creek Lookout, and so on. As the landscape allowed, Whitey and John began a slow decent, adjusting power and mixture settings as necessary, and came in over the little downhill ski area of Snowhaven, south of rural Grangeville.

In 1979, Grangeville, located at the southern edge of the rolling Camas Prairie, had a population of 3,600. Employment depended on farming, timber, and the USFS. In fact, the town was home to the USFS's headquarters for the Nez Perce NF and a satellite smokejumper base connected to the region's main base in Missoula. With the engines cooled down, the plane crossed over town and toward the airport situated to the north. John busied himself with the process of lowering the landing gear through a specified sequence of actuating a lever, latch, and monitoring a corresponding hydraulic pressure gauge. As the green light illuminated on the panel indicating the gear had lowered and locked successfully, Whitey and John verified the light by looking out their respective side windows for the main wheels, communicating: "I got a wheel." As John worked his side of the cockpit, they effortlessly swung the DC-3 into a left downwind pattern at the airport for a landing to the east. A gentle touchdown ensued and they taxied to the smokejumper loft ramp and shut the engines down—a routine flight.

• • •

Since the passenger manifest had dwindled to ten people and two dogs, they decided to load the cargo on one side of the aircraft and arrange passengers on the other side of the aisle. Because the plane was configured for smokejumping, the spartan interior was only two long rows of side-facing canvas seats against the walls of the fuselage. Cargo was stacked on the starboard (right) side, leaving ten passenger seats along the port (left) side.

. . .

Bryant watched the pilots and ground crew load the airplane and then grabbed his seat directly behind the cockpit. Other arriving passengers were greeted by Julie Hauger and Jan Blake, Moose Creek office staff based in Grangeville. Julie and Jan handed out paperwork and collected the necessary signatures for the flight. Bryant did not recognize any of the other passengers as they filtered in, taking seats and snapping seatbelt buckles. When the plane was nearly full, he had an odd feeling that he was forgetting something. Sure enough, his little beagle named Beetle! The beagle had been brought home by his dad while on a work trip and was intended to be a family dog. But Bryant and Beetle had bonded. With special permission granted from Art Seamans, the eight-year-old beagle had clearance to join Bryant at the station for the summer. With the sudden remembrance, he sprang up, exited, and ran to the car where his mother was waiting to watch the takeoff. He gave her a quick hug and a kiss goodbye, collected Beetle, and raced back. To his disappointment, his precious front seat was now occupied, and again he was relegated to the last seat by the rear cargo door. Beetle, knowing no different, jumped up next to him for the 30-minute flight.

Bryant could not complain. He could still see out the window slightly ahead of him, and across the aisle, because the cargo was not stacked too high to block his view. Aboard the aircraft from front to back on the bench seat: Kevin Leber, Don Easthouse, Bob Cook, Ron Hagan, Andy Taylor, Charlie Dietz, Catherine Hodgin, Patrick McGreevey, Thomas TerKeurst, Bryant Stringham.[2]

With everyone seated and the cargo secured, Whitey did a quick walk-through from the cockpit to the back of the airplane, checking seatbelts. He waved goodbye to Mike Uszuko from the rear cargo door and mentioned something about seeing him on the next leg of the flight. He closed and latched the rear door and returned to the cockpit. Mike then strode up to the left main landing gear, ducked down and pulled the chocks out from the tire and slung them over his shoulder. He walked out to the front of the airplane, made eye contact with Whitey, and gave him the all-clear signal. Whitey, perched in the aerodynamic nose of the Doug, leaned his head out the side window, his dark profile distinctive against the white, gray, and orange fuselage, and yelled, "Clear!" When Whitey flipped the boost pump on to prime the right engine, Mike heard a small humming noise. Then the three-bladed prop began to slowly spin, a rumbling sputter followed with a momentary gust of gray smoke which swept out into the prop wash. The engine caught and roared. Whitey again looked at Mike, pointed to the left engine, made a circling motion with his left hand and fired it off—it quickly caught. The pilots took another few minutes to check everything, and Mike and Whitey gave each other thumbs up. Whitey then eased the plane onto the taxiway toward the runway.

The plane departed Grangeville five minutes ahead of schedule at 0925 hours. For the first phase of the flight—takeoff and the initial

---

2 It is unknown whether Cook or Leber occupied the front seat or the third seat.

climb-out was just as Bryant remembered from the year before. The pilots announced over the loudspeaker mounted on the bulkhead at the front of the main cabin that passengers could come up and look at the cockpit. At least two of them took advantage of the opportunity, the last being Tom TerKeurst, age 19, from Grand Rapids, Michigan, who was seated on Bryant's left.

Bryant settled in to enjoy the scenery and observe points of interest he had either been to or had studied on maps, places he wanted to explore someday. Beetle was calm, sitting at the edge of the canvas seat between his owner and the big cargo doors. His muzzle worked a slight breeze whirring through a slit where the doors hung in a frame of the fuselage and he seemed content. Bryant looked down at him and stroked him, with his other hand he held a leash connected to the collar. A minute or two later, Beetle jumped across Bryant's lap to see out the side window across the aisle and over the cargo toward the right engine. The dog then kept tilting his head, as if hearing something inaudible to human ears. Bryant kept watching him, trying to judge what was going on. "I thought maybe he was just sick. He hadn't flown before…I was trying to follow his eyes and all I could see was this section of [the right] wing…the other dog was really calm the whole time and did not do that. My dog kept looking funny and cocking his head. Once I got him on my lap, he would not look down at all. He only looked straight out." Bryant's focus on his dog and the scenery was broken by another announcement over the loudspeaker by a pilot indicating that they were experiencing problems and reminded people to fasten seatbelts and stay seated.

As the voice sounded, TerKeurst made his way from the cockpit back toward his seat. Bryant remembers locking eyes with him. "I didn't know the guy, but he seemed extremely scared. He sat down and was clearly panicked. Then one of the pilots came on the speaker again. During the majority of the flight I had my eyes focused on the outside, and I distinctly remember how much quieter it became when the left engine was shut down...then seeing it sputter to a stop out the window. Then time went by fast...it seemed like seconds after the guy next to me sat down and that the right engine caught fire... an orange explosion out the window. At that time we all realized how serious the problem was."

Since Bryant had focused his attention outside, he knew they had passed the Lochsa River and had entered the lower portion of the Selway River canyon. Although not a straight line of flight from Grangeville, it is a common flight path from Grangeville to Moose Creek for experienced pilots performing smooth ascents and descents in mountainous terrain. Being familiar with the area, Bryant believed there was nowhere to land the plane other than the river. He quickly accepted a crash landing.

One second Bryant was watching the left engine's propeller slowly turn in the wind, and the next an explosion on the right engine. The interior of the airplane flooded with smoke and the raw smell of aviation fuel, burning metal, rubber, and the pungent odor of an electrical fire. Reacting to the destruction of the right engine, the airplane shook violently. Suddenly the fire began sweeping across the right wing. Then, an ear-splitting "BANG!" and the right engine twisted off its mounts and plummeted. The pilots struggled to maintain a flight track that would take them toward the Selway River.

Vivid in Bryant's memory was the knowledge that they were going to crash: "When the right engine fell off, the plane veered awfully hard to the left. The pilot then swung the plane back over the river hard to the right, which was extremely impressive. We then began to lose altitude. I don't think we actually picked up any speed, but as we came closer to the ground it felt as though our speed increased. Unlike the seconds between the left engine being shut down and the right engine exploding, the last few moments in the air felt endless. There seemed to be a great deal of time to think and to pray. There is no doubt in my mind that there is a God…"

Bryant again focused on the terrain passing out the left side of the aircraft. "I remember seeing rafters on the river and hikers walking along Selway Trail on the north side of the river. They were looking up at us. Time was so slow. Then the trees began whizzing by. One of the pilots, I think the co-pilot or someone else up front started screaming back to us. 'Hold hands! Cover your faces! Take your eye glasses off! Open the hatches!' But everyone just sat there. Nobody moved or seemed to hear the pilot. Whoever it was yelled it two or three times. I didn't know anything about airplanes, but I somehow reached back and fumbled with the cargo door latch handle. At first I was afraid to pull on it for fear the doors would fly open. Of course it wouldn't have mattered. But I opened the latch and left it there. On impact the doors blew off."

• • •

One of the groups Bryant had noticed on the trail in the agonizing descent consisted of six young men hiking up the Selway River on a backpacking trip: Marty Hibbs, Norm Herdrich, Fred Herdrich, John Herdrich, Ron Zaremba, and Howard "Hal" Blegen. Hal was a photographer and employee of *The Spokesman-Review* newspaper. Along the trail below Hidden Creek, a tributary, the group stopped for a break and heard an airplane in the distance. Curious, they fell silent, and looked skyward. The plane came into view, flying low and generating excessive exhaust. Then as they watched, the right engine exploded. Unsure of what they were seeing, Hal scrambled through his backpack to dig out his camera. It had the wrong lens, but he pointed it upward. With racing heart, he tried to capture the outline of the aircraft, but for a few seconds the sun was at the wrong angle and obscured everything in his viewfinder. Then the airplane reappeared to the side of the sun and he snapped as many shots as he could. In disbelief, the boys watched the right engine turn into a bright yellow-orange blob and tumble from the aircraft, trailing heavy black smoke. The plane disappeared behind the walls of the river canyon.

Knowing it was in serious trouble, Hal and his friends jumped to their feet, threw on their packs, and began moving east up the trail as fast as they could go. As they crossed Hidden Creek, an oil slick floated by, and they presumed it came from the airplane. One of them guessed it was a DC-3. About two hours after spotting the airplane, the hikers began noticing debris drifting down the river, confirming their speculation. The boys pulled what debris they could to the banks: freeze-dried food, split firewood, food containers, gas cans. By this time, multiple aircraft were audible in the canyon and they knew rescue crews were searching for the downed airplane. This spurred the group. At Pinchot Creek, a red and white Bell Jet Ranger helicopter owned by Valley Aviation of Orofino, Idaho, swung in close to the trail and hovered. The helicopter was working the search. The group shared what they could with the pilot, Frenny Frensdorf, and Hal handed him the roll of film, requesting he deliver it to *The Spokesman-Review*. The next day on the front page of the June 12, 1979 *Spokesman*, Hal's amazing photograph revealed the outline of DC-3 148Z and a smoke trail streaming off the falling right engine. Looking back at the photograph some 30 years later, Hal softly commented,

"I wish the photograph which has brought me the most recognition would *not* have been that one. The whole thing was really too bad."

• • •

The rafters Bryant saw in the final moments of the flight were a four-boat party operated by a commercial outfitter, Western River Expeditions. River guide Al Moore was at the oars of the lead boat, beginning his eighth season as a commercial boatman on the Selway. On the final day of a multiday trip, he had four clients from Chicago on his boat. The crew was nearing the mouth of Ballinger Creek, regrouping after having run Class IV Wolf Creek Rapid.[3] It was a calm moment for everyone to enjoy a smooth stretch of water and prepare for the next Class IV rapid: Tee Kem Falls. Ballinger is one highlight of floating the Selway because it forms lovely falls close to the north summit of the mountains viewed from the river. In the distance an airplane was audable, which alerted one of the guests, who was a commercial pilot, and Al, who had parachuted from airplanes. Al recalled, "I locked onto the airplane. I'd guess from my experience of jumping out of planes it was at about 2,500 feet [Above Ground Level (AGL)]. The plane was trailing smoke, and then I saw a flash of flame. Seconds later an engine fell off the airplane. I had no idea the airplane was just a glider...we thought the other engine was still running. It was so surreal." By this time they were about three-quarters of a mile below Ballinger Creek when the engine, a ball of flames, flashed into view, sliced a tree on the north side of the river, then thumped to the ground before bouncing into the river. In

3   Whitewater rapids are rated on a scale of I to VI, with VI being the largest and most difficult to navigate.

complete shock, Al quickly maneuvered his boat to the bank of the river and beached before the river current carried them any farther downstream into Tee Kem Falls. "When I pulled up to where the engine went in, steam and bubbles were coming off the water and an oil slick started to form, but the engine was no longer visible owing to the depth of the river." The whole group went ashore, trying to piece together what had just happened. They extinguished a small fire that was smoldering among some pine needles on the forest floor. Al climbed up the steep riverbank about 20 feet and began tracing the route of the engine—a prop, oil lines, and cowl parts were scattered between the pack trail and the river. Realizing the importance of the engine, he went back to the boat and dug out some yellow rope to mark the spot. He placed one line in a tree at the impact area and another in a tree beside the trail at waist height directly uphill from the impact point. They rallied back at the boat and hustled down the river to report their story to a USFS official at Selway Falls.

· · ·

In the air upriver from Al and Hal—Whitey and John were combating aerodynamic impossibilities, maneuvering the powerless, wounded aircraft toward the Selway River. As the plane lost altitude flying upstream, the pilots had to negotiate a hard S-turn at Dry Bar. The oncoming topography rose through the V-shaped split windscreen of the cockpit. At 300 feet AGL, the altimeter continued to spin downward at a rate of 1,800 feet per minute. The canyon walls rapidly closed in, trapping the DC-3 with its 96-foot wingspan into an area of 400+ feet wide. Carrying a payload at near gross weight and attempting to maintain directional control, the pilots continued to point the nose of the aircraft downward at an airspeed of 90 miles per hour. Like prey trying to evade a predator, Whitey and John aimed the ship toward the best escape route: the lowest and most forgiving topography. It was a last ditch effort to straighten out the bend of the meander in hopes of at least reaching a relatively smooth, straight stretch of water. As their sought emergency landing site came into view, a tall tree protruding from a point on Dry Bar spiked into their left peripheral vision. No way to avoid it. CRACK!

At a final altitude of 200 feet AGL, the leading edge of the left wing impaled the tree approximately 15 feet inward from the wing tip. The pilots lost all control. In retrospect, Bryant commented, "It was a tight bend in the river to the left and had we missed the tree we likely would have made one of the only somewhat calm stretches of the river in that section in the canyon, and I've always thought the pilots were likely aiming for it. But when we hit the tree the nose of the airplane pitched down hard at a steep angle and then hard to the left. People naturally leaned forward and braced themselves. There was a tremendous crash. Things from inside of the plane were tossed about, and after what seemed like forever, the deafening noise of the impact stopped, and all became deathly quiet."

THE COOKHOUSE/OFFICE, MOOSE CREEK
RANGER STATION, 1975. (*R. Bosch*)

THE RANGER'S HOUSE, MOOSE CREEK RANGER
STATION, 1977. (*Seamans Collection*)

ART SEAMANS, WYLIES PEAK LOOKOUT,
OCTOBER 1979. (*Seamans Collection*)

CINDY AND NANCY SEAMANS, SELWAY RIVER
TRAIL, 1977. (*Seamans Collection*)

FRANK HILL AND CESSNA 180, MOOSE CREEK RANGER
STATION, 1983. (*Glenn Cruickshank, Lewiston Tribune Archives*)

BRYANT STRINGHAM AND BEETLE, JUNE 1979.
(Glenn Cruickshank, Lewiston Tribune Archives)

WHITEY HACHMEISTER AT THE CONTROLS OF A
REGION 4 DC-3/C-47, 1970S. (*B. Montoya*)

JOHN SLINGERLAND FLYING A CORSAIR IN THE SOUTH
PACIFIC DURING WORLD WAR II. (*S. Riggers*)

JOHN AND DEE SLINGERLAND AT BRUNDAGE
MOUNTAIN, 1975. (*S. Riggers*)

DEE AND JOHN SLINGERLAND WITH 148Z IN MCCALL, 1978. (*S. Riggers*)

CABIN INTERIOR OF A REGION 4 DC-3/C-47 (143Z), 1979. (W. Williams)

AN EXAMPLE OF A PROPELLER IN FEATHERED POSITION
ON A RADIAL-POWERED REGION 4 DC-3/C-47 AS SEEN
FROM THE PILOT'S LEFT SEAT. (S. McGrew)

AERIAL VIEW OF DRY BAR LOOKING UPSTREAM, JUNE 12, 1979. THE TREE STRUCK BY 148Z IS INDICATED WITH AN ARROW. THE CRASH SITE IS BETWEEN THE BEND IN THE RIVER AND THE TREE. (*Seamans Collection*)

AERIAL VIEW OF DRY BAR LOOKING UPSTREAM, JUNE 12, 1979. THE TREE STRUCK BY 148Z IS INDICATED WITH AN ARROW. THE CRASH SITE IS BETWEEN THE BEND IN THE RIVER AND THE TREE. (*Seamans Collection*)

THE DOUGLAS FIR STRUCK BY 148Z AS VIEWED FROM
BELOW THE SELWAY RIVER TRAIL FACING SOUTH,
JUNE 1979. (*Accident Report/USFS Collection*)

RICHARD H. HOLM, JR.

THE FUSELAGE OF 148Z LODGED AGAINST THE SOUTH BANK OF THE
SELWAY RIVER BELOW THE POINT OF IMPACT. (*USFS Collection*)

3

BECOMING A MOOSE CREEKER

*Kind friends all gathered 'round, there's something I would
say: That what brings us together here has blessed us all
today...Where strangers are as family, loneliness can't hide;
I've walked these mountains in the rain and learned to love
the wind; I've been up before the sunrise to watch the day
begin. I've always knew I'd find you, though I never did know
how; like sunshine on a cloudy day stand before me now.*
—KATE WOLF, "GIVE YOURSELF TO LOVE"

I n the world of summer employment with the USFS, the Moose
Creek District had gained a reputation by the mid-1970s as being
the leader in wilderness management and for having a culture
where the entire District worked as a team. Members of the team
became known as "Moose-Creekers."[4] Several factors contributed

---

4   Since Moose-Creekers did not hyphenate the term, the author has honored their his-
    toric usage.

to the District's success, but at the foundation was the physical location of the District within the 1.3-million-acre Selway-Bitterroot Wilderness Area. During the 1970s, the 560,088-acre Moose Creek Ranger District made up 4 percent of the overall designated wilderness in the US, and it was the only ranger district in the US located entirely within a wilderness boundary. Its only rival from the outset of the Wilderness Act was the Pinedale Ranger District along the western slopes of the Wind River Range on the Bridger NF in Wyoming, which was 95 percent wilderness.

The Moose Creek area was designated by the federal government as the Selway-Bitterroot Primitive Area in 1936 and in 1964 was one of nine Primitive Areas given immediate wilderness status with the passing of the Wilderness Act. Four years later, the Selway River corridor was designated a Wild and Scenic River, the only river to be included in both the original Wilderness Act and the original Wild and Scenic Rivers Act. Relative to other lands managed by the USFS in the early 1960s, the Selway-Bitterroot possessed an element of purity: no roads, no mining, and one limited-use commercial lodge. Lack of development meant it was among one of the more pristine, untouched watersheds left in the US. Although indigenous people inhabited the landscape for thousands of years, the area, for the most part, had negligible evidence of human use, other than a few private inholdings, USFS administrative sites, and a trail system. And, at the periphery of this remoteness, were hundreds of thousands of acres of forested land also managed by the USFS.

Another detail setting Moose Creek apart from other wilderness ranger districts in the national forest system was its air access. In the 1930s, at three points within Selway-Bitterroot Wilderness, the USFS had constructed landing fields permitting access. They were situated at Fish Lake, the former Phil Shearer homestead site, and at the Moose Creek Ranger Station. Of these three, the latter two were within the Moose Creek District.

Owing to its central location, the Moose Creek Ranger Station was developed in the center of the primitive area as an administrative site by the Agency, and the Moose Creek District's construction of a short, grass airstrip in 1931 further galvanized the place as the hub of managerial activities. After that, the Agency moved personnel and equipment in and out of the area to manage trails, fire lookouts, other neighboring administrative sites, and the network of telephone lines—with low impact on the ecosystem.

In 1921, the site was first established as a ranger station by District Ranger Jack Parsell. A year earlier, Jack became the first ranger of the new district. He set up his office in a tent and lived there with his bride, while he and several of his men built the first log cabin. The large, handsome structure became known to some as "The Honeymoon Cabin," now more commonly referred to as "The Cookhouse" or "The Office." Over the next several decades, the complex consisted of a barn, corrals, living quarters, and several support buildings. In 1957 to 1958 the airfield was modified to include a 4,100-foot cross-runway that could more easily accommodate larger aircraft such as DC-3s/C-47s. Although the airstrips affected the landscape, the Wilderness Act provided for such exceptions, and the Moose Creek landing field was considered a grandfathered use.

Beyond the attributes of the site and its remoteness, the personnel recruited to manage and care for it distinguished it from other wilderness areas during the 1970s. By this period in the District's history, it had developed an outstanding reputation for having solid wilderness-minded people from the top level down to trail crews and volunteers. Because the District was entirely within the federal wilderness system, management and the subsequent implementation of its plans solely focused on the one use they had to manage: recreation. In comparison, the other ranger districts in the USFS had to balance all the competing management objectives, such as timber, mining, and rangeland. Larry Keown commented, "The fact Moose Creek was 100 percent wilderness really set it apart. It was a unique mission. First and foremost was adhering to the Wilderness Act; it was the bible. The second priority was recreation: trail work for access, outfitters, horsemen, hikers, fishing and so forth, and then some rafting. The focus was so narrow that management directed it well. While admittedly unique, it was not a District where one was going to move rapidly upward either." For the more career-oriented civil service employee, ranger districts offering opportunities for experience in grazing, timber, and fire suppression were a more promising move. Yet Moose Creek retained some seasonal employees for decades, and many did use it as a stepping stone for other fields in the Agency. Instilled in all who were willing to work hard, moreover, was a true appreciation for wild places.

Bill Worf and Tom Kovalicky oversaw the Moose Creek District from the Region 1 office in Missoula and can be credited with much of the District's success. Bill was the director of recreation and land, and his assistant Tom was in charge of wilderness, wild and scenic rivers, and special areas. Two more wilderness-minded men the Agency could not have wished for. Wilderness was originally lumped under "recreation," but Bill and Tom pressed to treat wilderness as its own resource, a management persuasion that took time to ingrain.

The two men met in 1962. Bill was the Bridger NF supervisor, and Tom a junior forester detailed to wilderness study areas on the forest. At the time of their meeting, Bill was tapped by Edward Cliff, the chief of the USFS, along with three others, to develop and write the Agency's wilderness management program. As a consequence of his involvement with the early wilderness management team, Bill returned to the Bridger NF and enlisted Tom in restructuring the management of the Pinedale Ranger District to a defined wilderness approach, which was possible because the District had only 22 miles of frontcountry road. This launched the all-wilderness management concept, meaning a strict constructionist interpretation of the Wilderness Act—no motorized vehicles, tools, equipment; no utility devices mounted on wheels, such as wheelbarrows—only traditional tools and transportation to maintain trails and move about the land. During the first summer the new model was applied, Tom remembered, "We had a formal two-week training session before we turned them loose. Each wilderness ranger was given a saddle horse, a pack mule, and a wall tent camp outfit. One ranger to a camp, spread out over the west slopes of the Wind River Range for a total of about 65 miles." In 1966, Tom became the district ranger of the Jim Bridger Ranger District, consisting of the combined former Green River and Pinedale ranger districts. The wilderness program crystalized. The only other program in the nation evolving at the same pace was Moose Creek, and the two districts collaborated on methods and management ideas. Once Tom joined Bill at Region 1 in the 1970s, the Moose Creek Ranger District rapidly became the premier leader in wilderness management.

Individuals such as Bill and Tom were supportive at the regional level; it was at the District level, however, where the exceptional wilderness culture and management innovations developed and contributed to Moose Creek's success. This spirit was fostered by the leadership of District Ranger William "Bill" Holman, and encouraged by those succeeding him, such as Art Seamans and Barry Hicks. Early Moose Creeker Mike Oliver gave Holman much credit for the District's wilderness leadership: "Bill [Holman] was a person who took to the District and dived into the whole concept of wilderness—practically and philosophically. He essentially tried to live there [Moose Creek] year-round unless someone put him in a full Nelson and forced him to Grangeville. He really stressed the notion of wilderness as a state of mind...he revolutionized the District." Holman was the first of the district rangers to start the educational outreach to public schools to teach about the importance of wilderness. His first audience was Gary Newell's high school sociology class in Grangeville.

Oliver added, "I was in the class and worked for Bill [Holman] the year before on the District. It was a pretty dicey idea for the time in conservative Idaho County to present to high schoolers on a topic thought to be 'liberal.'" According to Oliver, Holman pulled ideas from hands-on experience and from Roderick Nash's revolutionary book, *Wilderness and the American Mind.* The outreach programs grew with each Moose Creek District ranger, and at its zenith extended from elementary to high school students in local public schools, as well as to higher education, with students at colleges and universities. As the education program developed, it incorporated wilderness skills and traditional tool-use. In 1978 and 1979, the District even wrote and produced more than a dozen Public Service Announcements (PSA) aimed at educating people on low-impact camping and wilderness stewardship. The PSAs narrated by then Moose Creekers aired regularly for several years on Grangeville's KORT radio station.

Emil and Penny Keck carried the message from the district ranger to other employees from the late-1960s through the mid-1980s. The

Kecks were the glue bonding all of the young workers who began to call themselves "Moose Creekers." The Kecks worked at Moose Creek for a combined 24 years. Emil first came to the District at age 50 in 1963, after many years of logging, along with a background in firefighting. Proving a jack-of-all-trades, Emil shared his skills concerning traditional tools. He prided himself in completing tasks considered impossible, while working within reason of wilderness standards. Initially, his official title was Moose Creek fire control officer. As his role changed, the District tailored a job more to his skills: construction and maintenance officer (CMO). In 1967, he hired Penny Kummrow, the District's first female employee, as the lookout on Shissler Peak. Penny was every bit as resilient and knowledgeable about the outdoors as Emil, and in 1968 the two married. Once they were married, owing to USFS regulations prohibiting nepotism, Emil could no longer be her boss. Penny resolved the problem by simply volunteering for her husband on the District. In praise of the Keck's reputation and of their shared time at Moose Creek, colleague Steve Wright wrote in 1982, "Emil and Penny Keck are Moose Creek's conscience and—though irascible at times—were a powerful force in the District's program. Their work ethic was a benchmark by which others could measure their own efforts."

After the 1980 season, Emil reached mandatory retirement age, and he and Penny switched positions. She became the supervisor of the construction and maintenance program; he became the volunteer. The couple often lived year-round in the wilderness: building bridges, repairing structures, running pack strings, working trails. Emil's personality came across as gruff and Penny's as no-nonsense, but to those who knew them well and worked for them they were loyal and kind, and fostered a family-like atmosphere. Mike Oliver encapsulated this: "The Kecks were hugely influential to us. To most, other than maybe our own fathers, we had this indescribable respect for Emil. He was just so influential to our lives." The Kecks became well-known and revered figures at Moose Creek; they earned an enviable stature in the backcountry. In fact, the Kecks were the subject of many local, regional, and national newspaper and magazine articles, and they were the feature of a June 1986 NBC television documentary *The American Story with Bob Dotson.*

• • •

Wilderness as a statutory designation was decreed in 1964, but the language intentionally left room for some interpretation, and unlike other areas managed by government agencies, managers at differing levels tied to the Moose Creek District recognized the difficulties associated with implementing strict guidelines for the Act. As a result, much leeway was given to the people who were in the field day-to-day. The Moose Creek crews enjoyed wrestling with the concept of wilderness, as well as its practical application. Management evolved to meet the new demands.

On the District, the title of district ranger remained the top position. He reported to the forest supervisor. Because most District tasks came under the umbrella of recreation, roles below the district ranger were modified. The ranger still had an assistant ranger (or resource assistant), but the new position of wilderness ranger was established at a lower level, and they were in charge of "portals," specific entry points bordering the wilderness. Former guard station administrative sites were now managed by wilderness rangers with their own crews.

Bill Worf was responsible for the concept of the wilderness ranger position, which became a staple in the national wilderness system. In

1969, Richard "Dick" Walker became one of the first wilderness rangers on the Moose Creek District, and the following year he headed the program as the wilderness resource assistant. For more than five years, he tailored the program to the District's needs and selected and hired the candidates for the job. Three wilderness ranger positions became the norm, one each at Moose Creek, Selway Falls, and Lost Horse. Among early wilderness rangers: Clem Pope, Dick Lowe, Gary Koehler, and Warren Miller. The position was distinct from that of district ranger, which had administrative duties. The wilderness ranger's role can be described in short as the eyes and ears of the backcountry. They are not enforcing regulations or laws, but rather educating the public, monitoring campsites and outfitter permits, and being a general presence in very remote areas. When clarifying the two distinct roles, Tom Kovalicky laughed, "One other way to look at this is the district ranger generally has descriptive four-letter words in front of his title, while the wilderness version is more associated with romantic visions of Aldo Leopold striding across the mountains with a pack string." Longtime Moose Creek employee Warren Miller noted, "Managing a wilderness is kind of an oxymoron. Wilderness by definition doesn't need to be managed, wilderness manages itself. And what wilderness managers really are doing is managing people and mitigating the impacts of people on the wilderness resource. And so most of that is education, some of it's law enforcement for the recalcitrant people who refuse to be educated. So it makes sense to talk to people before they go into the wilderness, and try to encourage them to use low-impact camping methods, and try to instill in them a little bit of a sense of what wilderness is, although, again, that's a subjective sort of thing. So it made sense to move the wilderness rangers to the external portals to contact the public."

Trail crews, then mainly comprised of two people, were divided into sectors of the District—primarily associated with the respective portals. A usual "hitch," or block of work, was ten days in the field, followed by four days off. Under Holman and the Kecks, the trail maintenance moved away from big crews supported by pack strings, which required larger camps and meadows for grazing. Instead, low-impact, self-supported backpack crews, consisting of two per crew, were spread out across the District. In the fall of 1963, the District started experimenting with backpack crews, and gradually phased in the practice. Each person carried his own provisions; the tools were divvied up. Equipment encompassed: crosscut saw bent in a U-shape and carried over an aluminum Kelty pack frame; wedges, oil to grease the saw, shovel for tread work, Pulaski for grubbing, two axes. A Moose Creek employee at the time, John McCarthy, noted, "A backpack crew could camp close to the work section. The Kecks and senior crew members knew where to find water from springs and how to stagger camps at short intervals to limit morning and evening hiking distances. Camping only a night or two in one spot with only two people and naturalizing any fires or other touches on the land meant minimal impact to the site. The intentional light touch led to the "Leave No Trace" concepts, where campers strive to leave no signs of having been there. No wood piles, no cut stumps, no hanging ropes, no fire pits, and of course no trash left behind." The innovative concept became such a mainstay for wilderness management that in 1971 the Moose Creek District was asked by the Missoula-based USDA Forest Service Equipment Development Center to participate in the production of an educational film on the subject. The 13-minute reel titled, "Backpack Trail Maintenance," demonstrated equipment necessary to perform backpack trail maintenance on a ten-day hitch.

The film featured Moose Creek's own Dick Hulla and Steve Sorensen as the two-person crew.

Backpacking as transportation on the District not only greatly reduced impact on the land, it also reduced the costs of pack strings. Although backpackers did not eliminate the district packer, the packer's job became more specific, transporting supplies or specialized heavy tools to projects like a new bridge or a trail reroute. Other upper management positions included a fire management officer, but since wilderness fire management policy was changing, they largely managed two-person backpacking field crews to inventory and map fuels, as well as staffing for fire lookouts.

• • •

There are many other unique innovations that illustrated the extent Moose Creek was willing to go in an effort to better interpret and apply wilderness management. One example occurred in 1972, when Emil approached Bill Holman about moving the District's fire dispatcher from Moose Creek Ranger Station to the Shissler Peak Lookout, four miles northwest and 3,000 feet higher. At the time, there was no central fire dispatcher on the forest, and therefore the dispatch job was vital. Holman agreed, and for the summer Paul Conger and his wife Fran lived on the lookout, doubling as fire detectors and as fire dispatchers. They had to leave in August, and Mike Oliver filled in for the remainder of the season. Mike said, "They reasoned it pulled the dispatcher out from the station and placed them in the landscape as part of wilderness where fire was playing a role…the environment of which they and fire were a part of. They felt the dispatcher would not only develop a wilderness mindset and gain a better understanding of the landscape—geographically, but also be better equipped to

55

know weather conditions and fuels." The dispatcher/lookout combination proved beneficial to all District communications because the person on Shissler could more easily handle morning and evening check-ins from crews in the field and relay messages from the portals on the periphery of the District. The arrangement was considered a success and lasted into the early 1990s. Laura Mae Jackson, who staffed Shissler from 1980 through 1991, commented, "It was a unique arrangement in the USFS to have a lookout person also be a dispatcher and a radio relay. In the years that I was there the old number nine phone line from Shissler to the ranger station was still maintained, so I had a good connection with whatever staff was there, without tying up the forest radio system. We also used channel two on the forest system a lot because geography meant the Moose Creek District was on the radio routinely more than other districts. Shissler also served as a radio repeater site for folks in the field to do their required morning and evening safety check-ins with me."

Another example was introduced by Art in 1977 at the annual fall meeting of wilderness rangers. In attendance were Emil and wilderness rangers Warren Miller, Dick Kuhl, and Tim Rich. Once gathered in the Moose Creek bunkhouse, Art opened up discussion to the group on a new concept, whereby he believed the District's wilderness rangers could establish a better rapport with public and commercial stock users (mainly hunters) if they, too, used horses instead of inspecting camps on foot with a backpack. The horses, Art argued, would provide a shared link between the District and this user group. From the outset, the group had mixed opinions as Tim remembered. "Warren was sort of for it, Dick was sort of against it as he was a strong, fast hiker and just saw stock slowing him down, and Emil was totally against it. I was the youngest of the crew and just stayed quiet, although in the back of my mind I thought learning about and riding horses sounded pretty cool. But when Emil took the floor everyone listened, and he said something to the tune of 'Well, Art, if it's true that an outfitter will show more respect and listen to someone on a horse, then the next time someone from the USFS wants to talk to a logger they better drive up in a D-8 Cat [bulldozer]. It's that ridiculous." Much to Emil's consternation, Art's idea was tried for a few seasons with positive results and became a lasting management practice well into the late-1980s. The program did prove to not only foster better relationships with users, such as hunting outfitters, it was also useful because wilderness rangers could backhaul garbage from old camps, pack out smokejumper gear, or resupply a project camp.

Yet another progressive example of Moose Creek's management was its willingness to hire and integrate women. Several Moose Creekers pointed out that even in the late 1960s and early 1970s it was uncommon to have women working in the field on ranger districts across the nation. But Moose Creek was different, and it started in 1967 when Emil hired Penny. Thereafter, the number of women on the District increased annually. In 1971, the District made history by employing and implementing the first all-female backpack trail crew in the nation. The crew was comprised of two of Penny's friends from Oregon and led by Cherry Spurlock. The following year, Mary Helen Ferguson and Mary Paczesniak made up another all-women crew, working the Selway River corridor trail. Mary Helen was appointed to the position after having worked on the District for four seasons, split between lookout duty on Shearer Peak and Shissler Peak, and as the last cook for the Moose Creek Ranger Station. Mary Helen recalled, "I felt I had to prove myself. It was an exciting opportunity and I knew it was unique. At the time I had a lot of pressure to do a good job. Along the way I bumped heads with my male counter-parts...and I gave it my all. I was raised to have a strong work ethic and was taught if you work hard, everything in life will work out. It was a similar ethic Emil really reinforced at Moose Creek, and I knew if I could earn the respect of Emil, it would validate my skills and leadership. It was an exciting and fulfilling time in my life."

• • •

People drawn to the seasonal jobs on the District had to be tough. The positions were not eight-to-five, as in some ranger districts, where one could drive to and from work. A day's work was measured by the amount daylight, not by a wristwatch. People who lived and worked in these wilderness environments formed bonds and learned dif-ferent perspectives. Other than the communications radio and an occasional listen to a portable radio, it was an isolated place with no distractions. As one Moose Creeker put it, "In the 1970s and 1980s when you were at Moose Creek you were at Moose Creek. It was a lifestyle, and it was a self-contained community."

Moose Creek molded its crews of self-reliant individuals into a team. "We were all very impressionable," recalled early Moose Creeker Clem Pope, "and we were all living in an isolated place, working together, and a culture formed." While you may not have worked day-to-day with one another or even in the same field area, everyone was working toward a common goal—wilderness preservation. Bill Holman, Art Seamans, and Barry Hicks recruited hardworking young men and women, typically either in college or just out of college. The young people who gravitated to Moose Creek tended to be those who could withstand living in a remote and primitive environment with no conveniences, and who were either really interested in wilderness or wanted to know more about it. Clem further explained, "There was a seed planted there [at Moose Creek] during that time. A lot of things seemed to come together. The Regional Office was really supportive, and combined with the leaders of the District, everyone had incredible vision and brought us together as a team in which we all cultivated and shared wilderness ideas and ethics. Moose Creek was not for everyone. People who went there did so for a reason: to be in wilderness or to learn about it, or both. Wilderness is a mind-set, and for most it becomes super meaningful—a place where you return again and again."

• • •

As with any business, positions and objectives are driven by demands. Applying a basic business model, if the Moose Creek Ranger District were a business, the resource of wilderness was the product, and the consumer was public users. To better manage the business, regular surveys were conducted to meet consumer demands. For example, in 1977 the products highest in public demand were well-maintained trails: 57 percent of the users identified as hikers/backpackers, 20 percent horse users, 12 percent aviators, and 11 percent floaters. The aviators rarely left the vicinity of respective airstrips (Moose Creek or Shearer) and were mainly there to camp and fish. The Moose Creek veterans called them "the fly-in-park-and-fish folks," and many were day-users. By the late 1970s and into the 1980s, Emil had become an icon, and it was common for pilots to make annual visits for his companionship and stories. Penny described her late husband: "Dynamic. He could talk to anyone. He could have talked the Pope into swearing. He was very outgoing, and he talked to everyone coming and going."

Since the most valuable resource to users was trails, Moose Creek focused its efforts on them. In the 1970s, an estimated 500+ miles of main-line trails existed on the Moose Creek District. In a given season, most of them were cleared of trees and downfall, and some received a higher level of maintenance, such as tread work, erosion control, blasting, and rock cribbing. Visitors came from all over the US. The 1976 visitor-use survey reported users from 43 states, along with Canada and France.

Minor users not specifically identified in these annual surveys were academics conducting research during this era. Among purposes of the Wilderness Act is the preservation of "ecological, geological or other features of scientific, educational, scenic, or historical value." A number of Moose Creek employees were involved with studies associated with fisheries, acid rain collection in high mountain lakes, and wildlife research projects. In connection with the designation of the Selway-Bitterroot Wilderness, the United States Geologic Survey (USGS) studied the region during the RARE II (Second Roadless Area Review and Evaluation) process to determine potential mineral resources. University of Montana professor Dr. James Habeck, a specialist in botany and plant ecology, conducted a number of studies in the Selway-Bitterroot Wilderness, more specifically on the Moose Creek Ranger District, studying the regeneration of old growth western red cedars, as well as general fire ecology of all tree species. Stephen Arno, a forest and fire ecologist, also had research-related projects there. Wildlife biologist and former Moose Creeker Gary Koehler, along with his mentor Maurice Hornocker, studied fire effects on marten habitat at the north end of the Moose Creek District in the drainages of Rhoda, Lizard, and Wounded Doe creeks. In the mid-1980s,

Hornocker founded the Hornocker Wildlife Institute, with a base at Running Creek. The Institute continued research projects on threatened and endangered species in the Selway area.

. . .

In addition to the structural management changes and development of new positions on the Moose Creek District, there was a need to slowly revert to traditional tool use maintaining the District's resources (chiefly trails). In the late-1960s, when some of the seasonal volunteers, trail crew members, and wilderness rangers arrived, employees were still using chainsaws and wheeled equipment. Deciding how to effectively and efficiently clear trails without modern tools was a unifying challenge. Much of the traditional equipment, such as crosscut saws, had long been disposed of. It was well enough to talk about clearing trails with crosscuts and other hand tools, but no one on the District in late-1960s knew how to use one, let alone properly sharpen it. Moose Creek again set itself apart from other districts in the country trying to accomplish the same goals. The Moose Creekers, through trial and error, persevered by experimentation and learning—gradually they developed the curricula and wrote the manuals that are still recognized as the authoritative source.

Reviving the crosscut saw along with the Kecks were Moose Creek employees Warren Miller and Clem Pope. They began experimenting with crosscuts on trail work. They then asked Emil how to sharpen one; he knew some things from his logging days, but not enough to help. Warren and Clems' curiosity sparked Emil to consider it further, and he tracked down Martin Winters, a saw-filer living in Olympia, Washington. Beginning in the 1920s, Martin filed for logging camps but had since retired; however, he maintained his skills by filing for contest sawyers. Emil urged a visit to Martin. So in the off season Clem, Warren, and Mary Helen Ferguson arranged a trip to Olympia. Martin welcomed them and spent a day teaching them all things crosscuts—from sharpening techniques to the different saw brands to general care. Before they left the shop, Martin reached under a workbench and pulled out two small gifts, handing one to Clem and Mary Helen and the other to Warren: a pair of specialized raker gauges handcrafted by him and crucial to saw-sharpening. They had been initiated into a waning craft. Elated, Clem and Warren returned to Moose Creek with a newly acquired skill. Warren went to work modifying a little building for the sole purpose of sharpening tools. He added a set of windows along one wall for natural light and below them a bench at the right height to sharpen crosscuts. To chase the natural light, through the changing seasons, the building was positioned on wooden skids allowing it to be easily moved. Since crosscuts of good quality had not been manufactured for years, Warren tracked down second-hand saws to keep the District stocked. He made two more trips to the Washington coast to scour old logging shops. Warren became a master saw-filer and soon started a side business sharpening saws for the District; his business grew nationally. He became well recognized in the field and was entreated by the Missoula-based Forest Service Equipment Development Center to write a crosscut saw manual, still the definitive book.

· · ·

To standardize the use of traditional tools for trail maintenance, the Moose Creek crew incorporated the tool-training into the USFS Guard School. For two decades, the Guard School had focused on forestry, fire suppression techniques, chainsaw use, and safety training. By the mid-1970s, Moose Creek slowly transformed the Guard School into a multiday training session covering some of the old topics, but with an emphasis on wilderness ethics, philosophy, skills, policy, low-impact camping, visitor education, wildlife, pack animal use, law enforcement, natural role of fire, and traditional tool use and care. According to longtime Moose Creeker Gary Miller, the Guard School for a number of years was divided into two camps—one led by the Kecks for the hands-on application of trail work and tools, and the other by Jim Bradley, a district resource assistant, who preached no-trace camping and the intellectual aspects of wilderness. Bradley promoted educational outreach and wrote the popular public handbook promoting low-impact camping and wilderness ethics, *Selway-Bitterroot Wilderness Primer*. The title page describes it as "a handbook with drawings, checklists, field guides, stories, manuals, glossaries, and other handy information." By the end of the decade, the Bradley and Keck camps merged and became a cohesive curriculum. Art Seamans refined the Guard School by appointing district staff, and recruiting experts from the Regional Office and other government agencies to give instruction and presentations on specific topics. At the height of the program, 40–60 people attended. As a national leader, the Guard School became the standard all ranger districts required with wilderness-management training wanted to emulate. In 1978, Bradley reported, there were attendees from seven national forests.

Penny recalled, "Moose Creek at that time was beginning to have a name, it became a half-notch above the Bob Marshall [Wilderness], it became a picture of wilderness, and people recognized that." It also became traditional, at the conclusion of the Guard School, for attendees to gather for a group picture at the edge of the ranger station grounds with the historic log buildings in the background. Absent from the tradition was the year 1979.

• • •

Becoming a Moose Creeker involved more than just attending Guard School and proving one was tough enough or willing to try new things; it was also becoming a part of a family. The Kecks, who were essentially in charge of the summer crews, had high expectations and led by example. No job was beneath them; they asked no one to work harder than they did, and the Kecks were the epitome of hard workers. Whether out on a hitch or at the ranger station, everyone lived a communal life. They helped each other develop emotionally, socially, and shared good food, music, and literature. In the 1970s and 1980s, the seasonal employees compiled a lengthy tongue-and-cheek newsletter reporting on a variety of topics: news, cooking, travel, music, entertainment, arts, and environmental issues. Most everyone on the District—from the district ranger to trail crews—to the fire lookouts—contributed an article or editorial. The title of the newsletter went through several iterations: *Camp Mouse Creek Newsletter*, *Brusher's World*, *Moosenews*.

Music was a popular pastime for many on the District. The few times during the season people were together on days off or between hitches at places such as Moose Creek, Shearer, Selway Falls, or Lost Horse, a group of them gathered in the evening and performed music. Folk music predominated—whether it "old-timey" or contemporary. The years Gary Miller and Charlie Mabbott were present, they tended to be at the center of such activities. Looking back, Gary commented, "In the 1960s and 1970s, in the aftermath of the folk wave but before compact music devices such as CD players and iPods, it was common for all kinds of people to be playing some type of acoustical instrument, whether we were any good or not." He played the fiddle, guitar, and accordion. Other players who frequently joined in were Tim Rich (guitar), Gary Oye (mandolin), Dick Kuhl (harmonica), Steve Barrett (dulcimer/banjo), Charlie Mabbott (vocal/guitar), Carol Mytron (guitar), and Dave McDonald. Tom Van de Water and others have memories of Gary calling square dances with his accordion in the Moose Creek cookhouse. It was the place to gather because it had a communal cook area and tables for family-style dining. In later years, as technology advanced, a portable cassette player was introduced, and Gary, along with some of the crews stationed on the neighboring West Fork Ranger District, exchanged folk music on cassette tapes by mail. Artists popular among the crew included Woody Guthrie, Norman Blake, Kate Wolf, Judee Sill, and Robin Flower. John McCarthy added, "The cookhouse was a place to gather and socialize, including people often teaming up to fabricate or cobble together meals from oddities in their stores. Even those of us who had separate wall tents with rudimentary kitchen stoves and sink, like me and Mary [Butters], Charlie and Nelia Gindler, would come over in the evenings on the long days of summer to hang out, maybe hear some homegrown music, and get the news of the trail. Dick Kuhl was always good for a wilderness ranger story, and Charlie would keep pace with his packer tales."

More prevalent among Moose Creekers than music was reading. People on the District spent a lot time in isolated places passing time in remote cabins or tents. Anyone who worked on the District from out of a backpack has a story of being holed up in a tent during bad weather and reading. The District had a special arrangement with the Grangeville Public Library, whereby Moose Creek employees, even without a library card, could check out books for the entire summer. Discussing books and exchanging them with one another was endemic. Being omnivorous readers, they explored a range of genres and topics—from science fiction to history and everything in between. Of course, environmental books were ubiquitous—Aldo Leopold's *A Sand County Almanac*, Roderick Nash's *Wilderness and the American Mind*, and Stewart Udall's *Quiet Crises* became staples. Other popular authors on the District were John Muir, Bob Marshall, Rachel Carson, Wendell Berry, Annie Dillard, Edward Abby, John McPhee, Barry Lopez, Willa Cather, Jerry and Renny Russell, and Wallace Stegner.

For the era, the most read book was Norman Maclean's *A River Runs Through It and Other Stories*, published in 1976. The title story reflected their lives at Moose Creek, given the coming-of-age narratives and the settings, but the canon was the last story in the book, "USFS 1919: The Ranger, the Cook, and a Hole in the Sky." Maclean blended in his autobiographical experiences of working for the USFS in 1918 and 1919. Like the people at Moose Creek, he was posted in the wilds of the Bitterroot Mountains at Elk Summit, just 20 miles northeast of the Moose Creek Ranger Station, where he cleared trail, wrangled pack stock, and served as a fire lookout (Grave Peak). Closer to home, he worked on the Bear Creek Ranger District, absorbed in 1932 into the Moose Creek Ranger District. So many Moose Creekers hiked the same steps as Maclean. His admiration and respect for his boss, Bill Bell, was similar to how Moose Creekers regarded their own bosses, Emil and Penny. Describing Bill, Maclean wrote, "Bill was the best...he could swing an ax or pull a saw, run a transit and build trail, walk all day if he had to, put on climbing spurs and string number nine telephone wire, and he wasn't a bad cook."

Maclean's portrait of the forest rangers drew a parallel to Moose Creek during the late the 1960s through the mid-1980s. Moose Creek was a living anachronism. Those who worked on the District during this period were working in the woods as their predecessors had during the first 40 years of the twentieth-century. While the new generation continued to work and live much like Bill Bell's generation, by living in the same ax-hewn cabins, drinking from the same springs, streams, and rivers, and utilizing traditional hand tools to maintain much of the infrastructure they built, the connection ran even deeper. The early generation of the USFS built cabins, fire lookouts, carved trails, and strung hundreds of miles of number nine telephone line for communications. The only difference was that the new gritty generation was undoing much of the Bill Bell generation's work to meet the constraints of the Wilderness Act. Many Agency-owned structures no longer in use, as well as buildings located on isolated inholdings purchased by the USFS, were naturalized. Outfitter camps with old dumps and permanent structures were dismantled, burned, and packed out.

As the old-timers left their contributions to the landscape of the Selway-Bitterroot, so did the crew of Moose Creek: while their work and dedication to the land were equal, their efforts were dedicated to returning the surroundings to what they were when found by the earlier generation. After a hard day's work, time was spent doing chores—splitting firewood for the cook stoves and preparing for the next day's tasks. Even many of the lost techniques were learned and taught again. And like many of the old-timers, many of the new generation were so captivated by the Selway-Bitterroot that they sought year-round refuge there, often taking jobs during the shoulder-seasons or winters at the few remaining homesteads such as Running

Creek, North Star, and Selway Lodge. Some worked as cooks, others as ranch hands, and some as caretakers. Several people even worked for the Idaho Department of Fish and Game, living on the upper end of the Selway River in a wall tent at Indian Creek, tending to fish eggs (the site and job were popularized by Peter Fromm's acclaimed book, *Indian Creek Chronicles: A Winter Alone in the Wilderness*). But as longtime Moose Creeker Bruce Farling said of the book, "We all thought, 'big deal.' We lived out of backpacks in the wilderness for months on end, and we did not have to poach a moose to survive."

• • •

By 1979, Art Seamans included a four-page outline titled *Becoming a Moose Creeker* with each application acceptance he sent out to new hires. The summary detailed "The facts of life at Moose Creek," along with the specifics on the District's work stations, job titles, job descriptions, recommended clothing and suggested food for the season. The outline began with, "A Moose Creeker lives a spartan life isolated from many of the conveniences of civilization. He or she must be self-sufficient and independent."

The nickname "Moose Creeker" arose in the early 1970s on the heels of the success of the crews in the late 1960s and their interpretation of the Wilderness Act with their boots on the ground. Discussing the origins of the name, Mike Oliver laughed, "I first heard the term from friends who worked on other ranger districts of the Nez Perce [NF]. It was derogatory and no different from being called a 'tree hugger' or a 'flower sniffer.' To put it in perspective, in the 1960s the Forest Service was cutting about 1.5 billion board feet of timber annually, of which about 100 million came from the Nez Perce [NF]. Of course timber harvest was prohibited in wilderness, so Moose Creek did not contribute to the target. Moreover, managers were generally rewarded for their ability to 'get the cut out,' a phrase connected with meeting the harvest." The perception of Moose Creek being singularly managed for "recreation" implied its employees were a bunch of liberal, long-haired, left over hippies, or "Moose Creekers." "At first, I was taken aback by being referred to as a 'Moose Creeker,' but much to their dismay, we embraced it. We were proud to be Moose Creekers…once a Moose Creeker, always a Moose Creeker…I believe the term has evolved to epitomize a rugged individualist who exhibits great regard for the natural environment and recognizes the need to conserve lands where humans are only part of its ecosystem."

To most, the term applies to people who lived and worked on the District through the mid-1990s. The group, known to have an undiluted sense of the wilderness concept, developed its own culture and was perceived by many in the general public and branches of the Nez Perce NF to be "cultish." As one member commented, "It was a good tagline for our identity, and people used it in a positive way, but maybe there was reluctance to overuse it or to appear elitist or too Forest Service-centric. Of course we were elitist in our little club of wilderness warriors, but we didn't want to rub it in."

Most of the individuals on the June 11, 1979 flight were either "Moose-Creekers" or were going to become one.

MOOSE CREEK RANGER STATION'S AIRFIELD AND
BUILDING COMPLEX, 1975. (*G. Miller*)

MIKE OLIVER, MINK CREEK TRAIL, 1970. (*M. Oliver*)

BILL HOLMAN, PENNY KECK, AND EMIL KECK
AT BEAR CREEK BRIDGE, 1969. (*R. Walker)*

EMIL KECK BUILDING MINK CREEK BRIDGE, 1977. (*Seamans Collection*)

PENNY AND EMIL KECK, MOOSE CREEK, 1976. (*R. Bosch*)

L TO R: CLEM POPE, MARY HELEN FERGUSON,
MARY PACZESNIAK, NICK HAZELBAKER, AND PAUL JUDD.
LONG PRAIRIE CREEK, 1972. (*M.H. Ferguson-Pope*)

WARREN MILLER, 1985. (*B. Farling*)

SHISSLER PEAK LOOKOUT DISPATCH DESK, 1972. (*M. Oliver*)

LAURA MAE JACKSON, SHISSLER PEAK LOOKOUT, 1983. (*G. Miller*)

CREWS ARRIVE AT MOOSE CREEK BY REGION 4 DC-3/C-47 FOR THE 1978 GUARD SCHOOL. (*USFS Collection*)

GUARD SCHOOL AT MOOSE CREEK, 1978. (*USFS Collection*)

EMIL AND PENNY KECK (STANDING CENTER) TEACHING
AT GUARD SCHOOL, 1978. *(USFS Collection)*

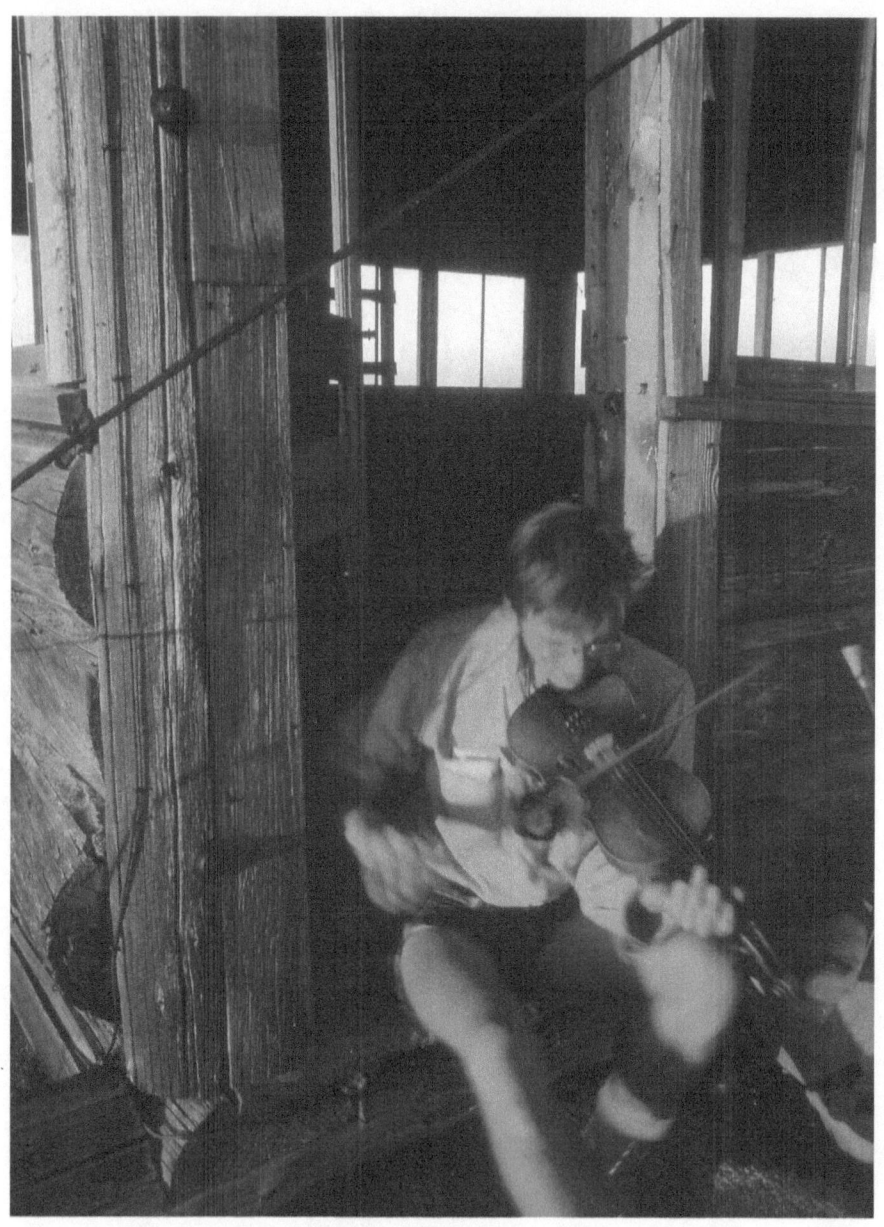

GARY MILLER FIDDLING, WYLIES PEAK LOOKOUT, 1977. (*G. Miller*)

1977 MOOSE CREEK GUARD SCHOOL.
STANDING AND SITTING ON FENCE (L TO R):
TIM RICH, LOCHLIN LOUD, CHARLIE GINDLER, DAN ZILKO,
DALE SWEE, WARREN MILLER, VIRGINIA FOX, PAT HART,
JAN BLAKE, RUSSEL BROTNOV, GARY MILLER, JOHN MCCARTHY,
PAM GOLDEN, RALPH FIREOVED, AND JOHN MACY.

KNEELING OR SITTING (L TO R):
PENNY KECK, NELIA GINDLER, ALAN CARROLL, GENE SANDONE,
BILL SAYER, DICK KUHL, LENNY BRENNAN, CINDY SEAMANS,
ART SEAMANS, DIANE BECKMAN, NANCY SEAMANS,
MARY BUTTERS, ROB NUCHOLS, DOLLY KOONS, JIM BRADLEY,
EMIL KECK, JOYCE SEAMANS, BOB MOHR, CHUCK NUCHOLS,
AND BRANDY SEAMANS (DOG). *(Seamans Collection)*

1981 MOOSE CREEK GUARD SCHOOL. STANDING (L TO R):
PENNY KECK, UNKNOWN, IAN BARLOW, DALE SWEE, DICK
KUHL, UNKNOWN, TOM VAN DE WATER, RALPH FIREOVED,
BETSY KEPES, UNKNOWN, PAUL MANDEVILLE, UNKNOWN,
MARY GRAMLING, CHERYL WARREN, STEVE WRIGHT, STARKER
WRIGHT, TIM RICH, CAROL HOLMES, RICHARD HILDNER,
UNKNOWN, LINDA HICKS, BARRY HICKS, SUZANNE HICKS,
CHARLIE MABBOTT, KATHY HICKS, AND JOHN POLISAR.

KNEELING OR SITTING (L TO R):
UNKNOWN, UNKNOWN, LAURA MAE JACKSON, WARREN MILLER,
EMIL KECK, MARY LANE PENNELL, DAVE MCDONALD,
BRUCE FARLING, ROBIN ZEAL, MARTIN HICKS,
UNKNOWN, AND UNKNOWN. *(B. Hicks)*

"No servant brought them meals: They got their meat out of the river, or went without. No traffic cop whistled them off the hidden rock in the next rapids. No friendly roof kept them dry when they mis-guessed whether or not to pitch the tent. No guide showed them which camping spots offered a night-long breeze, and which a nightlong misery of mosquitoes: which firewood made clean coals, and which only smoke. The elemental simplicities of wilderness travel were thrills not only because of their novelty, but because they represented complete freedom to make mistakes. The wilderness gave them their first taste of those rewards and penalties for wise and foolish acts which every woodsman faces daily, but against which civilization has built a thousand buffers. These boys were on their own in this particular sense." —Aldo Leopold

EXTRACT FROM ALDO LEOPOLD'S *A SAND COUNTY ALMANAC*, TACKED TO THE WALL OF THE MOOSE CREEK BUNKHOUSE, 1975. (*R. Bosch*)

4

VIEW FROM THE AIR

Fallen planes serve as sobering points of reference in the same
manner of shipwreck notations that dot mariner's charts.
—BRIAN MURPHY, *81 DAYS BELOW ZERO*

Word reached the Idaho County Sheriff's Department concerning the overdue airplane. Idaho County Sheriff Bud Walkup and his deputy Loren "Yogi" Schwartz responded by placing a call to Prairie Land and Timber, a local timber company. Located across the street from the Grangeville Airport, the company had a helicopter the Department contracted for search and rescue work. Bob J. Black, the pilot for the company, met the two of them at the helicopter—a small three-place F-28C Enstrom. Recollecting the day, Bob commented, "Bud hated to fly, and actually he never flew to my knowledge, so when he was sheriff one of his deputies was always appointed to ride along with me. As we got moving on the mission, I asked Yogi what kind of airplane we were looking for; he said a Forest Service airplane headed to Moose Creek. That was all he said. He never told me the size or the number of people on board and at that time he didn't know." Nothing else was communicated and Bob navigated the ship on what he considered the most logical course for an airplane to take from Grangeville to Moose Creek.

The 32-year-old Bob knew the Selway country well. His in-laws had owned and operated the Selway Lodge, located about 15 trail miles upstream from Moose Creek, for a number of years. His father-in-law, Sid Hinkle, was a known pilot in the area, flying one of the first Cessna 185s in the central part of Idaho. Sid pioneered many airstrips in the area, including those at Selway Lodge, Mallard Creek, and Dixie Town. Bob had taken notes and often helped him move supplies in and out of the Lodge with his father's Cessna 170. He then learned helicopter flying and instruction in the Army, and after a tour in Vietnam returned to Grangeville, where he flew for the timber company. Referring to the Selway-Bitterroot Wilderness, Bob explained "It's bigger and rougher country than most people think; it can swallow an airplane without a trace, and it has—at least for a while." Bob's estimate was correct—he was referring to the familiar disappearance of Joe Rosenkranz in October 1948, and as of June 1979, Rosenkranz, his passenger, and his airplane had yet to be found.

The Rosenkranz story had become a legend of the Selway country, and the story was woven into local campfire lore and included in the USFS's *Selway-Bitterroot Wilderness Primer*. Ironically, the second edition of the informational booklet had just been published, and a case of the newer booklets was aboard the DC-3. The Rosenkranz plane had departed three miles upstream from the Moose Creek Ranger Station from a private airstrip on Moose Creek, and it met its fate on the side of the Selway canyon near Glover Creek, approximately

14 miles downstream from where the DC-3 impacted the water above Dry Bar.

· · ·

On October 24, 1948, Joe Rosenkranz, a prominent Lewiston, Idaho, businessman and farmer, had finished a fall hunting trip at Moose Creek Ranches, a friend's guest lodge, and he was headed home. It was nearly dark, weather becoming an issue with low ceilings and obscured mountains. Joe left the airstrip about 45 minutes after his friend, Bert Zimmerly, of Zimmerly Air Transport, who was also headed to Lewiston with a load of elk meat. Joe was flying a new maroon Stinson 108 (NC6404) recently purchased from Zimmerly. Sitting next to Joe was W.J. "Bud" Bolick of Lewiston, who was hired by the guest ranch to wire the newly constructed hydroelectric turbine situated on East Moose Creek. The two were never seen again.

The next morning, pilot Dick Wagner flew a load of hunters to the ranch. In a casual conversation with others at the guest ranch lodge, he was asked what time Joe made it back to Lewiston? Wagner assured the folks that he never arrived. Within hours, a search was launched for the missing men and their plane. The USFS, Civilian Air Patrol (CAP), Idaho Aeronautics Department, several private individuals, along with Zimmerly employees, conducted the search. Bert flew several barrels of gas to the Moose Creek Ranger Station to establish a base of operations. They learned several hunting camps in the vicinity had seen or heard the airplane attempting to maneuver around the foul weather. The search planes combed the areas below the confluence of Moose Creek and the Selway in hopes of seeing a fire or any scrap of the Stinson. During this period, search planes made 150 landings at the Moose Creek Ranger Station in support of the efforts.

In retrospect, people involved with the search identified several issues that plagued the missing plane from the outset. Cooperation between the search agencies was cumbersome, search teams were going on hearsay from hunters, the search area was full of dense timber, and the airplane was deep maroon. Additionally, several pilots from southern Idaho who did not know the area well, but who had political ties with Joe, took charge, burning up the limited supply of aviation fuel furnished by the state. Before his hunting trip, Joe was mired in an election campaign, running as a Democrat from Nez Perce County for the Idaho state legislature. In his absence, he won. Well into November 1948, search parties continued to receive tips from hunters, including one group professing to have found broken treetops along a ridge. Every lead was investigated; rewards were offered. After weeks of searching, and with winter weather moving in, the hunt was called off. The following spring, a few additional searches were made, but nothing turned up.

Gossip, primarily generated by local media, stirred the story for decades. Since Moose Creek Ranches was known for its good times—heavy drinking and high stakes gambling—many were persuaded a large amount of cash was aboard the aircraft. Some people thought someone could have found the plane, taken the money, and never reported it for fear of being caught with the loot. Rumors circulated. The mystery went unsolved until early April 1987, when a former Nez Perce NF employee, Jay Jones, was antler hunting and found the airplane. The crash site was on the Glover Creek drainage off the north side of the Selway River. Jay, not knowing what he had found, removed the aircraft identification tag and reported the wreckage to the Idaho County Sheriff. Idaho County officials returned to the crash site, and the remains of the two men were found scattered about the wreckage, and they were positively identified. They were both killed on impact. Two decayed wallets were recovered within the wreckage. Remnants of the plane were hanging near a large rock, which explains why it was difficult to see the maroon painted aircraft from the air. The wreckage of the plane, with only 50 hours on its airframe and engine, remain at the site.

• • •

As Bob flew past Three Rivers, the confluence of the Lochsa and the Selway rivers, and upstream beyond Fenn Ranger Station, he thought about how hard it was to find downed airplanes in the tree-covered terrain, let alone sight people. He had flown dozens of missions for the Sheriff's Department, and it was not uncommon for a missing person to later report seeing rescue aircraft right overhead. Bob remarked, "It was not too far above Fenn that I started to notice debris in the water. At first I did not recognize what it was. The river was plumb full, busting at the seams with snow melt…but then we started to notice it more and more…the river was just full of shit…I then spotted a wheel sticking up out of the water on the south bank. I slowed down, and as a portion of the submerged aircraft appeared, it struck me! IT WAS THE FOREST SERVICE DC-3. I thought, Christ, here I was looking for a small airplane and it was the Doug. I never in a million years thought it would be a DC-3; hell, I had a little time in one, and they can fly around the world on one engine. Then it really hit me." Earlier that morning Bob had stood at his office window, looking out at the airport as he often did. He watched the USFS DC-3 line up on the west end of the runway, wind up, break ground, and make a nice gentle right turn bound in the direction of the Selway. "There was nothing I could do. We hovered around for a while looking for survivors from the wreckage downstream, but we spotted nothing. I felt terrible, but the river was so darn full, there was nowhere to land, not even the usual beaches were visible. The canyon is incredibly tight through that section. My mission was to report the plane found, and so I headed back home."

When Bob landed, he and Yogi were met by a number of law enforcement officials. Sheriff Walkup inquired about what they had found. Bob, with a blank face, looked the sheriff in the eye and said, "I don't know how many people were on board that aircraft, but you had better plan on having body bags to cover the entire manifest of souls on board." The sheriff replied, "Well, there were ten passengers and two pilots."

Bob asked who the pilots were, and because of their relationship, the sheriff told him. Just days before, Bob was flying over central Idaho on his way to Boise and talked to Whitey Hachmeister on 122.9 (the common air traffic frequency, or as some call it, the backcountry radio). The two had visited for a minute. Whitey mentioned that he would be in Grangeville some over the upcoming season. They signed off, agreeing to meet for coffee soon.

. . .

While law enforcement performed its duties, the USFS dispatcher offices at Moose Creek, Fenn Ranger Station, and in Grangeville buzzed with radio calls questioning the whereabouts of DC-3 148Z. Like passing ships, when Bob's flight for the Sherriff's Department was in the air, the USFS, after no response to multiple radio calls, launched its own search efforts once 148Z was 30 minutes overdue.

USFS fire dispatcher Dick Thompson in Grangeville called Grangeville Air Service, which they contracted for fixed-wing operations, and informed them of the emergency. The DC-3 left Grangeville at 0930 hours, and one hour later pilot John Moberly and USFS employee Homer Courville were in the air, flying a Cessna 206 (N7311Q) toward the Selway River. Homer was along to run the forest ground-to-air radios and provide a second pair of eyes. Moberly piloted the airplane by guessing the common route the DC-3 would have taken to reach Moose Creek. While traversing four or five miles west of the Moose Creek Airfield, Moberly and Courville picked up an Emergency Locator Transmitter (ELT) signal and began refining their search area. With nothing visually noted, they radioed the forest network their findings and requested another Grangeville Air Service airplane that was known to have better radio equipment to pick up ELT signals. At the same time, two helicopters on a "call-when-needed" contract with the neighboring Clearwater NF to the north were also dispatched.

The better equipped airplane was a red and white Cessna 180 (N42094) piloted by Frank Hill. Frank took off from Grangeville with USFS employee Chuck Nelson as spotter. In the air they met up with Moberly in the vicinity of the ELT signal. At about the same time, the other two dispatched helicopters arrived in the general area where the two Grangeville Air Service fixed-wing aircraft were circling around the ELT signal. One of the helicopters was a red and white Bell Jet Ranger (N584) piloted by Frank's friend and longtime area pilot, Charles "Frenny" Frensdorf. Working as a team, they began to narrow the search area. Just a little after 1200 hours, Frenny zeroed in on the area between Dry Bar and Pinchot Creek, where nearly hidden in the whitewater froth of Wolf Creek Rapid, a wing and wheel of the DC-3 were visible. At 1205 hours Frenny reported his findings.

There were no apparent signs of life on the ground or in the river. The Moberly-Hill-Frensdorf factions split up, and Frenny flew upstream to Moose Creek and consulted Art Seamans. Within hours, Art joined Frenny as a spotter in the survivors' search.

One might wonder how Bob J. Black spotted the wreckage so quickly in roughly the same span, and this group of equally experienced pilots and professionally-trained backcountry specialists did not. Any pilot or aerial observer will tell you how many times they have flown over the subject they were searching for without seeing it. So many factors are at play: amount of sunlight, shadows, angle of view, terrain contrast, weather, and so on. Depending on the situation, the factors can significantly compound. As for the disconnect in radio communications, between the Idaho County Sheriff Department and the USFS, in 1979, as today, in the Idaho backcountry and at surrounding rural airports, the airspaces are "uncontrolled"—there is no air traffic control. Pilots simply self-report positions among each other to see and avoid. Mountainous terrain and differing altitudes are usually another variable, since not all transmissions are overheard. Given the timing of the events, it is likely the information relayed by Frenny to the USFS coincided with the information obtained by Bob and Sheriff Walkup—all of it processed by two different agencies simultaneously.

Even with little knowledge of the situation on the ground at the site, word spread—the wheels of the federal government spun into high gear. Teams were mobilized from on-the-ground searchers to in-house investigators, all with a means and need to reach the remote area. From the moment Frenny confirmed the location of the downed DC-3 between Dry Bar and Pinchot Creek, the Selway River canyon flurried with activity. Throughout the daylight hours of June 11, aircraft from all sectors of the region, from Fenn Ranger Station to Moose Creek Ranger Station, a distance of 40 miles, began descending on the river corridor.

WOLF CREEK RAPID LOOKING UPSTREAM, JUNE 12, 1979. THE RIGHT WING AND LANDING GEAR/WHEEL OF 148Z IS VISIBLE DOWNSTREAM FROM THE HELICOPTER AND AGAINST THE RIVERBANK AT THE TOP EDGE OF THE WHITEWATER. (*R. Byars*)

THE TAIL (VERTICAL AND HORIZONTAL STABILIZERS) OF 148Z AGAINST THE SOUTH BANK OF THE SELWAY RIVER. *(USFS Collection)*

FRENNY FRENSDORF. *(R. Reel)*

5

BACK ON THE AIRPLANE

If you have lived a life that has thrown you in contact many
times with nature, you have already discovered that sometimes
you can deal with nature only by allowing it to push back
what until now you and others thought were its edges.
—NORMAN MACLEAN, *YOUNG MEN AND FIRE*

After the violent plunge into the Selway River, Bryant Stringham's world went dark. The roar of the river at springtime high water was thunderous. It was all that could be heard. He was upright and still buckled to the canvas-wrapped tubular seat frame and holding Tom TerKeurst's hand. The cargo straps used to anchor the gear had all broken. Coming out of his stunned daze, he looked up and found himself lap-deep in water. It was dark, but he could see the water was stained with blood. As he strained to look along the inside aisle of the airplane, "I saw several bodies, three or four is all I could see, mostly still strapped to their seats. As the water flooded in, the gear began to float around, slamming into me. Everyone was motionless, and to my inexperienced eyes…it seemed that they were all dead. The plane began floating downriver. I was not a strong swimmer, so my first thought was to stay with the plane until it lodged or beached itself. We went through one rapid, and I could tell it was only going to get worse. The plane started breaking up. I saw an opportunity to save my dog, and I threw him out the opening of the cargo doors. I was trying to get the seat belt off the person next to me. He was not moving. For some reason his portion of the seat sank lower, and I was unable to find the seat belt latch, or to hold his head out of the water. I was overcome with emotion…I watched his face slip beneath the red-stained surface of the waters within the plane."

The wreckage swept around another meander and another rapid into a short reach of even faster water. It forcefully breached the plane, and the airspace between the water surface and top of the shredded fuselage diminished. "I was again struck by several things that were floating free inside of the plane, and I knew I had to get out, or I'd soon be injured or trapped inside." Bryant plunged through the rear cargo doors. Again, he was afraid of the fierce current and the overwhelming strength of the whitewater, so he attempted to hang onto the plane, but the remaining void in the fuselage around the cargo doors formed a vacuum that tried to suck him back into the plane. In a last ditch effort, he broke away and swam into the fearsome current. As the river seized him, he submerged several times. In the struggle to keep his head above, he realized that the main section of the fuselage while behind, impelled toward him. The sight of the crippled airplane lodged in his mind. Ahead of the wing root, the nose bent and twisted like an aluminum can, cocked upward, the fuselage by then riddled with holes from rocks. He thought the metal mass was going to steamroll him.

While swimming for his life, the river propelled him toward the south side of the river—opposite the river trail. "I was sucked down into the river by an undertow at one point, all the way to the bottom of the river. I struggled against the current, and actually kicked against it using rocks at the bottom of the river to leverage myself against the powerful current. I finally managed to break free, and was swept farther downstream by a current that lifted me to the surface."

He succeeded in grasping some boulders and pulled himself out of the freezing water. Then he glimpsed the lower tail section of the plane scraping along the rock he was standing on. Amazed to this day at his reaction after his exhausting struggles, Bryant chuckling, says, "I somehow jumped over it and back onto the rocks. I had probably floated 300 yards since throwing my dog out. I then looked upstream and saw a man standing on a rock on the same side of the river, waving at me. He was not far upriver from me, but with the river noise I could not hear him. The terrain on the south side of the river in that area of the canyon is steep and full of little cliffs. With the high water, there was nowhere to walk along the shore due to the boulders, brush, trees, and terrain, so it took me a while to get upriver to him."

• • •

The man standing on the rock was 26-year old Charles "Charlie" Dietz. Charlie had long dark brown hair and a bushy beard, dressed in denim overalls and work boots. Large in stature with broad shoulders, he resembled the football player he was, having played two years at Kansas State University. Charlie was born in the small western Kansas town of Oakley and graduated from high school in Manhattan, Kansas, with a college football scholarship. In 1976, he met his future wife Julie, and the two married the following year.

Charlie graduated from college with a degree in natural resource man-agement and dreamed of working in a wilderness area for either the National Park Service or the USFS. Looking to get his foot in the door, he applied for a number of seasonal positions, and he received two offers: one from the National Park Service at the Colorado National Monument near Grand Junction, Colorado, and the other from the Nez Perce NF with a position on the Dixie Helitack crew. He and Julie chose the helitack job because it lasted several months longer. The Dietzes purchased a fifth-wheel trailer to live in for the summer and headed west. The summer of 1978 was wet, with little fire activity, and the helitack crew only fought one fire by helicopter. The season was largely spent clearing trails, along with helping on several fall fuel-reduction projects.

The job ended in November, and they hooked up their fifth-wheel and traveled south for the winter, where Charlie's sister was living with her boyfriend north of San Francisco. The boyfriend con-nected Charlie with a job working in a hose manufacturing facility. He loathed the work and could not wait to get back to the mountains. In the meantime, he applied for more seasonal jobs, and a wilderness opportunity opened with the Moose Creek Ranger District, with which he was familiar. He took it and was given the title of a wilder-ness information specialist (WIS). The position was informally known as the assistant Selway Falls wilderness ranger, and it included living quarters at the Selway Falls Guard Station, 15 miles from Highway 12, near the end of the dirt Selway River Road. The location is spec-tacularly beautiful. The forest in this area is lush, but varies from sparsely-studded slopes of ponderosa pine to dense brush-covered drainages, thick with fir and stately western red cedar. Immediately downstream from the USFS buildings, and south of the road, are the falls—breathtaking at any water level because they cascade through channels formed by massive boulders. In spring and summer, salmon and steelhead vault the falls in order to spawn upriver.

The Dietzes arrived in early June and moved into a wall tent located behind the main guard station cabin. It was a fine a place to live for the summer, and they found it comfortable. With them were their year-old Saint Bernard, Sacagawea and a house cat Sammy. The sturdy cabin was built in 1907 of hand-hewn logs with square-notched corners—symbolic of the West and the forest the Dietzes had come to work in. The site was selected in 1926 by the USFS after the road was built and extended past Selway Falls. The same year, the cabin was dismantled at its original site closer to the Fog Mountain Road junction. North of the cabin, near their wall tent, were a small warehouse, stock-shoeing shed, and corrals where pack animals were kept to service trail crews, as well as the remaining fire lookouts. The complex was strategically situated among campgrounds along the river road, and at a point where many trails headed into the non-mechanized world of the Selway-Bitterroot Wilderness. The main river trail begins at a trailhead at the end of the road—more precisely, Race Creek. Part of Charlie's job description entailed taking care of the campgrounds, providing information to wilderness users, monitoring the trailhead registry and, when not on site, he would be out in the wilderness clearing trails. Julie was more or less considered a volunteer, but she would fill in when Charlie was out in the woods; she also agreed to be a shuttle driver for the Moose Creek District river patrolman.

On the Dietzes travels to Selway Falls, they stopped in Grangeville for administrative purposes and to meet some of the District employees. They were warmly welcomed into the Moose Creek family. When

Jan Blake and Julie Hauger found out Julie would be living at Selway Falls with Charlie, they bought her a gift, a blue floral-print shower curtain. Both women commented that she needed "something pretty" at the station. The Dietzes then stopped at Don and Karen Easthouse's home, where Don briefed Charlie on early season plans and duties, including a preseason pack trip to the Moose Creek Ranger Station a week before the annual Guard School. Don thought the trip would give Charlie useful exposure to handling stock and to the trails. A few days later, as scheduled, district packer Ian Barlow and Don arrived at Selway Falls. The principal purpose of the trip was to leave the stock at Moose Creek, but on the way they also hauled supplies and checked camps. The three men spent the night at the ranger station; the following day they boarded a flight in a Grangeville Air Service Cessna back to Grangeville. Charlie then resumed work at Selway Falls until further training was required at Guard School.

. . .

Charlie did not recall getting out of the wrecked DC-3, but he found himself in the deep, icy water, and when he surfaced, he instinctively began swimming. When spotted a large floating backpack, he grabbed onto it. The last thing etched in his mind was Don Easthouse instructing the passengers with eyeglasses to remove and place them in pockets. Charlie removed his, snapping them into the top pocket of his overalls. Thinking about those last few seconds before the plane hit the water, Charlie later observed, "I just couldn't believe that he [Don] could maintain his composure like he did, it just amazes me. And then I realized my seatbelt was real loose; I'd loosened it to look out the window. So I said, 'God, I'd better tighten my seatbelt,' and the girl [Catherine Hodgin] beside me tightened her seatbelt, and I looked up and down the row and people were just staring to the other side of the plane, and some had their head[s] bowed and were praying to themselves…I was preparing myself to die, that's all I could think about…just thoughts in my head. My wife, and so on…"

• • •

On the riverbank, as Bryant approached Charlie, he noticed another man lying on a rock slab with his body half out of the water at the shoreline. He was 59-year-old Andy Taylor from White Bird, Idaho. Andy was a Nez Perce NF engineer based at the Supervisor's Office in Grangeville. He was flying to Moose Creek to work on the water system for the ranger station. After snatching the floating backpack, Charlie saw Andy alive and drifting ten feet to his right. So he worked his way over to Andy and yelled at him to grab onto the pack. With all of his strength, Charlie managed to get Andy and himself to the south shore. However, the men were not as physically lucky as Bryant. Charlie had suffered several injuries, a massively swollen leg for one, which Bryant thought was surely broken because he could barely stumble around. As for Andy, he was visibly in poor condition. Bryant added, "I helped Charlie pull the man out of the water, and Charlie then asked me if I knew first aid. I told him I knew a little, as I was an Eagle Scout. I felt from looking at Andy that he had some likely serious internal injuries and was going in and out of consciousness. So I was hesitant to give him any water to drink, but I did get a rag and after wetting it, gave it to him to suck on. We decided that we needed to splint his leg, which we did with a tree branch. As this was going on, I looked up and there was a man on the other side of the river yelling, but I could not hear him. We motioned to one another and walked parallel up the river to where we could kind of understand each other. He told me there was a bridge a few miles above us that I could use to cross the river. At the time, after what I had been through, I did not even consider trying to swim across to the trail."

Now aware of the bridge, Bryant quickly figured out exactly where he was because there was only one bridge that crossed the river between the Moose Creek Ranger Station and the end of the Selway Road. The previous summer, on one of his days off, he had hiked down to it at the mouth of Three Links Creek. It spanned from the north side of the river to Mink Creek on the south. The reason for his familiarity with the location was that the main Three Links Bridge across the Selway was being rebuilt by the Kecks. Bryant admired the husband and wife team and thought a visit would be an enjoyable overnight camp trip.

Bryant hustled back to Charlie and Andy. "We were on the opposite side of the river from the trail. There was a little bend in the river there, and we were surrounded by steep cliff-like rocks with trees above them. We knew it might be difficult to be detected by rescue planes, which both Charlie and I believed were sure to come. Also, the plane itself and most of the wreckage and floating debris had continued on downstream, and I thought it was likely that search efforts would be focused on the debris, wherever it ended up. So I told Charlie where we were, and asked if he wanted me to wait with him and Andy, or if he thought I should try to walk out to make sure help came. He told me to go ahead and walk out, that he would remain with Andy. I fished out several things that had washed up along the riverbank, such as clothing and a sleeping bag and laid them out to dry so that Charlie and Andy could stay as comfortable as possible."

Still high on adrenalin, Bryant began walking. Maneuvering along the south side was nearly impossible. He turned ninety-degrees away from the river and clambered about an eighth of a mile up the canyon wall. He clawed his way through thick vegetation. A dense canopy of grand fir, Douglas fir and western red cedar shaded him. He pushed his way through the chest-high spring foliage: yew, serviceberry, ninebark, thimbleberry, buckthorn, syringa. Breathing hard and sweating profusely, he finally reached a small ridge where the understory opened up. At a quickened pace, he pushed himself northeast toward the bridge. At times he was so far from the river that he could not see or hear it, but he knew he was headed in the right direction. He eventually scrambled down the Mink Creek drainage, but when he reached the creek, his heart sank. The mountain stream was swollen from the snowmelt, and he had to hike farther upstream until he found some logs to shinny across to the other side. He continued to move as fast as he could toward the bridge. When he arrived, he was greeted by the hiker who had shouted to him hours earlier.

The exhausted hiker offered Bryant a thermos of lemonade. Then he reached down to his side and said, "Hey, I found this dog." Bryant glanced down and to his astonishment it was Beetle, his little beagle! For the first time since the accident, Bryant felt some relief. Also for the first time, however, he felt serious bodily pain. It, combined with a growing awareness of the day's events, began to sink in. Taking some time to examine himself, he noticed his right hand ring finger from the knuckle to the tip, that he had wrapped earlier to slow the bleeding, was practically cut off. His body ached all over, and he detected a large bruise around his waist where his seatbelt had strained. His clothes, particularly his heavy work pants, were ripped to shreds. But even in the pain, he knew he was going to be okay. The hiker offered to help in any way he could, and the two agreed that Bryant should continue to hike the eight miles upriver toward Moose Creek for help.

• • •

Allan Greenleaf was the man who met Bryant on the bridge and helped him. At the time, Allan was a Ph.D. student in mathematics at Princeton University in New Jersey. He was on an extended road trip and came to Idaho to complete several backpacking hikes, although originally his plans did not include any Selway adventures. As it happened, his detour to the Selway was a happenstance. Initially, Allan and a friend, who was a kayaker, drove west with arrangements to meet some other kayakers from the East. He intended on camping with them for a few days before going solo backpacking. Sitting around a campfire one evening, they described a number of whitewater routes they had done or wanted to do, including the Lochsa and Selway rivers, of which he had never heard. Allan's first unaccompanied stop was a hike in the Idaho White Cloud Mountains, but shortly after leaving the trailhead, he encountered snow over the trail and decided, given his lack of equipment, he should return to his car and alter his plan.

His next endeavor was attempting lower elevation trails in the Sawtooth Mountains in central Idaho, 20 miles northwest of the White Clouds. This time, however, he injured his Achilles tendon and had to quit. After limping back to his rig, he looked at maps and decided to drive north to Montana, then over Lolo Pass into Idaho. As he followed the Lochsa River west, he recognized the name of the Selway on a sign, the river mentioned during the campfire conversation with his kayaker buddies. It looked like an inviting place to hike, and he drove to the Selway Falls Guard Station. He had no maps of that area, but he obtained a general overview map from Charlie and Julie Dietz. After some discussion with them, he thought as long as he stuck to the trails the map would suffice. Given his bad ankle, he wanted to stay on flatter ground and aspired to hike upstream along the river.

On June 11, Allan was making good progress when he saw the plane fly over at an alarmingly low altitude for the canyon, and then disappear beyond a meander. He knew it was in trouble; then he heard two loud explosions seconds apart. Within minutes, he saw airplane flotsam floating down the river. He considered trying to get in the river; however, he was about 200 feet above it, and the slope was precipitous and covered with slippery pine needles. Already favoring his ankle, he chose not to risk the descent. Reflecting on that moment later, Allan said, "Needless to say, it was very disturbing to see a large piece of the fuselage go past. With the velocity of the current, it and the other pieces of the plane went by at a good clip, and by then there was no way I could be of any help. There was no sign of life, but I have often wondered whether there was anybody still alive as it went down the river."

Allan continued east up the uniform trail, and soon he was able to drop to the riverbank, but he still did not see anyone. Soon enough, however, he looked across the river and saw the three survivors—one appearing okay, one with perhaps a broken leg, and one supine. He began shouting to them across the river and recognized Charlie as the man who had helped him with the map the day before at Selway Falls. After paralleling the river, and shouting back and forth above the noise of the whitewater about the location of the Three Links Bridge, he began a steady march toward it. Then out of nowhere, a wet dog began following him.

In 2017, Allan commented, "After all these years, this part is pretty fuzzy; I don't have clear memories of Bryant. He struck me as very young - late teens, in comparison to the other ambulatory survivor I had shouted to across the river earlier, who had a beard and seemed to be older. The north side of the Selway has a southern exposure and hasn't much undergrowth, but the south side, where Bryant had travelled, faces north and had a lot of brush. I do remember being surprised that he had been able to travel as far as he did to get to the bridge."

After conversing with Bryant, it appeared that there was not any more help Allan could offer. "This might seem strange in hindsight, but I think it was based on the difficulty of getting along the south shore to the other two with my backpack and my lame ankle, my lack of medical training or serious supplies, and figuring that help was on its way. I crossed back over the bridge and ascended a trail toward some hot springs, although I never got close to them - I just found some place to camp."

On June 13, Allan was headed back down the Selway River Trail and encountered a wrangler running a pack string of mules. Upon a closer look, Allan, two thousand miles from home, saw the man sitting in the saddle on the mule and recognized him as Ian Barlow. While growing up in New Hampshire, Ian was a neighbor. Of course, Ian was less surprised than Allan. After all, Allan had signed in at the Selway Falls trailhead, leaving his name and address in the registration box, and he had left a car there with New Hampshire license plates. "Running into him [Ian] was truly surreal. Ian, in fact, was a best friend of my older brother, who passed away at the end of high school. On that day, I hadn't seen Ian in six years, and to have him suddenly pop up on a mule on the trail as I was walking back downriver was bizarre. I haven't seen him since." The two chatted for a while. In light of the recent events, however, the conversation mainly concerned the accident. Ian was supposed to ride out on the DC-3 from Moose Creek to Grangeville to collect shoeing supplies for the livestock.

He had recently moved from Alberta, Canada, and it was his first year on the Moose Creek District as a packer. The events surrounding the crash had rattled him. Allan told him his side of the story, and Ian encouraged him to report it to the USFS. As a result of this synchronicity, Allan became a key eyewitness of the accident. By the time he returned to his car at the trailhead, a note had been left on his windshield by a USFS special agent, requesting he give a witness statement. Nearly 40 years later, after being contacted about his role in the events, Allan wrote, "Not more than a few days ever go by that I don't think about the accident."

• • •

Once Allan and Bryant parted, Bryant made stout strides for Moose Creek. At mile two a Cessna airplane buzzed overhead. The pilot circled back, and at a low altitude wagged the wings of the plane, letting him know he had been seen on the trail—another reassurance that he was going to be safe. At about mile six, Bryant saw a pack string coming down trail toward him. As it drew nearer, he recognized the two people leading the string: his friends, the Kecks. He spoke briefly with them. They had many questions because they only had pieces of the story that had come from radio communications at the station. The Kecks knew a few of the people on the DC-3, and they asked him if anyone else had survived. He thought it was possible that others exited the plane, but he could only confirm two. Conscious of how tired he was, the Kecks gave him Art Seamans' government horse, Trigger, to ride the remaining two miles to the station. Confirming he was "okay," the Kecks continued downriver in hopes of helping other possible survivors.

At the top of the trail that climbs from the confluence of the Selway and Moose Creek onto the shorter of the two Moose Creek Ranger Station airstrips, Bryant dismounted. Realizing he was going to encounter station workers, he did not want to be embarrassed by underwear exposed by his tattered pants. He took off his shirt and wrapped it around his waist. Now shirtless, he swung back into his saddle and Trigger began trotting across the green meadow of the airstrip and up to the ranger station complex at the far end. Cindy Seamans was sitting on the steps of the ranger's house. She happened to be looking out across the airstrips, and watched Bryant emerge from the dense timber at their far edge. "Non-horse people would probably call Trigger a white horse, but he's a gray. For me, I think of heroes as riding white horses, mainly because I associated my dad, who was my hero, riding Trigger. But on reflection, the emotion was far more than that, and so appropriate when I realized it was Bryant, a survivor. Popularized for centuries in folklore and litera-ture, the white horse is a symbol often representing a hero, freedom, and strength, but at that moment to me it represented a sign of hope in a very desperate and unknowing time." Acquainted with Cindy, Trigger trotted up to her and halted. Bryant eased out of the saddle and awkwardly greeted Cindy as if he had had a normal day. Cindy remembered little of their interaction, but etched in Bryant's mind was her telling him, "Well, you better get up to the office, my dad is going to want to talk to you."

When Bryant arrived, Moose Creek employee Alan Carroll was

sitting on the step with Cindy. He reminisced that folks tuned to the forest radio knew a survivor was on his way to the ranger station. "We were all waiting and pacing around the station. It took a long time for the whole event to sink in…it was so hard for us to believe something so tragic could happen in such a place of innocence. My emotion at seeing Bryant was more relief than awe, like seeing a ghost." Alan distinctly recollects Bryant was mortified by his tattered clothes and was apologetic about being late for work. "He thought he could stay and go to work the next day, as though everything would work out."

When the three were done with the brief visit, Cindy took Trigger, and Bryant walked to Art's office. With relief in his voice even 40 years later, Bryant commented, "Art was absolutely terrific. One of the first things he said was, 'You have to call your parents to let them know you are okay.' He then looked me over to make sure I was not hurt." After a quick physical inspection, Art's response was, "Well, your shorts are still white, mine sure wouldn't be."

Although Bryant appeared to be in fairly good shape, Art arranged for an airplane to pick him up and take him to Grangeville for a medical evaluation. An hour after having arrived at the station, Bryant was being coerced back into an airplane—this time a Grangeville Air Service Cessna 206. Bryant was understandably nervous and obviously reluctant to fly again, "But I was nothing like my dog! It took three grown men to contain and wrestle Beetle into the airplane. He wanted nothing to do with it." The pilot of the airplane was later approached by a local newspaper for an interview. He reluctantly gave in with the caveat that he remain anonymous. In the succinct conversation, the pilot commented, "[Bryant] Stringham didn't seem scared, he was looking at the ground as we flew back and told me, 'Don't crash.'"

Bryant was met at the airport by his parents and was taken to the hospital, where a doctor tended to his injured finger and told him to get some rest. He was housebound in Cottonwood for a week. To pass the time, he read magazines and watched TV, but he was also inundated with phone calls from the media requesting interviews, and by government investigators. While Bryant never would be comfortable flying in airplanes again, he could not wait for that grueling week to be over in order that he could return to Moose Creek for the summer. On day seven, he convinced his parents he was fine. With Art's approval, his folks drove him back to the Grangeville Airport with his gear and dog, and they flew to Moose Creek in the same 206 that flew him out a week earlier. Once more, while Bryant was able to force himself to fly again, his dog had to be wrestled into the plane. Bryant worked the remainder of the summer and returned to high school in the fall, where he played football and graduated with the class of 1980.

148Z FUSELAGE DAYS AFTER THE ACCIDENT. (*USFS Collection*)

CHARLIE DIETZ AT THE SELWAY FALLS GUARD
STATION, 1979. (*Dietz Collection*)

ANDY TAYLOR, 1970S. (*L. Walters*)

THREE LINKS BRIDGE RECONSTRUCTION PROJECT
NEARING COMPLETION, 1978. (*Seamans Collection*)

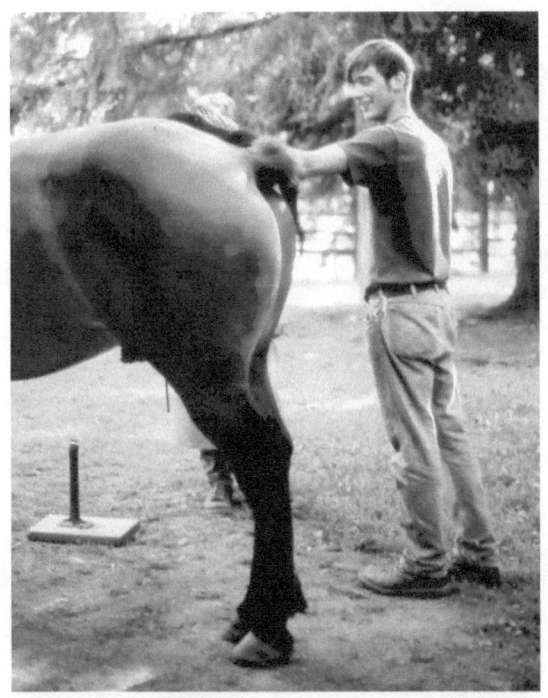

IAN BARLOW, 1980. *(USFS Collection)*

TRIGGER, MOOSE CREEK RANGER STATION WITH
AIRFIELD IN THE BACKGROUND. *(Seamans Collection)*

6

THE RESCUE—
EVERYTHING IN ABSTRACT

It is like that in the woods and even in the wide world generally—
the rescue of men and women, alive or dead, comes first...
But most people think they can be of help, and some even
seem born to rescue others, as poets think they are.
—NORMAN MACLEAN, *YOUNG MEN AND FIRE*

A row of dominoes began to cascade as word of the downed USFS DC-3 intensified. In Missoula, the Region 1 smokejumpers were organizing for the fire season with the second round of refresher training, combined with training for new hires. A few months earlier, Missoula had detailed some of the seasoned jumpers to Alaska and Silver City, New Mexico. It was a wet spring across the Southwest Region of the US, and half of the crew sent to Silver City returned to Missoula to assist with training. The loft, located at the northwest corner of the municipal airport, among other buildings collectively known as the Aerial Fire Depot, was quiet on June 11 when the call came in at 1140 hours requesting a rescue jump, including EMTs, be dispatched to the accident site on the Selway.

• • •

Helicopter 584 picked up Ranger Art Seamans at Moose Creek and flew him downriver to search for survivors. At 1205 hours, Art reported locations of the wreckage at Wolf Creek Rapid and upstream. Years later, Art wrote concisely of his flight observations: "I was told that there were three survivors on a boulder on the south side of the river. When we arrived, there were only two on the rock, Andy [Taylor] and Charlie [Dietz]. Andy, a good friend, waved at me, and I waved back, one of the more frustrating experiences of my life because we couldn't get close enough for a rescue." Art further explained that they could not get closer because there was not enough clearance for the helicopter's rotors owing to a stand of big cedars. And the rock was adjacent to the south bank. Then a few of the Missoula smoke-jumpers arrived by trail and rendered first aid.

• • •

For Art, seeing the wreckage kindled memories of his own near-death in an aircraft accident only 19 years earlier. During the preliminary construction of Bruce's Eddy Dam (Dworshak Dam), the US Army Corps of Engineers lacked the requisites for the project and in the fall of 1960 requested support from the USFS. The USFS assembled a six-man timber cruising crew. Because the area was so vast, a camp was established at the confluence of the North Fork and the Little North Fork of the Clearwater River. To efficiently move the crew from site-to-site, Johnson Flying Service of Missoula was employed to keep a helicopter at the camp, along with a fuel truck. Ken Roth was assigned as pilot for the Bell 47J (N2890B).

Cruise points were selected from aerial photographs. These locations were then mapped. The crew flew to each point, surveying timber from the low-water mark of the river to the estimated high-water mark of the incipient reservoir. For the narrow sections of the river, where the helicopter could not land, the points were marked from the air by dropping a bag of white lime powder. With the site marked, Ken would find the nearest upriver landing spot. Two men would then float downriver using an inflatable raft. Once the survey was completed, Ken retrieved the men from the next best downriver landing site.

Only two of the six men in the team could swim—Art and Al Langfield—so they became the designated boatmen for difficult survey points. Ken, Art, and Al eventually tired of the day-to-day routine of inflating and deflating the raft, unloading and reloading gear. Toward the end of the day with one survey point to complete by raft several miles below Big Island on the North Fork of the Clearwater, Ken suggested to Art and Al that he could squeeze into a tight spot on a sandbar. Enticed by saving time, they all agreed. Ken neatly landed the helicopter facing the bank of the river and signaled that he would keep the copter running while he waited. The first passenger left the copter on one side and Art on the other. As Art gathered his gear, the copter's landing skid closest to him gave way in the sand. In slow motion, the helicopter tilted toward him. Ken attempted to right it by lifting the tail over the river, but it dipped. The tail rotor struck the water and caused the copter to spin and tilt further. Unable to control the craft once the rear rotor blade was damaged, the tail swung around and smacked Art in the head, knocking him flat. Out of control, the aircraft lurched into the air and then fell back toward the river. The main rotor blades, constructed of laminated wood, thrashed the surface of the water and shattered into thousands of pieces. Powerless, it grounded itself in the icy river. When the hot engine was immersed in freezing water, it made a deafening blast. The Plexiglas windshield imploded and hit Ken in the head but resulted in an easier exit, although he struggled to free himself from his seatbelt. He finally waded ashore where Art was trying to comprehend what had happened. He had been knocked out momentarily and recovered in time to see the helicopter hit the water. Looking back 50 years later, he said, "I thought I'd seen death...I kept telling myself this is what it feels like to be dead. It is still a very blurry but vivid memory." Confoundingly, the helicopter had pivoted around Al, who never moved. "Al just stood there flabbergasted and watched the whole event."

The three men gathered their wits and realized they were a long way from nowhere with minimal rations. Ken and Art were soaked. A quick inventory revealed a handful of waterproof matches, but in the mayhem, the pump for the raft and the paddles had vanished. Someone suggested hiking upriver four miles to the Big Island airstrip. Once there, however, they had no means of communication. Suddenly, the cold still November air was ruptured by the sound of a motor. Out of the blue, a little outboard powered aluminum boat appeared, working its way downriver toward them. At the tiller, a small man with an angled white beard. His wife was in the bow. The couple beached their boat and explained that they had heard an explosion and had come to investigate.

Within 20 minutes of the crash, the three men were taken upstream by boat to a warm cabin. Wondering why they had not seen this little camp from the air, they perceived this polite couple operated a substantial moonshine still. When not actively working their mining claim, "the business" served for secondary income. The bootleggers had noticed the helicopter buzzing around the last few days and switched to working at night. Everyone entered an unspoken agreement. The kind couple even boated back down the river and found the other four members of the timber-cruising party and boarded them for the night. The bootleggers, who lived at the end of a dirt road, loaned Ken and Art their pickup to drive the 50+ miles southwest to the town of Orofino where they received medical attention and made a few phone calls. Ken's medical examination revealed a major gash on his scalp. Art's diagnosis revealed a hairline fracture of his skull. He was told it would heal in time.

Days later, Ken returned the pickup and then flew another helicopter south from Missoula to finish the job. Remains of the copter were later salvaged by paid log-drivers with a raft of wooden logs. After the timber cruise was completed, Art contemplated: life is short and life is chance. His close call persuaded him and his fiancée Joyce to move their wedding date from June 1961 to Christmas Day 1960.

• • •

Art's mind flooded with these memories, as the Selway helicopter hovered, him watching the two men islanded on the rock: his friend Andy was obviously in dire need of medical attention...Charlie, who he realized was the enthusiastic young man hired over the phone... both helpless...and the whereabouts of the others? Had anyone else survived? Art knew or had hired these passengers on the DC-3, and he felt personally responsible. The helicopter pilot nudged him, pointing out two other men—smokejumpers—wandering their way through the boulders along the south bank. He assured Art there was nothing more they could do. They headed back to Moose Creek.

• • •

Twenty-three-year old Wayne Williams was starting his third season as a Missoula smokejumper, and he was one of the crew who had returned from Silver City. He remembered the sequence of events well: "I was walking through the loft, and Bill Meadows [a more senior smokejumper] hands me two water bottles and told me to fill them up and then walked off. I fill the bottles and he walks back by me, collects his bottles and tells me I'd better fill mine up and gather my gear. I ask if something is up, and he just says, 'well kinda.'" For the Northern Region, June is early season and with training going on, no jump list had been formally put together, and the only people milling around the loft were the stragglers from Silver City and "the Overhead," meaning the base manager, foreman, and the squad leaders. "No one is saying anything, I grab my personal gear bag and everything else I need, and we gather in the ready room. Discussion about the mission starts to unfold, but we are in a hurry, so the briefing is carried on as we are loading into the plane. The briefing is led by Larry Eisenman [base manager] and Lowell Hanson. We are informed the mission is a rescue jump to a downed USFS DC-3 on the Selway River, and we are flying to its last known location. People are asking questions…How many people aboard? Just the pilots? Are they jumpers?…Larry says, 'Forest Service employees are on board the aircraft with pilots. We don't know much else.'"

In fewer than 20 minutes after the call, 14 jumpers, two spotters (Steve Clairmont and Norm Kamrud), rescue gear, and equipment were loaded on an Aero-Dyne DC-3 (N74589) bound for the accident site on the Selway.[5] The leaders of the mission continued to develop an action plan. These jumpers were positioned toward the tail of the aircraft, near the large open cargo door, in order that they could be early in the jump cue and also, as soon as the aircraft was over the site, better able to observe the situation on the ground. The EMTs of the group were among the men nearest the doorway, so they could be among the first on the scene as well. They were Lowell Hanson, Jeff Kinderman, John Nichols, and Larry Eisenman.

As soon as the DC-3 maneuvered over the river corridor, their strategies were abandoned. The only visible portion of the wreckage was the tail section wedged into the south bank of the swollen river. "The jumpers toward the front of the airplane could not overhear much of the planning discussion led by Larry and Lowell. 'Too noisy,'" Wayne explained, "You have to put the situation in perspective. This mission was not a routine fire call; we did not have the usual maps, reports, and briefings. Everything was in abstract." Adapting to the situation, they decided to split into two groups—one for the north side of the river, the other for the south. It was evident that once they were on the ground, there was no way to cross the river to reach the wreckage. After lots of circling and more discussion, they decided to drop the first eight jumpers on the south side and have them send

5   The DC-3 used on the mission was built as a C-47A (224064 S/N 9926). The plane was purchased by Aero-Dyne Corp of Renton, Washington, in 1969. Aero-Dyne flew the airplane until 1984 when it was sold to Saber Cargo Airlines of Charlotte, South Carolina. The significance of the aircraft is that it was flown in Operation Neptune on June 6, 1944 as part of the D-Day invasion of Normandy, France, during WWII and again in Operation Market Garden from September 17-25, 1944. After flying several other noteworthy missions, the plane returned stateside in July 1945. It was surplussed and ultimately purchased by West Coast Airlines of Seattle, Washington, which filed the paperwork to officially convert it to a DC-3.

a ground report by handheld radio before releasing the remaining jumpers and equipment.

At 1400 hours, the initial eight jumpers exited the rear door, steering for the south side of the river. Larry was first out the door, followed by Lowell. Two more sticks (groups) followed, with two jumpers per stick, led by John Nichols. Bill Meadows was with John, followed by the others: Jeff Kinderman, Floyd Whitaker, Wayne Cook, and Steve Carstens. Avoiding the risk of a river landing, the jumpers flew their chutes to the low ridge paralleling the river. Several of them caught their chutes in trees, the others had clean landings. At the last minute, Larry decided to deviate from the designated jump site in order to land closer to the tail section. Once on the ground, they gathered their personal gear bags and other rescue necessities, leaving their chutes for later retrieval. The south-side jumpers shared a few handheld Motorola radios for communications—one of which stayed with a group of three, remaining on the ridge to tend to the cargo drops.

For the next 15 minutes, five jumpers slid and scrambled over rocks and through the densely covered north-facing forest toward the river. Overhead, the Aero-Dyne DC-3 continued circling, as information filtered up from Larry and the other men on the ground. Larry was the first to reach the tail section. He looked inside and saw no victims or survivors. The seats and the floor had been ripped away. As he stared into it, Lowell, Jeff, and John cut off from the hill above the tail section and started searching the upstream side of the riverbank. Travel was difficult because the terrain often cliffed-out, forcing them to climb steep embankments.

At the same time, helicopters were working the corridor. One reported survivors upstream from the main wreckage. Larry radioed that he would stay with the tail section while the other three headed upstream. Jeff set a good pace with John and Lowell. John noted, "We continued upstream, we tried to work along the bank as much as possible. The conditions did not allow us to work right up next to the bank because of the rocks and the brush and trees and whatnot. There were a lot of times when you actually had to get away from the bank and move up into the hill. We tried to watch the bank for possible survivors and for any wreckage pieces; anything that the helicopter may have missed." In the process of scanning, John glimpsed a dog swimming in the river. He did a double take. Then he walked out into the water and helped pull it ashore. It was a German shepherd-retriever mix, later confirmed to be Bess, the pet of passenger Catherine Hodgin. John comforted the dog and placed it in a safe area.

As John was helping the injured dog, Jeff found the survivors. First he saw Charlie Dietz, sitting in a small boulder-strewn reach with his back against a rock. Charlie had observed the helicopter and fixed-wing air traffic in the area and knew rescue efforts were underway. He expected help to come by way of the water, a raft or boat. Since he did not realize smokejumpers had parachuted and were on foot, when Jeff approached he startled him. Charlie explained, "A guy popped up from a rock behind us and scared the daylights out of me." Jeff had passed his EMT courses, but was not yet certified. He did a quick assessment of Charlie, who insisted he was okay, and then turned his attention to Andy Taylor, who was lying on a rock five feet away. Jeff knelt beside him and took his vitals, then hollered downstream for John and Lowell because they were more medically qualified and carrying trauma bags. In 1979 trauma bags were new to the Missoula jumpers. They contained extensive first-aid equipment. John was a certified EMT, who had experience as a navy hospital corpsman and was a CPR and advanced first-aid instructor and was the first-aid instructor for the Missoula smokejumpers. In his off time, he worked for an ambulance service. Lowell was a former Special Forces medic and was also a first-aid instructor for the jumpers. The two began to work on Andy. Their exam revealed he had extremely low blood pressure, indicative of shock. They also found he had a compound fracture of his right leg, multiple bruises and lacerations on his right shoulder, back, and abdomen. He was coherent and some-what alert, but they could tell he was fading. His condition was such that they immediately put him in MAST pants (military anti-shock trousers—a medical device used to treat severe blood loss) to control his bleeding and stabilize him.

Meanwhile, the rescuers discussed options over radio chan-nels. One of the helicopter pilots was Forrest Gue with Minuteman Aviation, who was nearby when Andy needed to be transported across the river: "We talked about doing a 'short haul' where a rescuer is put down on a long line with a basket for the rescue and retrieval. It would have been instrumental in that type of situation, but in 1979 they were not approved, nor were we really equipped, but again we discussed it—something ad hoc...we would have really been sticking our necks out as we were not legally approved and safety became a concern. Things were happening so fast dur-ing the first day of the mission, and we had to move on to the next best and safest option."

After an hour of administering to Andy, he lost his pulse. John turned to Lowell for advice, with thoughts of starting an IV as a last resort. Immediately, they began CPR. John inserted a tracheal airway and used a pocket mask for the respiratory part. While John did the breathing, Lowell and Jeff relieved one another doing the cardiac compressions. They kept Andy alive another 35 minutes. Ultimately, they lost him.

. . .

Robert "Andy" Taylor died at age 59. He was born in Cheney, Washington, in December 1919, and not long thereafter his family moved to Orofino, before finally settling in White Bird in 1926—a place he called home the rest of his life. In his youth he was an avid musician who played the violin. Upon graduating from high school in 1939, and until he joined the Army during World War II, Andy worked seasonally for the USFS. After the war, he returned to White Bird, built his own house, and farmed until 1962, when he became an engineer with the USFS. In 1972, he married Susie Acree, who had two children from a prior marriage. Andy had planned to retire from the USFS in December 1979 in order to travel the US with his wife in their new fifth-wheel trailer. In addition to Susie and her two kids, he was survived by a large extended family. Andy is buried in the White Bird Cemetery.

The purpose of Andy's trip to Moose Creek was to sort out the failing domestic water system at the ranger station. In the 1970s, ranger districts across national forests, no matter the remote location, were required to have their domestic water brought into compliance with federal drinking water regulations. At Moose Creek, the source was supplied from a spring box above the ranger station complex. The gravity-flow system had worked properly for more than 50 years, but under the new regulations it had to be chlorinated. By 1979, two variations of the system with an incorporated chlorinator had failed. Instead of finding a solution to the problem, the ranger station crew found it easier to put a drop of chlorine in the water bottles before they were flown to Grangeville for testing. Moose Creek employee John McCarthy elaborates, "When we got the mix too strong, we were caught spiking the test flasks. The system and operators needed improvements. After Andy was killed, they abandoned the project. Eventually, years later, another spring was tapped at its source; a pipe was punched into the hillside to create an enclosed system whereby the water was enclosed."

• • •

Attention then shifted to Charlie, who after watching Andy die, had become more despondent. A check proved Charlie's vitals still stable. Lowell, John, and Jeff monitored his pulse and blood pressure and made him more comfortable until a means of moving him was agreed upon. After deciding his injured leg was not fractured the men wrapped it; however, a large hematoma was detected. They then bandaged cuts on his left hand and to prevent further stress, they strung tarps to shade him. Lowell put his jump jacket on Charlie, several down jackets, and eased a sleeping bag underneath him. By this time, other jumpers were packing down the supplies from the drop site down to the river.

While Lowell and the other jumpers were busy with communications and moving supplies, John asked if he could retrieve the dog found earlier. Lowell said sure. He went back, picked up the dog and carried her to the clearing. She was laid on some padding. She had a fractured leg and right paw, and her left paw was badly lacerated. He patched her up the best he could and let her rest.

While John tended to the dog, the communications network requested support from the Army National Guard based in Spokane. Two Guard helicopters were dispatched to the site. En route, they landed in Lewiston and refueled. While in Lewiston, coordinates were furnished and the Guard was notified that Missoula smokejumpers were on the scene. After refueling, one Guard ship flew directly to the site; the other detoured to Coeur d'Alene, Idaho, for an administrative stop before proceeding to the river. Two helicopters were dispatched because of the number of people reported to have been aboard the DC-3. The Guard helicopter flew up the Selway River and upon seeing the jumper's chutes hanging in trees, recognized the location of survivors.

Once the Guard surveyed the site, they hovered over the river. A plan was agreed upon by the copter crew and Lowell and his jumpers on the ground. John McColgin, a trained helicopter aid and certified EMT, was lowered on a hoist to the clearing. McColgin talked to Lowell and John Nichols, and following military protocol made his independent assessment of Charlie, as well as of Andy, even though Andy was dead. He complimented the jumpers on a job well done. Since Andy had died, McColgin informed the jumpers that technically the Guard was not allowed to hoist a body unless there was no other way to remove it because each hoist maneuver must meet a certain criteria within a risk-assessment plan to keep the crew safe. McColgin later told investigators that the risk to removing the body was too high, stating, "You see, the main rotor and tail rotor were maybe 15–20 feet from the snags on that side of the river, and it's tough. You get a gust of wind or something like that, and it could blow the tail rotor right into the trees, and then you've got four casualties instead of one."

The rescuers lifted Charlie from the edge of the river in a Stokes litter basket, a metal caged stretcher designed by the Navy for evacuations. This took time to rig, and after extended hovering, the

Guard pilots were concerned about having sufficient fuel to return to Lewiston. The communication network shared the pilots' fuel issue with the dispatchers at Moose Creek, Fenn Ranger Station, and Grangeville. Frenny Frensdorf, the pilot who was based at Fenn and flying a Jet Ranger on the rescue, volunteered the use of his Jet A fuel stored at Fenn. So the Guard ship left McColgin and flew 25 miles to Fenn to refuel. McColgin was then retrieved from the river by the second Guard ship, and they all rendezvoused at Fenn, where McColgin re-boarded the original helicopter in order to monitor Charlie on the flight to the helipad at Lewiston's St. Joseph Hospital. Following a quick examination by doctors there, the helicopter transported him to Sacred Heart Medical Center in Spokane.

After what Charlie has coined "the longest day of my life," he was relieved. Recalling the events decades later, Lowell joked, "I'll never forget I overheard Charlie telling one of the guys at the rescue site that day referring to me, 'I knew when I saw the old gray-haired smokejumper, I would survive.' I thought if I ever meet that smart-mouth kid again, I'd punch him in the mouth. And to think he also stole my jump jacket!" Lowell commented that he had been on eight other rescue operations as a smokejumper, including the 1959 Yellowstone earthquake, a suicide attempt, and a man who had blown himself up with dynamite, but this one was different, because it was the first time he had lost someone. Reflecting, John Nichols added, "I still think about the DC-3 accident often. It has become a part of my DNA and for good or bad has added to who I am today. There are things to be gleaned from it…positive things such as being more sensitive. The debriefings in those days were well meaning, but they aren't like they are today, and a lot of us ended up packing things around. I remember when I heard the news of Storm King.[6] My memories of the Selway DC-3 flooded back to me. I was in tears. But I remind myself, and others in this line of work do as well, that you don't want to go through these terrible things, but you don't always have a choice…we [first responders and firefighters] chose to go into this work. Of course, reasoning does not make the fact go away that I still feel bad that I could not save Andy.

THE REMNANTS OF THE HELICOPTER ART SEAMANS WAS ABOARD DURING THE NORTH FORK OF THE CLEARWATER RIVER TIMBER SURVEY, NOVEMBER 1960. (*Seamans Collection*)

---

6   Storm King (South Canyon Fire) occurred on July 6, 1994, near Glenwood Springs, Colorado. The wildfire killed 14 wildland firefighters. Among the victims were two McCall smoke-jumpers (Roger Roth and Jim Thrash) and one Missoula smokejumper (Don Mackey).

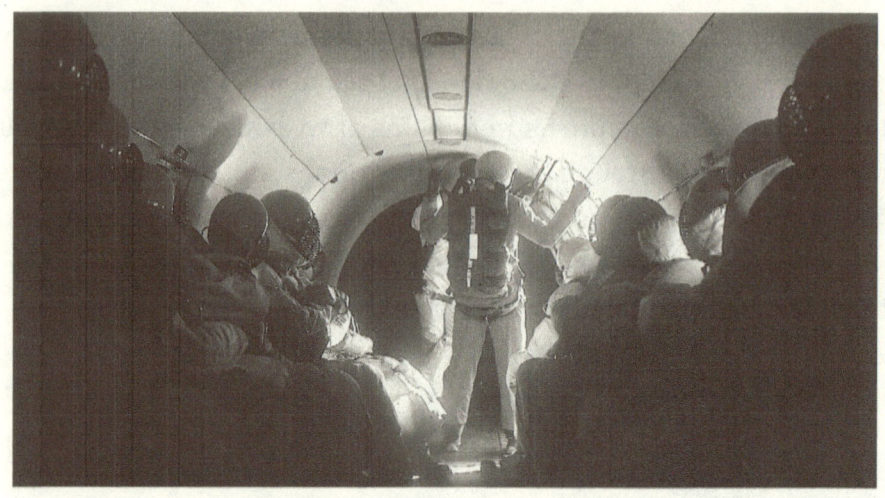

INTERIOR OF A CHRISTLER DC-3/C-47 LOOKING TOWARD THE REAR CARGO DOOR DURING A REGION 1 JUMP. *(W. Williams)*

WAYNE WILLIAMS, SHEARER AIRSTRIP, 1979. *(W. Williams)*

JOHN NICHOLS AND FLOYD WHITAKER, 1977. (*J. Nichols*)

FORREST GUE AT THE CONTROLS OF A BELL 206L1. (*F. Gue*)

CATHERINE HODGIN'S DOG, BESS, 1977. (*C. Mason*)

ANDY TAYLOR'S HEADSTONE, WHITE BIRD
CEMETERY, WHITE BIRD. (*R. Holm, Jr.*)

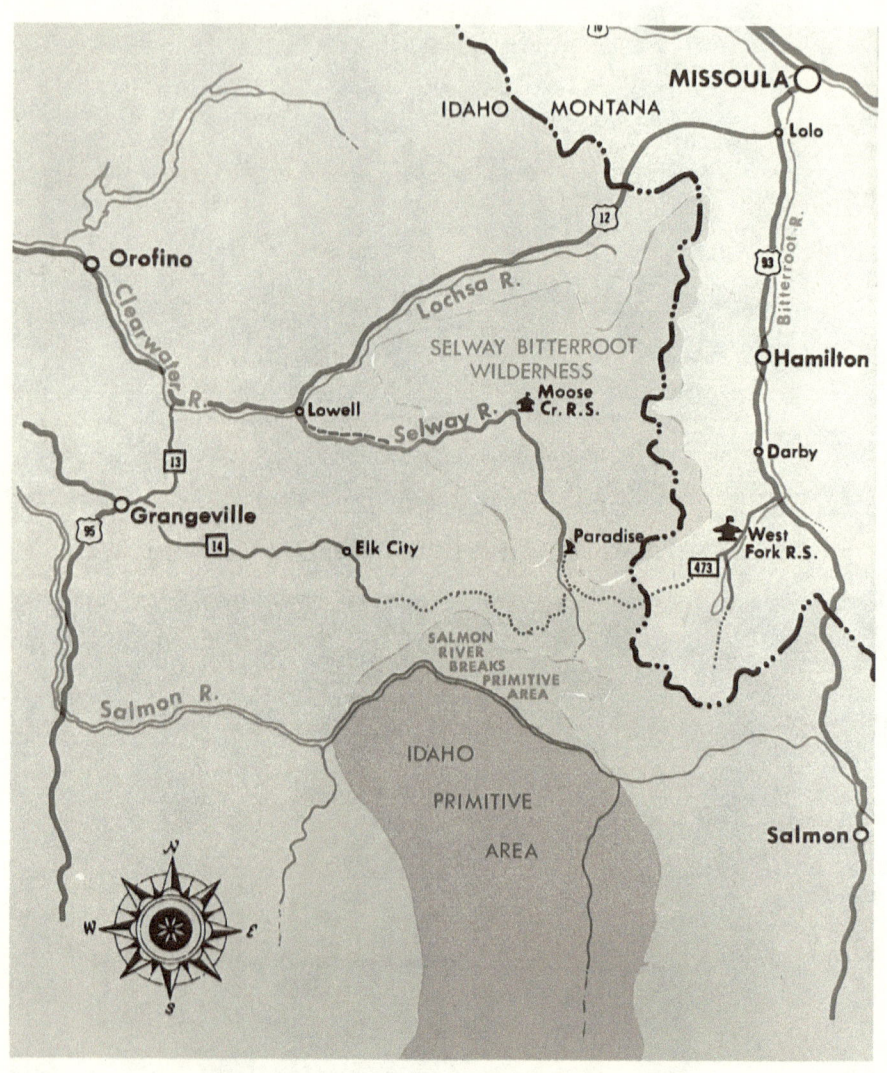

SELWAY-BITTERROOT WILDERNESS AND
SURROUNDING AREA, 1978. (*USFS Collection*)

7

NEARING THE END OF THE FIRST DAY

There is immediacy down in a canyon, particularly on a river
challenging to descend. So we tend to blot out the rest of the
world, or hold it in suspension while our attention is absorbed
in the day at hand, the hour, the moment. And these moments,
in recollection, define our passage and mark us forever.
—STEPHEN CUTRIGHT, "THE SELWAY PASSAGE"

As events unspooled on the ground with the eight south-side jumpers and information threaded to the circling Aero-Dyne DC-3, the spotters and remaining six jumpers in the plane selected a jump zone on the north side of the river with a south-facing slope in an open stand of mature ponderosa pine. The site afforded easier access up and down the river corridor by the trail. These jumpers included Wayne Williams, George Scott, William Duffy, Bernard Hilde, Steve Williams, and Dave Custer.

The north-side jumpers' mission was to search for survivors and victims, as well as clear out helispots as close to the wreckage as possible for logistical support. The first location was at Dry Bar, which became known during the rescue mission as "Survivor Bar." A second helispot was established near the mouth of Pinchot Creek, which was an open area with a sandy beach. This spot was a common campsite used by backpackers and river rafters. With all the jumpers on the ground, the spotters then made two separate cargo drops containing rescue gear and equipment—one on each side of the river. Evenly dispersed between the two sides were medical supplies and long boards that could be used as stretchers.

Wayne Williams was one of the last of the six smokejumpers to exit the Aero-Dyne DC-3; he was assigned the task of jumping with glass IV bottles. The bottles were carefully packed upright in layers of "Insulite," which was the latest type of foam pad. The layering mimicked an egg carton and cradled nine bottles. The casing was enclosed with a specially designed pack sewn by jumpers and was carried over the chest with forward facing shoulder straps. Wayne remembered, "George Scott was my jump partner, and he and Steve Clairmont told me again and again as we were getting ready to jump that I would not be able to see my feet once the chute opened because of the IV bottle-pack over my chest." From experience, George and Steve also instructed Wayne to forego a ground landing and head for a tree to avoid breaking the bottles. He did as advised and steered his chute into the wide spacing of branches of a several hundred-year-old ponderosa. He secured himself in the canopy of the tree 100 feet above the ground and George awaited him at the base of the tree. Then Wayne began lowering the IV bottles using his let-down rope. To keep controllable leverage and tension on the bottles, he strung the rope through a series of branches creating a makeshift Z-lift. Once George stashed the bottles safely on the ground, Wayne eased himself down with the same rope. The two then joined the others and began moving equipment to Dry Bar. Men set about their tasks, and once the helispots were cut out with hand tools and chainsaws, everyone started combing the riverbanks for survivors or victims.

The communication network informed the north-side jumpers of the situation across the river, and some of the jumpers on the north trail-side of the river went searching for the young man who had survived, and was reportedly walking up the trail toward the Moose Creek Ranger Station with a dog. Dave Custer handed Wayne a radio and told him to hike as fast as he could upstream. Wayne took off at a rapid clip. When Wayne had covered a half mile, Dave radioed him with a change of plans. The survivor had arrived safely at the ranger station. Wayne's new order was to flag down three rafts of commercial boaters headed downstream near him.

• • •

Lacking a way to move Andy across the river, the USFS checked the launch schedule of boaters who were on the Selway River above Moose Creek to see if they could aid. Moose Creek employee Warren Miller was flown two miles upriver at 1500 hours in a helicopter to where three rafts were beached above daunting Ham Rapid (Class IV). The floaters consisted of six commercial guides with American River Touring Association (ARTA), who were running the river on a preseason training trip. The guides had hiked downriver from their boats and were scouting the best route through Ham. Unable to land anywhere in the vicinity to communicate with them, Warren drafted a concise note and placed it in a bag attached to a clipboard with a streamer. The helicopter pilot maneuvered over the rafts and Warren dropped the message into one of the boats. It read: "FM—USFS, TO-ARTA, Stop at Moose Creek Ranger Station. We need your boat for evacuation of an air wreck /s/ Warren Miller."

The rafters already planned to stop at the station because with so much air traffic in the area they thought something might be amiss. In the fever of running Ham Rapid, however, they never saw the note until after stopping at Moose Creek and visiting with Warren and Larry Keown. who were waiting for them at the Tony Point Bridge below the Moose Creek Ranger Station. The ARTA group was comprised of Rick Byars, Steve Cutright, Jack Garnsey, Peter Grubb, George Wright, and Harvey Young. While all of them were experienced boatmen, one of the purposes of the trip was to license some of the guides who had never been on the Selway before in order to acquire the necessary experience to guide future commercial trips. Harvey Young, the lead guide, had been running the river since 1972, and the others deferred to him. The initial plan was to gradually work their way down the river from the Paradise Guard Station launch site to the take out above Selway Falls, 48 miles in three days. The pace afforded the group time to scout rapids, discuss the river's nuances, and examine good campsites. By the time the boatmen were docked below the Moose Creek Ranger Station they were already farther along on the first day than they had anticipated. But they were fatigued. They planned, in fact, on taking a full day just to scout and run the big rapids formed by the Moose Juice below the confluence of Moose Creek and the Selway. The flow of Moose Creek (more characteristic of a river) increases the volume of the Selway so much that it is called "Moose Juice" by floaters. Within these few miles are some of the more challenging rapids on the river—all Class IIIs and IVs—Double Drop, Wa-Poots, Ladle, Puzzle, Little Niagara, No Slouch.

Given the gravity of the situation and faced with the request for aid, Harvey and the other guides emphatically agreed, estimating three hours to reach the site. The ARTA team took off downriver, facing their toughest stretch of water. Harvey and Rick were in the lead boat, an 18-foot Green River raft, followed by Steve and Peter in the second boat, a similar-sized Avon Spirit raft, and George and Jack in the third boat, another Green River raft. Harvey stressed to the men at the oars of the trailing boats to stick as close together as possible in case there was an emergency. "It was a self-support trip. We were not wearing dry suits or even wet suits in those days, pretty much just regular clothes, good shoes, and a lifejacket. You did not want to swim in the cold spring runoff. Before we entered 'the Juice' it was 1, 2, and 3, then we shoved off...once you leave the shore you're gone and things happen fast. It was paramount to stick together."

Stress was further elevated by sunlit reflections from the water, making it more challenging to select runnable routes through rapids. After descending the first rapid, Harvey's apprehension was confirmed. The blunder is etched in Peter's memory: "I can vividly still see the sun coming down, lots of whitewater, and watching Harvey's boat out ahead of us going to one side of a major rapid, and we were entering it on the opposite side—where we did not want to be and knew we shouldn't be. I thought, 'Oh shit.' It was a scramble like that the whole way down." With skill, grit, and luck, the two trailing boats, without scouting any rapids, escaped flipping.

• • •

A mile and a half above Dry Bar, Wayne saw the ARTA boats and dropped off the trail toward the river to flag them down. By the time he picked his way down to the water the first boat with Harvey and Rick had passed. But Rick noticed Wayne's movement below the trail as they swept on, and he whistled back to the other two boats. By this time, Wayne was also waving and shouting and was able to flag the boat rowed by Jack and George, who stopped to pick him up. As he jumped in, Wayne introduced himself and donned a lifejacket. He then filled them in on the rescue and settled back. For the first time in hours, he had a few minutes to breathe. He studied the two boatmen and did a double take. The rower looked familiar. Wayne: "You look familiar, but I just can't place you." George said, "So do you." The two conversed for a couple of minutes and suddenly...Wayne blurted, "I'm the hitchhiker you picked up earlier this spring in your Volkswagen bus on Parrotts Ferry Road south of Vallecito [California] by the Stanislaus River near Columbia [California]." The two laughed in disbelief. Here they were in one of the more remote wilderness areas in the Lower 48 on an intense rescue mission when their trails crossed yet again.

As the three boats approached the upstream end of Dry Bar, Harvey and Rick were still in the lead, followed by Steve and Peter in the second boat. With Harvey at the oars and Rick in the front bailing, both focused downstream and saw the smokejumpers motioning to them.

"Harvey was really honking on the oars to position the raft at a 45-degree angle to the shore—we did not want to overshoot the landing." As the Dry Bar riffle picked up speed, Rick, in the stern of the boat started yelling. Harvey awkwardly glanced rearward over his right shoulder, and out of the corner of his eye saw an airplane propeller blade emerge vertically from the water. With no time for him to maneuver, the tall blade jacked the boat up on one side. The sharp blade had pushed its way up through the floor of the raft! As the boatmen awaited the dreaded sound of ripping neoprene, the boat eased down unscathed, and the propeller vanished into the void of the river. They were free.

As the two swiveled to look back, another blade of the propeller slowly rose again "like a ghost" and then disappeared. Rick explained, "There was no doubt what it was, but it took a few seconds for it to register. I was right next to it when the boat hit it...the blade came up on an arc and when it was straight up, we ran into it—right in the middle of our boat. The tube was pressed in quite a bit, and for a few seconds I thought we might wrap, but then the boat and current overpowered it. Then another blade came up behind us, and then we saw it no more. It was one of the strangest experiences of my life... just so bizarre you can't make it up." Harvey again focused on reaching the shore. The other boatmen behind were equally astounded.

With all three boats at the site, the boatmen were briefed by the smokejumpers—most notably about the need for a boat to transport Andy's body across the river to the helicopter landing near Pinchot Creek. The magnitude of the accident weighed on their minds, but the need for action left little time. From the interaction with the jumpers, Peter best remembered the overwhelming mutual respect, "They were impressed at the risk we had taken to reach the accident site, and we were equally impressed they had jumped out of an airplane into the dense forest, all in an effort to help each other."

Andy's body was loaded onto the front of one of the ARTA boats and rowed downstream to the heliport. A helicopter then flew his body to Moose Creek, and it was in turn met by a fixed-wing aircraft for the final flight to Grangeville.

• • •

At about the same time as ARTA, the USFS's Selway River Ranger Peter "Pete" Mills arrived at Pinchot Creek by helicopter with his boat in a sling. Pete, fit, slender, dark-haired, with wire rimmed-glasses, exited the copter and helped the pilot release his boat and gear. As the helicopter throbbed off into the distance, the ARTA crew began to set up camp for the night and gestured for Pete to join them. As he hauled in his gear, he recognized the voice of Harvey Young. He knew Harvey from the Middle Fork of the Salmon River, where they both guided for competing companies, and the two had also run a private float trip together in the Grand Canyon years earlier. They made themselves comfortable and swapped stories while preparing dinner.

For Pete, Monday June 11, 1979 was to be his inaugural launch for his second season on the Selway. Everything changed when he walked through the door of the West Fork Ranger Station in Darby, Montana. West Fork was his customary stop on his way to the Paradise launch site at the upper end of the river in order to visit with Lloyd Reeseman, the head of the river program on the West Fork Ranger District of the Bitterroot NF.

Pete, a graduate student at the University of Montana in the College of Forestry, arrived at his summer home at Selway Falls a few weeks earlier, where he lived in one of the wall tents erected behind the USFS's Selway Falls Guard Station. The early season trips on the Selway are dependent on the flow, which is measured on a gauge located in the river at the Paradise Guard Station near the launch site. Readings of six to eight feet on the gauge are considered high, with occasional readings running as high as 11 feet. Normal flows for the Paradise gauge range from two to six feet from mid-May to mid-July.

Most commercial outfitters on the river use six feet as the sensible upper cutoff and will launch trips then if the expected temperatures and trend indicate falling flows. As an agency, the USFS in the late-1970s issued safety guidelines specifying only large rafts be used for flow rates five feet or more, and small rafts at flow rates of two feet or less. What constitutes a "safe" craft also is linked to the operator's experience, knowledge of the river flows, and the quality of their equipment.

Pete agreed with the six-foot cutoff. In the spring of 1979, the river peaked at 7.5 feet on May 24 and progressively decreased through June 5, when it declined to 4.9 feet. Over the next several days, it dropped steadily, and on June 11 it was running an ideal 3.2 feet. Even in the three-to five-foot range, the Selway is still considered by seasoned veterans to be "challenging, but not overwhelming."

The Moose Creek District had two boats to run the Selway—one for early-season high water and one for late-season low water. The high-water boat was an 18-foot Green River raft built by Rubber Crafters that could safely carry four or five people with their gear. The low-water boat was a 13-foot Miwok raft built by Campways/Riken. Both boats had solid floors and were not self-bailing—if they ran through big rapids, they had to be bailed by hand (now modern boats with inflated floors self-drain). Pete usually had someone along to use a bucket.

He was already regarded as an experienced boatman, clearly a requisite for his job. Pete had come to river running through a friend he met during undergraduate studies at the University of California, Santa Barbara. Through this connection, he began commercial guiding with Ron Smith, the owner of Grand Canyon Expeditions on the Colorado River. The seasonality of river-guiding and the connections among boatmen led Pete to migrate north to Idaho, working several other rivers, such as the Salmon. While he was wintering in Missoula, a friend noticed an advertised position on the Selway River as a USFS river ranger on the Moose Creek Ranger District and urged him to apply. He held the position through 1980.

• • •

The Selway River Ranger program was newly inaugurated. Like the administration of other western rivers, the Moose Creek Ranger District realized the need to manage the popular resource of the upper wilderness stretch of the river with a supervisory presence.

The program began in summer 1972 under the direction of Moose Creek Wilderness Resource Assistant Dick Walker, who appointed Dick Hulla as the first river ranger. Hulla hiked the river trail to monitor canyon activities. At the same time, the Moose Creek District paid him to get whitewater training, as well as experience on the river from Elwood Masoner (commercial outfitter) and Cal Tasanari (USFS boatman on the North and South Forks of the Flathead River). By 1973, Hulla was running regular trips, mostly between Running Creek and the end of the road upriver from Selway Falls. He then drove his boat and equipment to Kooskia, where he was picked up by Grangeville Air Service and shuttled back to the private ranch airstrip at Running Creek. Much of the 1973 season was spent cleaning up decades of garbage collected from campsites, and hauling it out, along with segments of abandoned cable crossing rigs: one at Bear Creek, one at Magpie Creek, and one at Otter Creek.

The same year, he and Art Pope spent two weeks at the Shearer Guard Station on the upper Selway drafting a new management plan for the river. Art was Moose Creeker Clem Pope's brother, and he was associated with an outdoor program at the University of Oregon and had years of experience as a boatman on western rivers, including the Selway. Pope, Hulla, and Walker surveyed other western river management plans from places such as the Yampa (Utah), the Colorado (Arizona), and the Green (Utah) rivers and then tailored a plan to fit the objectives of managing the Selway corridor. The resulting policy outlined a number of new practices, but most noteworthy was the restriction placed on launches, especially for private parties. Owing to the demand for float trips the system established a lottery. Once established, the West Fork Ranger District of the Bitterroot NF managed the lottery and issued permits. The practice remains. The Selway has one of the more restrictive launch programs in the Wild and Scenic River System, allowing only one group per day, with no more than 16 people per group during the floating season. While the main launching site just below the Paradise Guard Station was on the West Fork District, the majority of the river's reach was on the Moose Creek District, and thus the establishment of the river ranger position.

· · ·

Although the job description of the ranger included checking on permits, illegal launches, and unlawful campfires, it also included administrative purposes, such as moving trail crews, smokejumpers, upper-level personnel, and keeping a supervisory presence. Because of the length of the river and the logistics of driving from Selway Falls over Lolo Pass by Highway 12 and then through the Bitterroot Valley via Highway 93 and then taking the long, winding dirt road to Paradise, trips routinely started on a Monday morning and ended on Friday above Selway Falls.

Funding for the program was limited, and Pete was the only paid employee from June through August-end. It then relied on a volunteer, who occupied the position largely as a shuttle driver who hauled the boat and gear from Selway Falls around to the upper put-in at Paradise. For the 1979 season, the volunteer was Julie Dietz.

• • •

As Pete closed the door behind himself at the West Fork Ranger Station, he sensed something was awry. Lloyd, usually rather casual, rushed out to greet him, asking whether Julie was waiting in the van. Pete assured him she and another person were in the tow vehicle, waiting. Then Lloyd gave a description of the morning's tragedy. Scant details were known, but he had confirmed that Julie's husband Charlie was on the airplane. Not wanting to worry Julie unnecessarily, he told Pete not to tell her about the accident yet, to tell her there was a change in plans. Lloyd said, "They need you and your boat at the accident site to help in the search for survivors. An airplane is waiting for you in Hamilton [Montana]. The plane will fly you and your gear directly to Moose Creek. Another airplane is there as well, and it is for Julie and the other fellow to fly directly to Grangeville."

As the news sank in, Pete spun around and headed back out to the van. He jumped in and told Julie and the other passenger, Terry Kincaid, that they needed him in Hamilton. Terry worked for the Bureau of Land Management (BLM) as the outdoor recreation planner at the Cottonwood Area Office in Idaho, where he also managed the Agency's river program. He and Art Seamans had met years earlier, when Art was with the Slate Creek Ranger District; their management objectives often overlapped. The two became fishing buddies, and through their professional and personal friendship, Art arranged for Terry to go along with Pete on the early season patrol.

The ride to the airport was silent. Pete focused on looking out the window observing the lush, stunning Bitterroot Valley in hues of spring—a contrast against the snowcapped Bitterroot Range to the west. The smell of the fresh grasses filled the air. Yet the view was secondary to Pete's thoughts and his questions about what lay ahead of him on the Selway. As Julie slowed to make the turn from the highway onto the rural road leading to the Ravalli County Airport, the sound of gravel kicked up by the tires of the van snapped him out of his trance.

They pulled the vehicle into the small airport proper—just a few hangars and a single paved runway. Two single-engine Cessnas from Grangeville Air Service were waiting on the ramp with pilots pacing alongside. The boat sitting on the flatbed trailer was partially rigged, so Pete began breaking it down and deflating the tubes of the raft. One of the pilots began grabbing the gear out of the van, hefting it to determine its weight and proper place in the airplane for a balanced load. Shortly the plane was fully loaded and Pete crawled across the pilot's seat to the right seat in front of the Cessna 206. The pilot followed him, closed the door, yelled, "Clear!" The engine cranked to life. The high-wing Cessna lurched and whined as the pilot taxied out to the paved runway and lifted into the air. Within minutes, the plane climbed over the vast Bitterroot Mountains. Once over the divide, the pilot started a slow descent, homed in on the Moose Creek airfield where he then maneuvered the plane into a tight circle and landed. As the wheels touched down, it was nearly 1600 hours. The airstrip

RICHARD H. HOLM, JR.

was teaming with activity—helicopters and numerous people—both uncommon sights at the remote outpost.

The plane was greeted by several Moose Creek personnel, who were glad to see Pete. A plan was promptly formulated among Pete, Art, and Emil. The discussion of launching the boat and its gear at the confluence of Moose Creek and the Selway just below the airstrip was ruled out. Pete recounted that launching from that point was a logistical nightmare for several reasons: "First of all, the gear needed to be moved down to the river—not a long trail from the end of the runway, but a steep grade, and a distance when one is carrying it on one's back. No wheels are allowed in a wilderness area. Also, I didn't have someone to help me bail, and I didn't want to run the Moose Juice without one." Sorting these snags, the group finally decided to fly Pete by helicopter with his boat and gear to Pinchot Creek.

• • •

Unaware of why Pete abruptly canceled the patrol and shuttle drive, Julie found herself sitting in the back seat of a single-engine Cessna owned by Grangeville Air Service cruising over the Bitterroot and Clearwater mountains from Hamilton to Grangeville. Terry Kincaid who was supposed to accompany Pete, sat up front in the seat next to the pilot. She said, "I remember clearly wondering why they kept looking back at me. There was a lot of radio traffic throughout the flight, and I think now they were checking to see if I was paying attention. I wasn't. I was oblivious." As Julie and Terry got out of the plane in Grangeville, they were met by Jan Blake and Julie Hauger from the Moose Creek office. The two ladies then informed her of the DC-3 accident. Charlie's condition

148

was not known. They then drove her to the nearby home of Don and Karen Easthouse, where other families and USFS personnel had gathered for mutual support.

Word now reached Julie that Charlie had survived and was flying to Sacred Heart Medical Center in Spokane. "I was overwhelmed with emotions. We were just kids, with barely a bank account." Julie's car was parked at Selway Falls, and she was in no condition to drive. Friend Yvette Martin swooped in. The Dietzes had met her and her husband Jon while living in their trailers at Three Rivers the summer before. Jon was a seasonal USFS employee on the Clearwater NF and a student at Washington State University in Pullman—both had ties to Washington. Yvette's parents, Chuck and Jackie Moran, lived in Spokane. Yvette drove Julie, along with two dogs and Yvette's two children, to the hospital—a distance of 180 miles. The couple reunited at 0300 hours in the morning.

• • •

As daylight waned, eight jumpers on the south-side of the Selway camped in the clearing next to the river. The area needed to be combed again in the morning and more gear brought down to the river from the landing sites on the ridge. In the last light, helicopters slung equipment across to the men: sleeping bags, water, food. ARTA also used its rafts to move material between the locations and to move the injured dog. When the dog was lifted out of the raft at Dry Bar, some were persuaded the humane thing to do was to put her down. On hearing the suggestion, Bill Duffy, who would later become a minister, stepped in and said, "Absolutely not!" He picked her up and carried her to the upper end of the bar where his gear was stashed. It was dark by then, and Bill fashioned a shelter and set the dog on blankets inside. At one end of the shelter he kindled a small fire and kept it going all night to keep the dog warm. He and Wayne Williams bedded down under tarps next to the shelter.

• • •

On that night as the Selway River canyon became cloaked in darkness, many USFS employees lit Coleman lanterns at dispatch desks across the Nez Perce NF. In preparation for what everyone knew would be another long day of unknowns, they continued to collect and share information. According to dispatcher logs, Fenn Ranger Station announced, "10-7" (out of service) at 2155 hours. Others followed: Larry Eisenman (Dry Bar) at 2200 hours, Moose Creek at 2312 hours, Grangeville at 0110 hours (June 12), and the Grangeville Smokejumper Loft at 2230 hours. The logs were abnormally extensive, with Moose Creek totaling 16 pages and others more. The final entry made by the dispatcher at the Grangeville Smokejumper Loft read, "End of day. 3 survivors, 2 OK now. 1 died on beach. No news on others. John Wayne died." The dispatcher's note regarding the pop culture news of John Wayne's death had also trickled into the rescue operations and had been a topic of conversation on the river.

• • •

Radio communications were reestablished the following morning at 0400 hours by Moose Creek when it declared "10-8" (in service). Bill and Wayne awakened by their smoldering fire and a large, freshly-cut Douglas fir. They were dumbfounded. They had not noticed the tree when they went to sleep. After inspecting its base, they saw it was splintered as if it had been sheared in a windstorm. Yet there had been no wind overnight. Then they looked overhead and realized they were standing at the foot of the tree struck by the DC-3 in its last few seconds.

As Bill, Wayne, and the other north-side jumpers began their day, the south-side jumpers did as well, and they trekked up the ridge and hauled down the last of their gear and chutes. At dawn, Pete Mills and the six ARTA boatmen broke camp and readied their boats to ferry the south-side jumpers and their gear to the north-side near Pinchot Creek for easier copter retrieval. The helicopters were back at work, and one of their first missions was transporting the dog to Grangeville, where a veterinarian met them.

At 1200 hours on June 12, the Missoula jumpers were informed that they would be relieved of their duties and were to return to their base for debriefings. Several of the regular jumpers asked to stay. As a result, John Nichols, Wayne Cook, Jeff Kinderman, Steve Carstons, and Wayne Williams remained. The other jumpers were shuttled by helicopter pilot Frenny Frensdorf in a Bell Jet Ranger to Moose Creek, where they were then flown by fixed-wing back to Missoula.

The ARTA boatmen, thanked for their work, continued their journey downriver checking each eddy along the way for possible victims. Pete Mills stayed on. He worked 13 days before making a complete routine river patrol. He also was crucial in general river operations moving people down the river. Pete was joined by Alan Carroll, a Moose Creek employee who had arrived early in the season for spring trail work. Alan worked with Pete on-and-off for nearly ten days— mainly running several miles of river below the wreck site to look for bodies and debris—usually as far as Coon Creek. At the end of the designated reach, a helicopter retrieved Pete, Alan, and the boat and flew them back to the upriver clearing.

RIGHT WING OF 148Z SUBMERGED AT THE HEAD OF
WOLF CREEK RAPID, JUNE 12, 1979. (*R. Byars*)

THE ARTA BOATMEN AT CAMP ON THE EVENING OF JUNE 11,
1979. L TO R: PETER GRUBB, HARVEY YOUNG, JACK GARNSEY,
GEORGE WRIGHT, AND STEVE CUTRIGHT. (*R. Byars*)

SLING LOAD OF RAFT GEAR TO PINCHOT CAMP, JUNE 1979. (*T. Kincaid*)

PETE MILLS, 1970S. *(C. Conley)*

USFS RAFT FERRYING PEOPLE NEAR ACCIDENT SITE, JUNE 1979. *(M. Hill)*

8

FATE?

To this day I have never looked up the Selway River without
saying a prayer to my older brother Patrick. He was my best
friend, and hero. A part of my heart is forever left on that river.
—EDDIE MCGREEVEY,
LETTER TO RICHARD H. HOLM, JR. (2024)

The phones at USFS offices rang continuously as word about the
crash rippled outward. Steve Waterman, the public affairs officer
for the Nez Perce NF, took the media lead and the initial calls from
relatives and friends. Within the first 48 hours, Waterman reported
that his office had been contacted by 43 newspapers, radio, and television stations about the crash.

USFS dispatch logs from June 11 and subsequent days reveal
the turmoil. Dozens of entries regarding inquiries from friends and
loved ones either on or suspected to be on the aircraft were common:
"Called Mr. Ken Jaseca in Chicago...told him his nephew Mr. Russo
was not aboard the a/c...Marilyn TerKeurst called. Is planning to

fly out 6.12. Will call back in morning...Howard Easthouse [Don's brother] called. Call him as soon as we know anything. Rbt. Cook's father called. Told will call as soon as we have any info. Chris Hayne called R-4 wanted info on pilots..." Art Seamans and Larry Keown took the principal roles in tending to the extended family of Moose Creek employees. Powerless and needing proximity, a handful of parents with children who were on the DC-3 gravitated to Moose Creek in desperation—among them the Lebers, McGreeveys, and Marilyn TerKeurst.

Kevin Leber's father, Walter P. Leber, understood the complexities of rivers and their hydraulics better than anyone on the search, rescue, and recovery mission. He was an engineer with the US Army Corps of Engineers and had traveled the world during World War II, thereafter working in the North Pacific and the Ohio River Basin. Most notably, he served as the lieutenant governor of the Panama Canal Zone, and later as governor. In an effort to assist, he and his wife chartered a plane to the Moose Creek Ranger Station and spent several days on the trail searching for their son and offering expertise.

Dolly Koons, part of the Moose Creek crew, and who was usually at Shearer, was at the station in the days following the accident. She spent uncountable hours comforting a mother of one of the unfound victims. There were no words, but Dolly filled their void by taking her on walks near the station and by sitting on the banks of the Selway with her.

Patrick McGreevey's family also chartered a single-engine Cessna with Minute Man Aviation to Moose Creek. Only five years earlier, Patrick's parents, Edward and Dollie, had lost their son Mark to an accident; the thought of losing another son was incomprehensible. Knowing Patrick's mental and physical toughness, they believed that he would be found alive. One of Patrick's younger brothers, Eddie, remembered, "Following the news of my brother's plane crash, my father and I sought permission from the Forest Service to participate in the search efforts that were underway. The Forest Service was reluctant to allow any non-employee into the area. Fortunately, after much deliberation, they said they would allow us into the area, contingent upon securing air travel to Moose Creek. From there, the Forest Service arranged a helicopter flight to get us to a sandbar near the accident site."

Eddie and his father were joined by two close friends, Steve Naprstek and Pat McGree. Once at Pinchot Creek, the four split into two groups so that they could search both sides of the river. Eddie and Pat searched the trail-less side of the river and hiked up to the Three Links Bridge, which they reached at nightfall on their first day. "At the pack bridge, we made a small fire and tried to get some rest. Nothing could have prepared me for what I would experience the next day. The river was swollen to its banks, making travel arduous. Since there were no trails on the south side of the river, the combination of downed timber, brush, and high water made travel along the river's edge almost untraversable. Several miles below the pack bridge we came upon the fuselage and spent the rest of the day working below it. Debris was scattered everywhere…a lot was pinned to the riverbanks by swift current or had accumulated in backeddies. Remnants of camping gear, clothing, shoes, sleeping bags, and other personal items were apparent. To say the least, it was a horrific sight."

On the morning of June 15, Eddie and his friend were about a mile below the crash site, still looking for his missing brother. They were two of the many searching along the river. Men in rafts and divers were also working the same stretch of water; they observed two divers lift a lifeless body into one of the rafts. "Although I could not make a distinct recognition of the body, I thought I could recognize my brother's burly moustache." Denying what he was seeing, Eddie happened to look across the river at two men staring at the same scene—it was his father and his father's friend. "My father had a clearer and closer view and was able to confirm that it was in fact my brother. The Forest Service then shuttled my dad and his friend to Moose Creek. Pat McGree and I were rafted across to the helicopter landing site, and boarded a helicopter for Moose Creek, where I was reunited with my dad. Needless to say, it was very somber when my father informed me that the body we both saw was my brother. Living in Missoula, and being an avid steelhead fisherman, I have passed the Selway River hundreds of times where it joins the Lochsa River. To this day I have never looked up the Selway River without saying a prayer to my older brother. He was my best friend and hero. A part of my heart is forever left on that river."

• • •

Disturbing stories began to trickle in to employees and volunteers on the Moose Creek Ranger District. In the succeeding days, months, and years many people contended that they had had a brush with fate by missing the 0930-hours' departure of 148Z from Grangeville on June 11. Some context is necessary. The Guard School was a multiday event with typically 40–60 people in attendance. Many were new hires, some were returning seasonal employees, some district management, many were experts who were invited as speakers or to conduct specific training. Moving dozens of people in and out of the backcountry takes considerable planning, and as anyone knows who has spent time coming and going from the remote region for work or recreation, more hours are consumed in the planning stages of the trip than time in the field. Owing to the logistics, people's plans were in flux leading up to June 11. Art's final handwritten manifest for the flight wavered around 14, but he anticipated as many as 20 people. To accommodate a spectrum of schedules, he left open the option for a second DC-3 flight, as had been done in the past, but on the preceding days he had also reserved multiple flights by single-engine aircraft with Grangeville Air Service. Thus, many people claimed they missed the flight. Nonetheless, there are stories of individuals who Art penciled in on his final list, and some stories from those who in the days and weeks leading up to the wreck had considered taking the 0930-hours' flight.

• • •

The winter before the fateful flight, Gary Miller and Dave Clarke skied deep into the Selkirk Mountains in northern Idaho to a remote parcel owned by Gary's family. The Selkirks are known for their rocky, craggy, high altitude, cirques and lakes. The previous fall, along the shoreline of one of these lakes, with the help of a fellow Moose Creeker, Curt Green, Gary had started the foundation to build a log cabin. Then from January through May, Gary and Dave cut trees, skidded logs, and started log work. The goal was to finish the walls and rafters and place the ridgepole before reporting to Moose Creek for the 1979 season. They were scheduled to be in Grangeville on June 11 to catch the DC-3 flight, but by the time each wall log was peeled and scribed, they were lucky to set four logs a day. Working 15-hour days, the two gradually realized they were not going to be able to set the ridgepole. Gary worried that if the ridgepole was left on the ground, it would begin to rot. Additionally, the cabin needed to settle over the summer before putting on the roof, and Gary did not want to prolong the project another year. On May 30, calculating the time and effort spent on the cabin and their aim, they decided to extend their stay another ten days and face the consequences of showing up late for Guard School. Since Gary and Dave were both seasonal USFS employees, they were able to borrow a radio from the local ranger district for communications. Their change in plans was relayed to Gary's father in Spokane.

The ridgepole was lifted with the last of daylight on June 9. The two men paused for a moment to snap a picture of their accomplishment. The next morning, they broke camp and hiked the strenuous six-miles through the sloppy snow with skis strapped to their packs, meeting Gary's father at the nearest road. It was late in the day, on June 10, when they were picked up. There was no time to drive to Grangeville and collect their gear, rations, and other supplies for the summer ahead. Therefore, Gary spent June 11 in Spokane, and Dave in Missoula, shopping for new gloves, trail pants, boots, film, and visiting local bookstores. News about the crash soon reached them. When Dave thinks back to June 1979, and looks at the photograph Gary took of him sitting on the ridgepole, he is humbled by life's convolutions. When the season ended at Moose Creek, Gary resumed work on the cabin and finished it. For decades thereafter, the two friends visited it on winter skiing excursions.

• • •

Dave and Gary were not the only ones with such a story. Other people underwent a change of plans. Bob McCue, who Art had hired as a member of the trail crew, called days before, telling Art he had taken another position with the Agency. Others on the list tended to be returning seasonal employees.

On the morning of June 11, Dick Kuhl and Mary Gramling met in Missoula intent on catching the first flight in. Dick had started at Moose Creek in 1974, and Mary had come to Moose Creek as a volunteer student in 1978, while attending the Sterling Institute located in Craftsbury Commons, Vermont, a private preparatory school for a college based on outdoor curricula. For the 1979 season, she was returning as a paid trail-crew employee. Mary, who credits her German heritage for always being punctual, had several personal matters arise that delayed their departure to Grangeville by several hours. Speeding along Highway 12 in Dick's Volkswagen bus, the two chatted and enjoyed the scenery. As they approached the turnoff to the Selway River, a large and lovely butterfly fluttered across the highway, paused in mid-air, collided with the bus, and splattered across their windshield. "Dick and I looked at each other shocked."' Forty years later, Mary reflected, "The butterfly was so beautiful! The moment of the butterfly in the sunlight in that place is ingrained in my memory...it was a strikingly odd moment of splendor and then it was over. Dick and I both thought it was a visible premonition of something, even then. Hours later, we learned about the accident and determined that about the time we had this premonition was when the DC-3 crashed. I still think about it."

Jan Blake and Julie Hauger usually attended the Guard School to help organize paperwork for employees. They were feeling overwhelmed because of the number of volunteers and new employees, and they declined the earlier morning flight—instead choosing one later in the afternoon or on the following day.

A new hire, Laura Till arrived in Grangeville on time, but decided to stop at the grocery store for the season's supplies. Knowing she was running late, she contacted Art and they agreed she could catch a later flight.

Carol Mytron, a returning trail-crew worker, happened to call Don Easthouse on June 4 to verify her seat on the DC-3 flight to Moose Creek for Guard School. He confirmed she was on the manifest, then out of the blue gave her the option to ride in early with Grangeville Air Service on Friday June 8 because after trailing in the District stock for the season, an empty plane was chartered to fly Charlie Dietz, Ian Barlow, and him out. She took the early flight, and she was with Warren Miller, monitoring the radio at Moose Creek, when the news reached the ranger station.

Vern Paulson, a new hire on the District, was listed on Art's final manifest as passenger number 14. His story for canceling is unknown, but at some point Art crossed off his name.

Two other Sterling Institute students, Cheryl Warren and Zannah Crowe, who were volunteers on the Clearwater NF and were encouraged by their supervisor, Mel Fowlkes, to attend the Guard School. They discussed flying in from Grangeville, then decided to hike in instead.

Don McPherson, a conservation officer with the Idaho Department of Fish and Game, who was scheduled as a guest speaker during the training, had a friend die unexpectedly. He canceled to attend the funeral.

Gary Power, a wildlife conservationist, also with the Idaho Department of Fish and Game, was scheduled on the flight to attend the Guard School. He canceled a few days earlier to take a personal leave-day because of stress related to his difficult divorce. To clear his head, Gary left Lewiston on Sunday morning June 10 and picked up his horses, which he boarded with an outfitter located at the confluence of the Lochsa and Selway rivers. He unloaded his animals and overnight camping gear at the Coolwater Ridge Trailhead. The next morning, he awoke on top of the ridge and looked out over the Selway River drainage. As he sat there, he watched the USFS DC-3 fly by in the distance, bound for Moose Creek.

Joan Caswell, a regular fire lookout on Sheep Hill, was another Nez Perce NF seasonal employee who had wanted to attend and canceled.

The morning of June 11, Jim Huntley, a surveyor on the Nez Perce NF based at the Supervisor's Office in Grangeville, worked with Andy Taylor and Ron Hagan. Spontaneously, the two invited Jim to join them on the inspection trip to Moose Creek on the DC-3, assuring him there was plenty of room. Although tempted, he was supervising a survey crew near Red River and needed to check on it, so he declined their invitation.

Tom Kovalicky, the assistant director of land for Region 1 based in Missoula, called Art apologetically on Sunday night, explaining that he would need to be "scratched from the presentation agenda." Tom's boss, Bill Worf, had instead asked him to fly to Washington, D.C., to brief the Chief of the USFS, Max Peterson, on wilderness. Time was essential because the Chief had to testify before Congress about wilderness lands under consideration in the western part of Roadless Area Review and Evaluations (RARE II).

Cheshire Peirce was scheduled for the flight and listed on Art's final manifest as passenger number nine. Following high school graduation in 1978, she worked for her uncle and aunt, Everett and Freddie Peirce, who owned Selway Lodge. The Peirces operated it as a guest ranch and hired Cheshire as the "cabin and kitchen girl." When not cooking and cleaning, she spent days off hiking and exploring the wilderness. Jim Bradley, the Moose Creek District resource assistant, happened by the Lodge one afternoon and in conversation learned her interest in hiking and encouraged her to apply for a job with the District for the 1979 field season.

In the spring of 1979, as Cheshire finished final exams for her freshman year at Bryn Mawr College in Philadelphia, Pennsylvania, nothing sounded better than ditching the East Coast and escaping to the Selway-Bitterroot Wilderness. Eager to head west, she booked her airline ticket to Missoula for Friday June 8, three days ahead of time for the June 11 flight. The extra days were for roaming around Montana and gathering supplies for the anticipated season. On the first day in Montana, she traveled south to Hamilton. Walking out of the grocery store with her arms full of supplies, Uncle Everett noticed her as he was walking in. He had flown his Cessna 185 to Hamilton from the Lodge to pick up the mail and buy supplies. Unaware of each other's travel plans, they embraced the joyful happenstance. "You are going back with me to the Lodge for the weekend. Your aunt will love to see you. On Monday morning, I'll fly you downriver to Moose Creek so you can report to work." She readily agreed. More than 40 years later, Cheshire commented, "Had either of us been 30 seconds different either way, I wouldn't be here. It was against all odds that I crossed paths with my uncle that day because mostly he was not in Montana."

• • •

Providential tales of fate were not limited to those listed on the manifest, or who had weighed the option to fly in for Guard School. Also included were people who had made life-altering decisions not to return to Moose Creek for the 1979 season. They, too, felt fate had propelled them in an inexplicable direction. Charlie Gindler, the

District packer from 1975 to 1978, was one example. Charlie enjoyed working at Moose Creek, but his wife was expecting a baby, and she was unwilling to care for it at a backcountry ranger station. He took a job with the BLM, as a historic site caretaker and recreation area manager, in Brown's Park, Utah. Charlie vividly remembered the day Dick Kuhl called to inform him about the DC-3 crash: "I had never been fond of flying. I had made a lot of flights in and out of Moose Creek, quite a few on DC-3s, especially flying supplies and feed in for the mules and horses. As a horse-mounted wilderness ranger on the Gila NF in New Mexico, I had been pulled off my horse and put on the helitack crew during the big fire burst of 1974, and flew into seven fires in ten days, the first time I had ever flown at all. On one fire, after dropping me and my crew off on a fire, the helicopter crashed, and on another fire a helicopter crashed on the way to pick us up. So, I felt that after the Moose Creek crash, which I likely would have been in had I returned that year, I had dodged a bullet three times."

DᴀᴠE CLᴀʀᴋᴇ ᴀɴᴅ Gᴀʀʏ Mɪʟʟᴇʀ ʙᴜɪʟᴅɪɴɢ
Gᴀʀʏ's ᴄᴀʙɪɴ, Aᴘʀɪʟ 1979. (*G. Miller*)

DᴀᴠE CLᴀʀᴋᴇ sɪᴛᴛɪɴɢ ᴏɴ ᴛʜᴇ ʀɪᴅɢᴇᴘᴏʟᴇ ᴏғ Gᴀʀʏ
Mɪʟʟᴇʀ's ᴄᴀʙɪɴ, Jᴜɴᴇ 6, 1979. (*G. Miller*)

BOB McCUE, 1980. (*B. McCue*)

CAROL MYTRON. (*G. Miller*)

DICK KUHL, 1977. (*G. Miller*)

LAURA TILL, 1979. (*G. Miller*)

CHESHIRE PEIRCE, SECOND FROM RIGHT, WITH HER
FAMILY AT SELWAY LODGE, 1978. (*C. Augusta*)

CHARLIE GINDLER, 1976. (*C. Gindler*)

CHERYL WARREN. (*G. Miller*)

MARY GRAMLING. (*C. Goodman/USFS Collection*)

Tom Kovalicky riding Trigger,
Moose Creek, 1985. (*USFS Collection*)

9

FROM RESCUE TO RECOVERY

*We do not pray for immortality, but only not to see our acts
and all things stripped suddenly of all their meaning; for
then it is the utter emptiness of everything reveals itself.*
—ANTOINE DE SAINT-EXUPERY, *NIGHT FLIGHT*

With the departure of nine of the 14 Missoula jumpers, other
leaders took charge according to their positions within the
USFS. From the Washington Office on down, the accident consumed
everyone connected to it. At the local level, the on-the-ground leaders
from the Nez Perce NF emerged: Neil Walstad, forest aviation officer;
Bob Wickersham, fire management officer; and Art Seamans, Moose
Creek District ranger. Art ran logistics from Moose Creek. Neil and
Bob took charge of crews on the recovery efforts. Neil was a former
smokejumper, and like Tom Kovalicky from the Regional Office, was
a Higgins Ridge survivor.

The five remaining Missoula smokejumpers—John Nichols, Wayne
Cook, Jeff Kinderman, Steve Carstons, Wayne Williams—were joined

on and off by Moose Creek and Selway ranger district employees, divers, investigators, and helitack crews from Fenn Ranger Station and Missoula. One of the earliest tasks was to establish where the pieces of the airplane had ended up in the river—eventually, four major parts were identifiable: the left engine, a center portion of the fuselage with the tail section, the right wing with the right main landing gear, and the right engine. The rest of the airplane either disintegrated into fragments on impact, or the hydraulics of the Selway River shredded them. Each of the four main components became common references in the operations.

The DC-3 crashed into the Selway River at the upper end of Dry Bar, and as the wreckage drifted downstream and twisted apart, the left engine grounded in the main river channel adjacent to Dry Bar. It became lodged in sand and rocks at a depth of six to eight feet. Current carried part of the fuselage with the tail section of the wreckage another 1,500 feet and wedged it into rocks along the south bank. The largest intact piece of the aircraft became tangled up in Wolf Creek Rapid about two miles below the impact point, and it was visible only because the right main landing gear and wheel were sticking up through the whitewater. The right engine was the farthest downstream wreckage. It fell off the airplane and submerged three-quarters of a mile below the mouth of Ballinger Creek. This creek enters the Selway on the north side of the river, about three miles below Dry Bar.

In the early stages of the operations, the fast-flowing river distributed debris from the accident along the length of the Selway, all the way to its confluence with the Lochsa River—a distance of more than 20 miles. As a result of the debris sightings, employees and volunteers from Fenn Ranger Station and Selway Falls worked the shores of the rivers for any evidence of missing persons. After the first 48 hours, however, the search zone narrowed to an eight-mile reach of river extending from Teepee Creek up to Dry Bar, and then within 72 hours, was refined to a four-mile section. Even with the contracted search area the steepness of the canyon dictated the base of operations and limited the areas in which helicopters could safely maneuver. The only two feasible camps with enough open space were at Dry Bar and Pinchot Creek. The Pinchot Creek site became the main base of operations because of its open area for the heliport. Within a few days, it resembled a fine-tuned fire camp with makeshift tents, sleeping bags, tools, and equipment. Geographically, Pinchot was crucial to operations as mid-point between the four identified parts of the wreckage. At one time, the site was occupied nightly by nearly 20 people. Some were shuttled in and out daily to Orofino and Grangeville; others, such as the Missoula smokejumpers, were put up overnight in bunkhouses at the Fenn Ranger Station. For two weeks, when weather permitted, the camp had a rhythm. The rescue and recovery operations extended into mid-July, and official cleanup of smaller pieces of the wreckage stretched into the 1980 season.

Once the most identifiable parts were located, Neil's team also put together the ever-evolving retrieval plans. Two primary objectives emerged and were conducted simultaneously: assist the recovery team in the search/recovery of missing bodies and recover the two engines to expedite the accident investigation. To carry out the approved plan, Neil and his crew assisted three other distinct teams that formed within the days of the accident: the accident investigation team, the Clearwater County volunteer divers, and the salvage experts. Other management issues were absorbed by USFS personnel on the West Fork Ranger District, the Moose Creek Ranger District,

and the Selway Ranger District. For example, one was providing public outreach to hikers and backpackers at the trailheads to inform
them of the activities on the river. Several times during the operations, especially during the aerial lifting of the wreckage, the trail
was closed for safety. Another example was intercepting private and
commercial boaters on the river to inform them about the hazards
of the wreckage, as well as the general operations in the sections of
the river below Dry Bar. Owing to the limited permits for the Selway,
parties continued to launch every day after the accident through July
31, but several times during the recovery and salvage efforts boaters
were waved off the river to wait for removal operations.

The investigators, salvage experts, divers, smokejumpers, and
other support people were rowed about by Pete Mills in the USFS
boat, along with two BLM boats run by Terry Kincaid, Winston
Cheyney, Bob Michels, and Jeff King. The BLM cooperation resulted
from Terry's friendship with Art, and his being with Pete when their
river patrol trip was canceled. When Terry left the Grangeville Airport
after being diverted, he called Art and volunteered the use of BLM
resources; consequently, four boatmen and two rafts participated.

Helicopters on contract with the USFS ferried all of these groups
up and down the river corridor, and carried out rescue and recovery
missions from June 11 through June 18. Two of the primary rotor-
craft were a pair of Bell Jet Rangers (Bell 206) flown by two different companies—one Minuteman Aviation of Missoula, piloted by
Forrest Gue, and the other Valley Aviation of Orofino, piloted by Ray
Reel and Frenny Frensdorf. The pilots used all the legally acceptable flying time each day as weather allowed, and over the course of
the mission each flew a little more than 30 hours, more than any of
them had flown on a single mission in 40-year careers. The flying

involved a lot of hovering over the river, looking at pools in slanted light, and divergent elevations, trying to detect bodies and pieces of the plane. They shuttled a lot of people from Moose Creek, Pinchot Creek, Selway Falls, and Fenn. Forrest commented, "As far as a large-scale rescue operation, it was smooth, everyone worked well together, but Ray and I just had a hard time helping anyone, just not much we could do toward the end, and so we moved on."

Both pilots had frequently flown over the area; but the Selway River country was a special place for Forrest. This river corridor 14 years earlier was where he discovered his interest in aviation. At the time, he was a college student and had been hired to staff the Gardiner Peak Lookout on the Moose Creek District. Before moving into the lookout, part of his training was attending the annual Guard School. As a result, his first flight on an airplane was from Grangeville to Moose Creek in a Cessna piloted by Frank Hill, essentially the same flight and event tied to the subsequent disaster. While stationed at Gardiner, he also took his first helicopter ride, and it ignited his desire to become a career helicopter pilot. Arriving on the scene with Forrest and his helicopter were Jim Scofield, a regional helitack specialist, and Lloyd Whitaker, a helitack foreman, both of them with the Regional Office in Missoula. The two men were integral to the helicopter operations. Lloyd's twin brother was also on the mission as a Missoula smokejumper.

The day following the crash, everyone involved was simply trying to recover missing bodies. Large ground patrol parties consisted of persons from the USFS, Idaho County, Clearwater County, and rescue units deployed along sections of the river below Dry Bar. A 24-hour watch was stationed at the O'Hara Bridge above the Fenn Ranger Station. At night, lights mounted on the bridge illuminated the water. From the onset it was thought possible that one or more of the bodies could be pinned in or under some of the identifiable pieces of the wreckage. With this in mind, large holes were punched in the tail and fuselage sections by rescuers, without results. With the resources exhausted from aerial and ground searches, Clearwater County Sheriff Nick Albers was contacted regarding the use of the county's relatively new volunteer diving team. He agreed. Beginning on June 13, under his direction, his team searched long and thoroughly until June 17. They returned at lower flows in July, and often were joined by other diving units from the nearby areas. Dive teams consisted of four to eight people, depending on conditions.

The high reconnaissance patrols were done at about 100 feet AGL at higher airspeeds; low-level patrols at no more than 30 feet AGL and at airspeeds from stationary to 30 knots. The Bell Jet Ranger is capable of carrying four passengers and its pilot, but at low altitude it was kept lighter. Water clarity varied greatly. A case of polarized sunglasses was flown in and glasses were handed out to crews.

On the morning of June 13, the helicopters started flying river patrols at daybreak. Within the first two hours, someone on the ground reported seeing reflections of submerged airplane parts and saw bodies in a backeddy near the mouth of Ballinger Creek, three miles downstream from the impact. Immediately divers from the Clearwater County Sheriff's rescue team were ferried by helicopter to the site. The bodies of John Slingerland, Don Easthouse, Tom TerKeurst, and Ron Hagan were recovered from a deep pool.

That meant five others were still missing. Pilot Forrest Gue in his Jet Ranger was dispatched to the site to see if he could help carry the victims to the Fenn Ranger Station. With him were Lloyd Whitaker, Wayne Williams, and Wayne Cook. Once there, he hovered while he considered a sliver of sandbar by the eddy. He slowly lowered his craft toward it as the other men briefed each other over the intercom. Wayne explained, "In those days there was little regulation. We simply got shit done. Our decisions were based on experience and working as a team. We all did what we thought was safe, was within our abilities, and did what we knew we could do safely." Within seconds, Forrest hung the tail rotor of the copter out over the river, and with the skids inches above the slender sandbar, Williams and Cook leaped out with hand tools. To allow the helicopter blades more room to get in closer for easier loading, they hacked out the brush along the riverbank. Leaving his crew on the bar, Forrest flew the bodies out in two trips, then retrieved his men.

• • •

Thomas "Tom" TerKeurst, born in November 1959 in Pontiac, Michigan, and was the second son adopted by John and Marilyn TerKeurst. He grew up in Grand Rapids, Michigan, where his father worked as a negotiator for Holly Carburetor and automobile labor unions. Tom attended East Grand Rapids High School and worked a part-time job on an assembly line at Irwin Seating. He struggled in school. In an effort to find a solution to improving his studies, his mother consulted with her sister-in-law, Jane Johnson, a high school career counselor in Ann Arbor, Michigan. When visiting Jane's office, she noticed some brochures about Sterling Institute. In the fall of 1978, Tom took a break from school and became a Sterling student. During the spring semester, the director of the school, as well as one of Tom's professors, urged him to apply for a summer internship with the USFS. He recommended his friend, Art Seamans, on the Moose Creek Ranger District. On May 22, Tom received Art's acceptance letter for a volunteer position on the District. The letter said he was to "report for work on June 11 at 0800 at the Smokejumper Loft, Grangeville Airport. You will sign up as a volunteer and fly into Moose Creek for a week of intensive training."

After graduation from Sterling, Tom took a Greyhound bus to Idaho. En route, he stayed with his uncle and aunt, John and Ruthanne Hibbs, who lived in Denver, Colorado. John and Ruthanne recalled his wonderful visit. "Tom had been trouble as a kid and a teenager. He was doing poorly in high school and nothing seemed to interest him. Then he went to Sterling. The school and general experience there transformed him into a nice young man." During his stay in Denver, John took Tom sailing on nearby Cherry Creek Reservoir. The boat was a two-person Coronado C-15. John was an experienced sailor, but an unexpected wind gusted across the reservoir and capsized the boat, sweeping John overboard. Tom, with little experience, righted the boat and retrieved his uncle. John also loaned Tom his new Honda 350 motorcycle, "I'm not sure why I set him free on it. He was truly a changed person and found his calling in the outdoors. He had a wild time on the motorcycle." After several enjoyable days, they dropped him off at the bus station for his final leg to Grangeville. Driving back to their house they had an uneasy feeling—that it would be the last time they would see him. Days later they were informed he had been killed. Awareness of the premonition stayed with them for years, but they were comforted by knowing he had finally found happiness.

Haunted by the loss of their nephew, John and Ruthanne talked about visiting the accident site for closure. In the summer of 2016, after 37 years, the trip came together, but during the planning they were disappointed to discover, given their physical limitations, they would be unable to reach the accident site. An alternative plan evolved, and they drove to Idaho, where they chartered a single-engine airplane to take them to Moose Creek. At least they were able to see the destination of Tom's flight and the memorial at the ranger station. Tom's older brother, Jim, remembered him as "a strong athletic young man who was incredibly passionate. He was wonderful with animals, and enjoyed testing himself physically. He excelled at acrobatics, and when we lived on a farm in Wisconsin he would jump off the wooden roof beams into the hay to practice landing—eventually he would jump out of second floor windows. He was fearless in pretty much everything he did. Sterling was a really transformational place for my brother. He went there with a lot of frustrations, and the people and outdoor work really helped him find his future."

• • •

Ronald "Ron" Hagan, age 37, was born in March 1942, in Kellogg, Idaho, to Milton and Alice. At the age of four, the family moved to Laurel, Montana, where Ron graduated from high school as the valedictorian. Then in 1967, he attended Montana State University in Bozeman, where he graduated with a degree in civil engineering. His employment with the USFS began the same year. As an engineer with the Agency, he moved several times before settling in Grangeville. In 1971, he married Beverly Lufkin, who also worked for the USFS. Since Ron had two children from a previous marriage (John and Julie) they merged two families because Beverly also had three children from a previous marriage (Wendy, Betty, and Richard). The memorial service at the Noland Funeral Home was officiated by the pastor of the Trinity Lutheran Church in Grangeville.

• • •

Hours after the victims were recovered from the eddy below Ballinger Creek, another body was located from the air, upriver from the mouth of Teepee Creek, about eight miles below Dry Bar, and it was recovered in a torpid reach of the river. The body was that of Catherine Hodgin.

• • •

At the same time the divers and support teams from Moose Creek were working along the river, the accident investigation team was trying to decipher what had caused the crash. The USFS accident investigation team was made up of managers from several departments in Region 1 with titles such as safety manger, aviation safety officer, aviation maintenance specialist, law enforcement, and deputy regional forester. Led by Tom Coston, the team was comprised of Jeff Sirmon, Jim Hocking, Larry Houtchens, Gene Imlay, Nels Jensen, Roy Keck, Gordon LaFournaise, and Chub Riggleman. After assembling, it had flown to Moose Creek on June 11 and arrived by 1730 hours. Originally they were going to hike downriver to the accident site, but it proved to be too difficult logistically, so they spent the night and were ferried down by helicopter the following morning. The investigators all had individual assignments. The aviation men concentrated on examining the engines, and each of the major dismembered pieces, while the others tracked down eyewitnesses. Some members of the team came and went from the accident site before finally leaving on June 18 to pursue other aspects of the investigation.

• • •

On June 13, after a fruitful day, the divers were optimistic about finding the remaining four people on the 14th. Based on the results of the day before, divers concentrated on eddies, deep pools, and sandbars. Divers, however, struggled with the swift current and cold temperatures, estimating the water averaged 38 degrees. To overcome the strong currents, divers strapped on lead weight belts of up to 80 pounds, and when that was not enough, canteens filled with sand were added. Regardless of the difficulties and fatigue, the divers worked systematically and indefatigably, but no more recoveries were made that day.

Other crews labored together on trying to put cable rigging on the plane's two engines for retrieval, without success. The water was too fast, powerful, and relentless. Neil's group went back to the drawing board. Based on the day-end debriefing, Damon Rust of Boise, a whitewater salvage expert who was located through Agency channels, was asked to join the effort. On June 15, he arrived. The crews were hopeful he could offer expertise on how to move the four major pieces of the wreckage. Not only would it help the investigation team, there was speculation within the recovery team that bodies could be pinned in the biggest piece of the wreckage at Wolf Creek Rapid. Damon might assist all of the crews.

• • •

On the morning of June 15, the divers were flown in by helicopter from Orofino to the heliport at Pinchot Camp. They and their equipment were loaded on to rafts and ferried to points along the river. A few hours into their operations, the body of Patrick McGreevey was found in a deep pool about a half-mile above the Class II rapid formed by Pinchot and Coyote creeks, a mile below where the airplane had struck the river.

Patrick, age 24, was one of the few people on the airplane who was not a volunteer or employee of the Moose Creek Ranger District; rather, he was attending the Guard School to learn skills for his summer position in the Gospel Hump Wilderness area of the Red River Ranger District on the southern portion of the Nez Perce NF. He found the job through a friend, Dick Blodnick, a biologist who was based in Grangeville.

Patrick was the eldest son of a close-knit family comprised of six siblings. Quiet by nature, he was known for his sharp intellect and reliable sense of humor. He found solace, as an avid outdoorsman, in the tranquility of nature, no doubt fostered by the summers he spent with family at their mountain cabin located at the base of the Anaconda Pintler Wilderness in Montana. He enjoyed skiing, fishing, hunting, and hiking, often in the company of his younger brothers and two sisters. Patrick's long-held goal was to become a doctor. To that end, he began his academic journey at Carroll College, Helena, Montana, and later at Montana State University, where he earned a master's degree in anatomy and physiology. He was to begin medical school at Kansas City University in the fall of 1979.

Five years earlier, Patrick suffered the loss of his younger brother, Mark, in an unfortunate accident. It had a devastating effect on Patrick and on his family. The strength and resiliency he demonstrated during this time left a legacy cherished by all who knew him. Surviving relatives included a son Corey; parents Dollie and Edward McGreevey; brothers Eddie and Greg; sisters Leslie and Laurie Johnson; maternal grandparents Nellie and Achille Santini, and numerous aunts, uncles, and cousins. Funeral services were held at St. Paul Catholic Church in Anaconda, Montana, and he is interred at the Mount Olivet Cemetery in Anaconda.

• • •

On Friday afternoon (June 15), the Missoula jumpers were informed that they would be relieved of their duties. After dinner that evening, the jumpers were flown out by helicopter to Moose Creek, and then picked up by a fixed-wing aircraft and flown to Missoula. It was a bittersweet departure for the Missoula jumpers, because they wanted to stay on and help finish the mission. They knew the topography, knew what areas had been searched, and knew which had not. They sensed that the transition would lose precious time as their replacements were brought up to speed by other teams. However, some of the managers were persuaded long hours were risky. Summing up his time on the mission, Wayne Williams commented, "We were assigned a task and we had to get it done. At the end of the day it was a job, and it was not personal for me...I didn't know any of the victims we were recovering. But others on the job, such as Neil Walstad and Art Seamans did. They were much less fortunate than I."

• • •

Fresh out of recurrent training, the Grangeville smokejumpers were brought in as the relief crew to work under Neil. This team was led by Terry Williamson, who was a squad leader. Assisting him was jumper Mike Hill, who had been with the Grangeville jumpers since 1972 and taught school during the rest of the year. He was also the son-in-law of pilot Frank Hill, who was involved with fixed-wing flying associated with the accident. Beyond assisting Terry and Neil with the ongoing recovery and retrieval plans, Mike was assigned to document the efforts with a daily log, photographs, and filming with an 8mm movie camera.

As divers and recovery teams searched the river, Damon Rust was boated to the sites of the engines and the wreckage. He studied each one. At first, he was unsure that anything could be done until the river level dropped. But that evening he consulted with other experts and was persuaded there was a possibility with vertical movement that the pieces could be extracted. The only piece of equipment regarded capable of such lift was a Vertol helicopter manufactured by Boeing. The heavy-lift, tandem-rotor helicopter powered by twin turboshaft engines had proved itself as a military aircraft during the Vietnam War. The ever-evolving plan was again updated by Neil and submitted to his superiors in the Agency, requesting approval to contract with Columbia Helicopters, a commercial operator of Vertols in the region, which happened to be working on a logging operation in northern Idaho. The request was approved. Even with the authorization, however, the ground crews still faced the challenges of rigging all the components for the lift. By the following day, a Columbia Helicopter Vertol was on standby in Grangeville.

With the Vertol in Grangeville, crews concentrated their efforts on preparing the biggest portion of the wreckage for lifting—the wing and landing gear wedged in Wolf Creek Rapid. If anyone knew how to move massive objects with cables, chokers, and blocks, it was Emil and Penny Keck. Based on Emil's knowledge from his old-school logging days, the husband and wife had with minimal tools built a number of massive timbered bridges in the Selway-Bitterroot Wilderness. Beginning in 1965, Emil rebuilt the Moose Creek Ranches Bridge, and along with Penny, undertook the bridges known as Tony Point, Three Links, Bear Creek, and Moose Creek. Other smaller bridges with spans shoter than 45 feet, included those at Cupboard, Ballinger, Meeker, Halfway, Dog, Pettibone, and Goat creeks. Their skills would prove invaluable in moving the Wolf Creek wreckage.

Art asked Emil if he thought it was possible to move the wing with cables, and Emil responded, "If you give me enough cable, I'll pull Christ off the cross." Art replied, "Tell me how much you need and we'll [Moose Creek Ranger District] buy it."

The principal mission was to rig the wing with cables and necessary lift points for quick and secure attachment to a line descending from the helicopter. In setting the cables, they decided that the force of the water would not allow for a clean lift from directly above. After much consideration, the Kecks suggested trying to move the wing horizontally out of the major portion of the rapid, toward the southern edge of the river. Using a spider web of cables and related equipment, several attempts were made at coaxing the wing shoreward. The basics of the system included a Homelite XL chainsaw with a two-ton capacity winch attachment. Cable could then be run from this attachment through additional blocks, multiplying the power of the chainsaw by a factor of two, thus one block gave a capability of four tons, two blocks eight tons, and so forth. The Keck's system and equipment had the capability of generating a pull of more than 50 tons. Given the remote wild country, the Kecks usually relied on boulders or trees for anchorage, and ran long lengths of cable if necessary to connect all the points. Of course the boulders and trees were rarely at the right location, so it was a process of deciding where to fasten them, and then wrap a cable around each for the block. The cable running through the winch was only a quarter-inch thick (and the chainsaw engine had to be cabled to a rock or tree as well), but as the force was multiplied, they also had to increase the size of the cable, thus there was a lot of splicing of successively thicker cables to each other. The Kecks called this a "farmer's splice," as opposed to a "logger's splice." Their system never exceeded half-inch cable. The narrow canyon and the tall trees surrounding the site on the south side of the river posed further complications.

Under the direction of the Kecks and Grangeville-based smoke-jumper Mike Uszuko, cables were rigged and prepared for attachment to the wing submerged in the rapid. It then became the job of Damon and his team of Boise-based divers—Gene Peterson, Jerry Gould, and Marving Tullis. These four divers, with the cable in tow, formed a human chain through the raging rapid. They were able to half anchor themselves to a rock in the middle of the rapid and then work on attaching the cable to the wing. By the end of the day, several attempts were made to move the wing using different points, angles, and techniques, but every time heavy loads were placed on the system, the cables started to tear through the attachment points, causing them to release the tension. On the final attempt of the day, so much force was placed on the landing gear it almost ripped away from the overall wreckage. At 1500 hours lifting the wing was scrubbed and the Vertol reduced to standby.

• • •

On Sunday, June 17, a low pressure cold system moved into the Selway-Bitterroots, but the weather and natural light on and in the river proved sufficient to continue all missions. The major focus of the day for the investigators and support teams was to try to move the left engine out of the deep channel near Dry Bar and rig it for lifting. All efforts, by early afternoon, however, were diverted to assist the diving crews who had located two more victims—Kevin Leber and Robert Cook. Both bodies were found above Pinchot Rapid in a deep pool in the same place Patrick McGreevey's body was found two days earlier. The two divers who recovered the bodies, Mick Pollock and

John Bryant, relayed to their supervisor Sheriff Nick Albers what they had found. The two victims still had their seat belts fastened and were secured to major portions of seating structures—at least six seats—which had embedded in sand. Unable to budge the metal framing, the divers sawed the seating from the wreckage to free the bodies and pull them ashore.

· · ·

Philip "Kevin" Leber was born in 1955 in Alexandria, Virginia, to Walter and Bernice Leber. He had two older siblings, Randy and Bonnie "Fig." His father was prominent in the US Army Corps of Engineers, which resulted in travel and many childhood homes. From a very young age, Kevin had an interest in the outdoors and was a Cub Scout and Boy Scout. Before Kevin was in high school, the family moved from Panama, where his father was the governor, to Fort Belvoir in Virginia, just outside of Washington, D.C., because he had been assigned command of the Ballistic Missile Defense System. It was during this assignment that Kevin attended high school at Stephen's Episcopal School. Besides loving the outdoors, he was known among his family and friends as having a light-hearted temperament. Laughing, his sister Fig commented, "He played on the football team during high school and muddled his way through academics. I remember going to see him play football, and I had asked him what his jersey number was so I could keep track of him on the field. He gave me the number of a different, really good player. So I was thinking he was this great football player when it wasn't actually him. He definitely had a great sense of humor."

Although an average football player, Kevin maintained his interest in nature, and during his senior year spent two weeks hiking the Blue Ridge Trail in Virginia. He wrote of the experience for his thesis project and won an award. Post-graduation, his father retired from the military and purchased a home in Stuart, Florida. To improve his grades, Kevin enrolled in the University of South Florida in Tampa. While there, he discovered forestry and wildlife management and knew they were the fields he wanted to pursue. With improved grades, he applied to the University of Idaho and was accepted for the fall semester of 1976. While living in Moscow, he suffered a compound leg fracture in a motorcycle accident and missed a semester. By 1978, he was excelling socially and academically. He had a girlfriend, and he earned a student-intern position in winter recreation management on the Holy Cross Ranger District of the White River NF in Colorado, from December through mid-April 1979. From there, he applied for a trail-crew position on the Moose Creek Ranger District, and he was elated to be a part of the elite wilderness program. Before reporting to Grangeville for the summer season, he and his girlfriend, Joni McKeighan, traveled to Florida to visit Fig and her family. The two then drove back to Idaho, sightseeing along the way. The trip was a sendoff for Kevin. They visited his older brother, Randy, an Air Force pilot living in Midwest City, Oklahoma. Reflecting on the last time she saw her brother, Fig said, "He was such a kind and caring person. I am so happy that I got to see him happy. He had found his niche. One of my questions to God is why do we have to get old to get smarter about what the important things are in life? I often wonder what he would have been like as a grown-up. When he died, I figured God needed someone up there to take care of his forests and wildlife."

Kevin's father delivered his eulogy at a memorial service held in Kirkwood, Missouri, at the Grace Episcopal Church. The succinct farewell described Kevin as a smart, outgoing, cheerful, upbeat person who set high standards for himself and others. "He knew what it means to climb a mountain, turn back temporarily, and then return to conquer the toughest part. Kevin knew himself and he knew his world—he was at peace...Kevin was not one for long goodbyes or for windy speeches...always looking forward—never backward—as indeed we all must do." Kevin is buried at the Sunset Memorial Park and Mausoleum in Affton, Missouri, with his paternal grandparents, and later with his mother (1996) and father (2009).

Two years after the accident, Kevin's brother Randy was assigned a mission flying a Boeing E3 (AWACS) from McChord Air Force Base in Tacoma, Washington, to Tinker Air Force Base in Oklahoma City, Oklahoma. The route placed him in the vicinity of the Selway River, and with permission from air traffic control, he deviated from the flight plan and made a high-altitude, 360-degree turn over the river corridor below Moose Creek to see where Kevin had lost his life. Ten years after Kevin's death, Randy retired from the Air Force as a lieutenant colonel, and then flew another 16 years for Boeing as a flight instructor on the 737, 757, 767, and 777. Referring to his long aviation career and the loss of his brother, he explained, "At times in my life I have had high-risk jobs and have had lots of acquaintances and friends killed along the way. To deal with the risk and loss, I put things in compartments...it is a way to cope and come to terms with difficult experiences. BUT, the loss of my little brother I have never been able to put in a compartment...it is something I've never gotten over and I'm not going to...The whole deal was bullshit. My brother was very special. I'm sure the other kids on the airplane who died were special too...it is the sum of the whole that is important to remember."

Like Randy, Kevin's sister, too, wanted to see the area where she lost her younger brother. In the summer of 2021, plans for the long anticipated trip came together in conjunction with a cruise on the Columbia River. She and her husband drove to Grangeville and chartered an airplane to Moose Creek. The pilot flew them over Dry Bar, and they paid their respects at the memorial at the ranger station.

• • •

Robert "Bob" Cook was born in August 1958 to Stephen and Dorothy Cook in San Rafael, California. He was raised in Mill Valley with a sister, Mary, and two brothers, Sam and John, and graduated from high school in 1977 from Tamalpais High School. He earned his Eagle Scout the same year, and several months later he was awarded the Young American Award from the Boy Scouts of America. He was active in his teenage years, receiving a community service award, was a member of the Golden Gate Council, American Youth Hostels, and of the North Coast Model Railroaders. In the spring of 1979, he had finished his freshman year at the College of Marin in Kentfield, California.

Before reporting to his summer job, Bob flew from San Francisco to Lewiston, and visited his parents, who had recently relocated to nearby Asotin, Washington. He compared the feeling of leaving California to "a bird being let out of a cage and set free." While staying with his parents, he explored the local area, bought his summer supply of freeze-dried food for "80 days in the woods," and visited an 85-year-old family friend named Charley Bowens. In a letter to his girlfriend, Bob described Charley as a "Creek Indian now known as a Seminole from Oklahoma." Bob enjoyed listening to his friend's outdoor adventures from the old days.

Then in preparation for Monday's flight to Guard School at Moose Creek, his parents drove him to Grangeville on Sunday, where he spent the night at the smokejumper loft. Before going to bed, he wrote a several-page letter to his girlfriend, "Tomorrow I will be flown into some of the most beautiful land that these eyes of mine have ever seen...As I drove with my parents to Grangeville today, we drove through the Camas Prairie...Eastward in the distance could be seen the Bitterroot Mountains rising out of the land with their peaks capped with snow. The sky above was like a watercolor scene on canvas. Clouds and light blue sky melted into each other to create the liquid appearance of watercolor." He closed the letter writing, "Here are a few words Charley left me with as I ended my visit with him—Tasamn hic—It means in Creek Indian, love to you my friend."

Jean Barnard, the mayor of Bob's childhood town, spearheaded the movement to rename a section of the Pacific Coast Trail in his honor because he was instrumental in building a section of it as part of his Eagle Scout project. In fact, Cook grew up hiking on the nearby Cataract Trail with his family, and as a teenager distributed a mimeographed flier around Marin County soliciting volunteers to help with the trail project: "Come get a sun tan and dig on the mountain. Learn trail construction by helping to complete the final link of the Pacific Coast Trail." Coordinating with the governing agency of the Golden Gate National Recreation Area managed by the National Park Service, he enlisted the help of the Boy Scouts, Girl Scouts, Tamalpais Conservation Club, Sierra Club, the Lions, and several church youth groups. The memorial portion of the trail extends from the west side of Mount Tamalpais and connects the Golden Gate National Recreation Area to the Point Reyes National Seashore. In 1980 it was dedicated, with a bronze plaque set in a bench fashioned of native rock. It details

Bob's dedication to the scenic 4.3 miles of the trail. The Bob Cook Trail runs between the Matt Davis Trail above Stinson Beach and McKinnon's Gulch.

Funeral services for Bob were held at Pilgrim Hall of the Congregational Presbyterian Church in Lewiston, and he was buried in the nearby Normal Hill Cemetery. In July 1980, his parents hiked the Selway River Trail and camped at Ballinger Creek. The goal of their trip was to reach the accident site, but Dorothy had to turn back at Pinchot Creek. Stephen pressed onward to Dry Bar and the scene of the crash. Bob's parents later returned to the Selway to visit the memorial at the Moose Creek Ranger Station.

• • •

With Leber and Cook accounted for, the divers had successfully recovered eight of the nine missing victims—leaving only Whitey Hachmeister unfound. Helicopter pilot Ray Reel flew the two recently recovered bodies to Selway Falls for transport. By the end of the day, the river canyon socked in with low clouds and steady rain. Crews were forced out of the river and returned to camp. Again, even though the day saw some success, they struggled to remain optimistic. While sitting around camp, members of the teams brainstormed and shared ideas about the rigging on the engines, and where to search next for Whitey. With several areas eliminated, the group consensus on one hand was that Whitey's body might be pinned in the wing section at Wolf Creek Rapid. The divers, on the other hand, had reason to believe that the fluvial dynamics of the river were moving debris from the crash site in and out of the big eddy above Pinchot Rapid— stressing bodies were found there on two separate days, and they observed lots of pieces from the aircraft buried in the sand. Some of the divers tried to move big sheets of aluminum, but they did not budge. The divers even considered dredging the sand to see if it might uncover something.

On June 18, the crew at Pinchot Camp awoke to colder and wetter conditions than the day before—the canyon shrouded in low clouds with intermittent rain. The diving crews did not fly that day. They stayed in Orofino to rest and repair equipment. Richard Mauer was sitting in camp with the crew—a reporter from the Boise-based *Idaho Statesman*. From the onset, local, regional, and national newspapers were covering the story daily. John M. Willis, a freelance writer for the Associated Press, was the first reporter on the ground at the site. He hired two professional guides, who packed him and his photography equipment by horseback for the day (June 13). However, until Richard's visit, no other paper had been willing to put a reporter in the area for more than 12 hours, probably because of the cost. Richard, an avid outdoorsman, recalled pitching the story to his boss was difficult, and when he was granted permission, the assignment did not include a photographer, and he had to reach the site downriver from the end of the Selway River Road at his own expense.

He decided to hike in over the weekend, camp two nights, and hike out. He had been covering the story extensively since the day it occurred and was eager to see everything in person. His reception at camp was routine, because everyone else was too busy, but Richard observed and listened. He took notes and quotes from Neil Walstad, diver John Bryant, Mike Hill, and others. Many of the quotes resulted from conversations he overheard while sitting around the evening campfire. Richard latched onto those speculating about forces and loads placed on the wreckage from the river and mechanical lifting. BLM boatman Winston Cheyney, who was sitting around the fire the same evening, recollected 40+ years later, "We were running numbers, wing sizes, water weight, the force of this and the force of that…it was of course complete and utter BS. There was not a licensed engineer within a hundred miles. But it made us feel good that we were trying …trying to help even in times when we were forced to be idle on the mission."

Richard's article appeared in the June 19 *Statesman*. It sensationalized aspects of the story, but it did capture the drive, temperament, and troubles experienced by those involved up to that point. "The frustrations mounted through the weekend. Saturday night, the stars disappeared and on Sunday, leaden clouds descended into the valley. That night it rained, and the moods of the 17 men and one woman camped at Pinchot jury-rigged shelters were lifted only slightly when a fire boss brought in a case of beer and a bottle of 151-proof spirits. Even out in the woods, the bureaucracy of the government kept a presence. Terry Williamson, whose job was to keep a detailed account of whatever was loaded into a helicopter, sat drying his manifests by the campfire. 'I ought to throw them in,' he said. 'Nobody's ever going to see them.' 'You better not,' Walstad said. 'All these things are going to be looked at when they have an inspection.' Monday morning dawned gray when the camp was rousted out of bed at 5. Emil Keck, a veteran firefighter, didn't want to take any chance with fate when he saw a young worker start to dump the coffee grounds that had been mellowing in the pot for a few days. 'Don't throw them grounds away!' Keck said. 'On a [forest] fire, if you throw the grounds out on the first day, you'll never get it [the fire] out. We don't need that kind of luck here.'"

By late morning, the weather lifted with enough visibility for some on-and-off helicopter activity, allowing crews who remained on the river to work on finishing the rigging on the two engines and the two pieces of wreckage. If these tasks were accomplished, the Vertol waiting in Grangeville could perform its final lift. Everything over the course of the day, however, took longer than anticipated. The crews split up their usual tasks. The investigation team and the Kecks, along with other support members, focused on trying to get the rigging set on the left engine. If it could be moved to the south bank, where the velocity of the river wanted to carry it, then it would be easier to lift with the copter, and rigging could be re-set with minimal damage. Three attempts using the Kecks' chokers, cables, and grappling-hook systems, failed. Nels Jensen, from the investigation team, was maneuvered over the engine in a raft, tethered on each side of the river by a cable. USFS boatman Pete Mills provided a snorkel mask, and Nels put his head under water and confirmed that the three bladed propeller, nose cone, and cylinders were still attached to the engine. More significantly, he established the propeller blades were in the feathered position. A "feathered propeller" is one where the blades have been increased in pitch by a lever in the cockpit to turn them parallel to the oncoming airflow. In this position, drag from a non-operative engine is minimized. This was important because it validated eyewitness' reports of the left engine being inoperative. The pilots had shut down the engine on purpose.

By mid-afternoon a steady rain fell. The crews slowed. The Vertol waiting in Grangeville was again put on standby. Without much sunlight, the river darkened. Diving became ineffective. The salvage crew, the Kecks, and the investigators were discouraged. Everyone was stressed and exhausted, working from dawn to dark. One member of the investigation team fell ill and requested to fly out. Damon Rust said there was nothing more to do until the water level fell.

With the rain the river rose to four feet on the Paradise gauge and after June 14 began a slow decline—but not enough to make a difference. The hydraulics simply outmatched the equipment. Everyone decided to take a break and regroup once the flows subsided and the weather faired. Despite their somber mood, the crews had accomplished a great deal, especially given the weather and water. All of the remnants were rigged and set for lifting. As well, each of the parts had been tentatively anchored with cables to points along the shore—hazardous to floaters, since one location had a low steel cable strung across the width of the river. Crews notified personnel at Moose Creek and Paradise to inform floaters. Then the mission was officially placed on hold.

At the end of the long and discouraging day, Pete Mills wrote in his USFS Diary, "M [Monday]. 6-18. Sat at Pinchot. Team attempted to retrieve D.B. [Dry Bar] Engine. Guard equipment at Pinchot. Everyone out. BLM out. Tu [Tuesday] 6-19 Alone at Pinchot."

· · ·

By June 20, the cold front had expired. The river had dropped, with the Paradise gauge reading 3.3 feet. The seven-day forecast predicted continued snowmelt. A crew of divers from Clearwater County and from Lewiston returned to the river. Based on what they had seen on June 17 in the deep eddy above Pinchot Rapid, they strongly suspected that part of the DC-3's nose section was buried in the sand in the pool and might contain Whitey's body. The divers brought along shovels and a gas-powered dredging machine equipped with three-inch diameter hoses to move sand away from the area.

When they reached the bottom of the pool where they had spotted significant debris three days earlier, all had changed. Old debris was gone; new debris was present: clothes, suitcases, lawn chairs, oxygen masks, an AM-FM radio. They proceeded to dredge. After several hours, they had moved 170 cubic yards and decided theirs was an ineffective effort. The sand replaced itself with more sand. It reclaimed debris before it could be removed. The divers concluded the bedload sand was saltating too much at the present flow. They proposed the bar and eddy be searched weekly as the river dropped. A summary report compiled by Selway District Ranger Darrel Kenops on the diving operation through June 20 stated, "To date the diving effort has been very effective. They have done everything we have asked and more. The information given by them at the evening debriefing sessions has been a tremendous help to our planning effort and the success of this operation. The water is cold [average 45 degrees] and current is tricky. However, the major problem is sand...They have offered to come back at our call anytime. They are strongly devoted to finding the remaining missing person."

Convinced they had exhausted all avenues in looking for Whitey's body, the volunteer divers were excused until the river subsided significantly or if new clues emerged. As a safeguard, a person was stationed around the clock at the O'Hara Bridge near Fenn to watch for the body.

When the recovery mission was temporarily suspended on June 18, the Vertol helicopter on standby in Grangeville was released for another contract. The salvage crews led by Emil and Penny Keck spent June 20 rigging and preparing the two engines for lifting. Crews were confident the Kecks' rigging capabilities would allow a Bell 212 (N84FC) from Boise to make the lift, and on June 19 one was brought in on contract. During the interval of foul weather, Emil and Penny re-engineered one of the grappling hooks, convinced longer extensions from the attachment points to the bottom of the hook would give them more bite. Once Emil settled on the final modifications, it was taken to Dye Machine Shop in Grangeville and machined to the Keck's specifications.

On June 20, with the river flow unchanged—still holding at 3.3 feet on the Paradise gauge—the Kecks, equipped with their cable system and modified grappling hook, along with their support crews, were able to get enough purchase on the rigging of the left engine in the deep current at Dry Bar to winch it to the south shore, where it was further rigged for aerial lifting. The Bell 212 was then dispatched and arrived at Dry Bar at 1230 hours. Piloted by Lee Young and John Shested, with a support crew of Shep Johnson, Rick Clay, and Gilbert Ball, the copter lifted the engine to the end of the Selway River Road, where it was loaded onto a two-ton flatbed truck.

Having successfully retrieved the left engine, the crews moved downstream to the site of the right engine below Ballinger Creek. Emil Keck floated down with two BLM boatmen, Vern Grussing and Scott Fasken, along with one of the investigators, Glenn Haney, and Chub Riggleman with the aviation team. Similar to the rig for the upstream engine, a cable was strung across the river and the raft tethered to the line. To retrieve this engine, Emil looped a long cable and attached a dozen heavy end-wrenches around it adding more weight, making it sink in the fast current. The top of the loop was closed with a choker so that once it caught, he could then lasso the engine. Scott remembered that once the boat was maneuvered over the engine, Emil yelled, "Drop." Then he pulled the choker and cinched the cable around the engine. The crew on the riverbank slowly inched the engine through the current using a series of come-alongs. The engine, re-rigged with cables and a simple hoop, allowed crews to quickly attach the modified grappling hook at the end of the line lowered by the helicopter to the rigging.

At 1800 hours, the right engine was hoisted from river and flown to the end of the Selway River Road where it, too, was loaded on the same flatbed truck as the left engine and transported to the Grangeville Airport. The following day, the engines were placed on a DC-3 and flown to Steward-Davis, Inc. in Long Beach, California, for teardown and analysis. Chub Riggleman and Tex Wright of the USFS aviation investigation team oversaw the teardown process there for four days in order to photograph and document the findings for the Agency's in-house accident report.

While the engines were being transported to California, the salvage crews were back at work on the Selway. Impressed with the Bell 212's capability to hoist the two engines, the crews intended to rig and lift the tail section resting along the south side of the river (1,500 feet beyond the point of impact). Using cables and the same grappling hook, the tail section was freed from the river by 1330 hours and slung to the end of the Selway River Road. An hour and half later, crews moved downstream to the wing section in hopes it too could be moved by the Bell 212. During the rigging process, they encountered several problems, including getting the grappling hook snagged in the wreckage, which took several hours to dislodge. At 1900 hours the operation was called off and crews returned to the Pinchot Camp.

Another effort was made on June 22, using the Bell 212. The river had receded to 3.1 feet on the Paradise gauge and rigging was completed by mid-morning. In this section of the river on the southern bank, large fir and spruce trees grew to the water's edge, and for the helicopter to position itself over the wreckage, the pilot had to hover close to these trees. The snags, and even the live green spruce, were weak, and the downwash from the rotor blades caused serious concern for crews. Penny Keck added, "The downdraft from the helicopter was tremendous, and there were a lot of snags around, even the green trees were considered dangerous. Someone was looking after everyone involved on the recovery from start to finish. This was no exception. The whole time everyone was risking just a little bit, what we were trying to do was minimize the risk." The helicopter was called to return to Pinchot Camp while crew members cut and felled the hazard trees. Fallers included the Kecks, Mike Uszuko, Shep Johnson, Gilbert Ball, Scott Fasken, and Moose Creek employee Gary Miller. Once the hazard trees were cleared, the helicopter repositioned over the wreckage, and the lines were attached and secured. Everyone was disappointed when the Bell 212 at full power could not budge the wreckage. The operation was called off; again the crews waited three more days, until the Vertol was available.

By June 25, the river flows withdrew to 2.8 feet. With lower water and the superior power of the Vertol, crews were optimistic. Several attempts, however, were made with the Vertol with an estimated 10,000 pounds of pull, but the wing did not move. On one attempt, the grappling hook pulled the landing gear from the wreckage. Other endeavors were likened to clawing at the wreckage—just breaking little bits and pieces off at each tug. The Kecks and support crew, including Pete Mills and Moose Creek employees Alan Carroll and Dolly Koons, along with others re-strung their cables, adding another side-force, while the helicopter pulled vertically—the Keck's cables alone were estimated to have exerted 40 tons of pull. The cables snapped. The wing was obviously immovable until the water retreated further.

Eleven days later, on July 6, Mills, the Kecks, and other support

202

crew returned to attempt moving the wing still stuck in Wolf Creek Rapid, and possibly uncover Whitey's body. The water on the Paradise gauge leveled at 1.8 feet from July 4 to July 8, then began a downward trend each day through July 30, reaching 0.6 feet. Lower water, exposed more of the wing surface. The crew again rigged the wing, planning to move it to the south bank where it would be more easily rigged to the Vertol for lifting. Unlike the other efforts, this time the concept was to inch it in small horizontal progressions with little verticality. By morning of the following day, the wing was secured along the shore. Penny recalled, "It was when the wing was finally moved I really understood the hydraulics of water. The amount of force water can create is amazing and most people have no idea. The hydraulics were pivotal, and once the river receded, we moved the wing a little at a time, never exceeding a two-to-five ton pull each time we moved it [the wing] before the rigging was re-set."

Mike Hill, who had also returned to the site to photograph the wing removal, recalled that during the crew's debriefing of the June 25 failure, it was hypothesized that not only were they trying to overcome the fluvial dynamics of the river's hydraulics, they were confronting the water weight trapped inside the wing. In an effort to overcome these factors, schematics of the wing were obtained and holes were punched throughout it to drain the water. On July 10, nearly a month after the accident, the Vertol returned to Wolf Creek Rapid and successfully lifted the wing. There was still no sense of closure, however, as Whitey's body was not found. Penny, reflecting on the moment and the post-accident operation, commented, "From the beginning, we were trying to make certain first and foremost families were taken care of…they were our main concern…and the airplane was always secondary."

• • •

Four days after the noise of the big Vertol helicopter faded from the remote canyon, a group of river rafters glimpsed a partially submerged body near the mouth of Cupboard Creek, four miles downstream from the impact. As soon as possible, the float party reported its findings to the USFS, which then notified the Idaho County Sheriff's Department. Officials from the county flew in by helicopter to the Cupboard Creek area the same day. Fred Noland, a mortician from Grangeville, began walking along the rocks downstream from the mouth of the creek and saw the body. He reached into the back pocket of the victim's green trousers and pulled out a wallet with information identifying him as Marvin Earl "Whitey" Hachmeister. Finally found, just two days before his fifty-second birthday. The body was recovered and flown to Fenn Ranger Station, where it was then transported by vehicle to Grangeville. Whitey is interred at the Fort Douglas Cemetery, Salt Lake City, Utah. His grave is marked with a traditional Vermont marble military headstone, inscribed as "Marvin E. Hachmeister, Major US Air Force."

Among the reverberations of the accident, Bruce Spotleson, a journalist with the *Lewiston Morning Tribune*, wrote an ode to Whitey, whom he greatly admired. Before his job at the newspaper, Bruce had spent six years on a USFS hotshot fire crew based in McCall and was a regular summer passenger on aircraft piloted by Whitey. "To us, Whitey was a guardian angel, comforter, source of both strength and confidence, and bush pilot—all rolled into one. Older smokejumpers who'd flown with Whitey before we came along told all kinds of tales about his experience in the war, but we never really knew which war…All we knew was that he was the best DC-3 pilot around." In the decades that followed Whitey's untimely death, Bruce would not be the only one to hold him in heroic regard. Barrie K. Gilbert, a wildlife biologist specializing in grizzly bears, is another admirer. Barrie credits Whitey with saving his life in 1977, after Barrie was mauled by a grizzly at a remote mountainous area in Yellowstone National Park. Whitey was the pilot of the DC-3 that dropped the smokejumper rescue crew.

LOOKING DOWNSTREAM WITH PINCHOT CAMP TO THE RIGHT, JUNE 1979. (*W. Cheyney*)

RAY REEL WITH A BELL JET RANGER, EARLY 1980S. (*R. Reel*)

A TWIN OTTER USED FOR SHUTTLING RAFTS AND GEAR
TO MOOSE CREEK RANGER STATION AS PART OF THE
RECOVERY AND SALVAGE EFFORTS. (*T. Kincaid*)

RECOVERY AND SALVAGE OPERATIONS AT THE END
OF THE SELWAY RIVER ROAD. (*T. Kincaid*)

RECOVERY AND SALVAGE OPERATIONS AT THE END
OF THE SELWAY RIVER ROAD. (*T. Kincaid*)

HELICOPTERS AND A BLM RAFT USED DURING RECOVERY AND
SALVAGE OPERATIONS BELOW THE ACCIDENT SITE. (*W. Cheyney*)

MIKE HILL AND PETE MILLS WITH THE FUSELAGE DURING
RIGGING STAGES OF THE SALVAGE OPERATION. (*M. Hill*)

WOLF CREEK RAPID LOOKING DOWNSTREAM FROM THE SELWAY RIVER TRAIL. PETE MILLS ROWING THE USFS RAFT (CENTER) AND OTHER CREWS VISIBLE ON ROCKY BAR (LEFT) AND CLIFF (RIGHT). *(W. Cheyney)*

RIGHT LANDING GEAR AND WHEEL VISIBLE (FAR LEFT) AND CREWS ON ROCKS AT WOLF CREEK RAPID ASSESSING RIGGING. *(M. Hill)*

RIGGING ATTEMPTS OF RIGHT WING AND LANDING GEAR IN WOLF CREEK RAPID. A KAYAKER IS VISIBLE IN THE FOREGROUND. (*M. Hill*)

Divers in Wolf Creek Rapid at the right landing gear and wheel. (*T. Kincaid*)

Boatmen taking a break for lunch along the Selway River. L to R: Winston Cheyney, Pete Mills, Jeff King, and Bob Michels. (*T. Kincaid*)

BOATMAN BOB MICHELS FERRYING DIVERS. NOTE
TETHERING CABLE STRUNG BANK-TO-BANK. (*W. Cheyney*)

TOM TERKEURST. (*J. Johnson*)

RON HAGAN. (*University of Montana/USFS Collection*)

PATRICK MCGREEVEY. (*E. McGreevey*)

Kevin Leber. (*F. Dehlinger*)

Bob Cook. (*M. Goodson*)

EMIL AND PENNY KECK DISCUSS THE RIGGING OF THE
RIGHT WING WITH PETE MILLS (CENTER). *(M. Hill)*

GRAPPLING HOOK USED TO LIFT PIECES OF 148Z. (*G. Miller*)

A DIVER (L) AND MIKE HILL (R) PREPARE THE LEFT ENGINE
NEAR DRY BAR FOR AERIAL LIFTING. (*M. Hill*)

THE LEFT ENGINE BEING LIFTED, JUNE 20, 1979. (*M. Hill*)

FUSELAGE AND TAIL SECTION BEING LIFTED, JUNE 20, 1979. (*M. Hill*)

THE VERTOL LIFTING THE RIGHT WING FROM WOLF
CREEK RAPID, JULY 10, 1979. (*Seamans Collection*)

RIGGING THE RIGHT WING FOR VERTICAL LIFT BY THE VERTOL HELICOPTER. *(Seamans Collection)*

NEIL WALSTAD STUDYING THE RIGHT WING OF 148Z AT FENN RANGER STATION. *(Seamans Collection)*

WHITEY HACHMEISTER'S HEADSTONE, FORT DOUGLAS
CEMETERY, SALT LAKE CITY. (*Holm Collection*)

10

GRIEF AND GUILT

We enter now a different time zone, even a different world of time.
Suddenly comes the world of slow-time that accompanies grief
and moral bewilderment trying to understand the extinction of
those whose love and everlasting presence were never questioned.
—NORMAN MACLEAN, *YOUNG MEN AND FIRE*

On June 11, 1979, Steve Wright was sitting in his office on the campus of the Sterling Institute, located in Craftsbury Commons, Vermont.[7] Founded in 1958, the school began as an all-boys preparatory school for college. By the 1970s, the curriculum focused on outdoor leadership—which was loosely connected to Outward Bound. It evolved into a four-year, co-ed undergraduate program, with emphasis on environmental stewardship through ecology, environmental humanities, general outdoor education, and sustainable

---

7 Currently known as Sterling College, located in Craftsbury Commons, Vermont.

agriculture. The transition to higher education started with a short course in outdoor leadership. In addition to Steve's work as professor at the school, he collaborated with government agencies nationwide to place students in summer internships. In 1975, he and Art Seamans met over the telephone and forged a close personal and working relationship, resulting in the placement of a handful of Sterling students each season on the Moose Creek District. The internees returned with rave reviews. Thereafter, the internship positions at Moose Creek were saved for the best and brightest students, an arrangement that extended into the mid-1980s.

It was a cold, rainy, dreary day. Steve was depressed sitting in his office, and that was unlike the enthusiastic 38-year-old professor. All the students had departed for the summer; the campus was silent, and he had little to look forward to until fall. Before lunch, he left his office and trudged home to his small apartment. To lift his spirits, he sat down at his fly-tying desk. He opened a box with his completed flies, something he had not done for months. His inventory revealed a shortage of his favorite flies. Mulling the mystery of missing flies, his mind wandered to a Montana and Idaho fishing trip he and a friend had taken the previous summer. It included an excursion to Moose Creek and on this side trip; he had parted with the flies.

While on the road trip out West, Steve decided he really wanted to visit Moose Creek after hearing so much about it from his students and Art. So he and his buddy drove to Grangeville and chartered a flight with Grangeville Air Service. He was smitten by the Selway. They fished for about three days, visited students and staff, and familiarized themselves with the area. In the evenings, they sat around and enjoyed the lively conversations over dinner. During these sunset chats one young person in particular made an impression on

Steve—Bryant Stringham. Bryant grew up fishing and was captivated by fly-fishing. Every evening, Bryant quizzed Steve about the flies he was using, the species and size of fish he was catching, and their location.

Engaged in reminiscing, Steve realized as they boarded the airplane on their way back to Grangeville, he had given a handful of flies to Bryant, including the most successful pattern of the trip—the Grey Wulff. At that moment, Steve was overcome by a surge of an odd feeling. It bothered him, but he could not identify it until that night when a friend, who also worked at Sterling, called him and asked if he had seen the *CBS Evening News* with Dan Rather. Steve had not. His friend informed him that a USFS DC-3 had crashed in a remote Idaho river and most people aboard were unaccounted for. The friend inquired, "Does this mean anything to you?" Steve's response: "You better believe it means something to me!"

Just months earlier, Steve had inveigled Art's right-hand man, Don Easthouse, for a few student intern slots at Moose Creek. Easthouse could only reserve one; however, nine other students were placed on the Nez Perce NF and neighboring Clearwater NF in 1979. For the Moose Creek spot, Steve chose Tom TerKeurst. After gathering all the information he could, he learned that a former Sterling student, Mary Gramling, who had been a volunteer on the District and had recently been hired as a paid seasonal employee, missed the plane, but Tom was aboard and presumed to be dead. Steve called Tom's family, then the Sterling administration. All agreed that he should book a flight to Idaho as soon as possible. On the morning of his flight, he hurried to his gate at the Chicago O'Hare International Airport. As he walked past a newspaper stand, he saw the front page of a newspaper, above the fold, was the photograph of the DC-3 with the tumbling, burning engine trailing a smoke plume. He snatched a copy and continued to the gate, only to be informed that the door was closed and no further boarding allowed. "I was a bit stirred up by that and put the front page of the paper in front of the person in charge of boarding. I said, 'See this? I am on the recovery team and you have to get me on that plane!' The person looked at the photo and said, 'Get the pilot to pull back to the gate.' It worked."

In the whirlwind of emotions, phone calls, gathering facts, travel, and trying to figure out how he could best help, Steve realized that about the time the airplane plunged into the Selway River was when he was staring at his few remaining Grey Wulffs. The coincidence haunted him for the rest of his life.

He arrived in Idaho and fulfilled the needs and requests of the TerKeurst family—an immensely sensitive task. He not only became responsible for collecting all of Tom's belongings, he also helped Marilyn TerKeurst with the family's request to spread Tom's ashes near the accident. Because of logistical complications, Steve coordinated with Art and they chose an alternative site two miles inside the Selway-Bitterroot Wilderness boundary, at the confluence of Renshaw Creek and the Selway River. Here the stream joins with the Selway at a serene, sandy beach framed by majestic western red cedars draped with bearded lichen. Steve invited the other Sterling students in Idaho that summer to join him on the hike to honor Tom. He led the group, which included Cheryl Warren, Zannah Crowe, and Craig Lang. On June 17, 1979, Steve stood alongside the merging waters, spoke kindly of his former student, and scattered him there.

Many Moose Creekers from the 1979 season credit Steve with modifying the mood of the post-accident mourning. He became the mainstay for so many who needed someone to talk to and listen to during their grieving. His background as an educator furnished these skills. Art recognized his ability. On his way out of town, Steve stopped by Art's office in Grangeville. Art sat him down and offered him the opportunity to fill the vacancy left by Don Easthouse's death. After days of discussion, they reached an agreement whereby Sterling allowed Steve to work for Art on a two-year temporary leave. Steve recalled it as the best two years of his life: "It was glorious. Those two years became the foundation of my career." According to him, the Moose Creek District was distinctly set apart from the other areas he placed students. It was an accolade. "Moose Creek had the courage to dare…dare to do something different and try new things, both on the ground and administratively. There are times when people come together and create a certain synergy. It is more than one-plus-one-equals-two, it is bigger than that. At Moose Creek, we were doing God's work, in one of God's most beautiful places. The students and employees were tough when they got there—mentally and physically—and when they came back or moved on, they were even tougher. It was an honor to be a part of it."

· · ·

Don Easthouse was the District's most hopeful future wilderness management leader. Don had come to the Moose Creek District a few months before the accident and immediately made a promising impression on all of his peers. That promise was considered pivotal to future wilderness leadership on the District and the forest. During his fleeting tenure, he led an impressive and effective campaign to shape a wilderness education program for local public schools, something he also had strived to implement while attending the University of

Montana. His wilderness program expanded from primary school to college.

Don was born in September 1949, in Watertown, South Dakota, where he spent his first 12 years before moving in 1961 with his family to Wilcox, Arizona. The Easthouses grew to a family of three boys and seven girls. Two years after high school graduation, Don married Karen Berryman, and then, until 1971, served several years in the Marines. The following year, he enrolled in the School of Forestry at the University of Montana and worked seasonally for the USFS, mainly on the Bitterroot NF's Stevensville Ranger District as a wilderness ranger. His emphasis developed into wilderness management and education. He graduated from the program in 1978, briefly took a position with the BLM in Medford, Oregon, before accepting the Moose Creek position and moving to Grangeville, where he planned a career in wilderness management, along with raising his children, Dylan and Krystal.

He is buried in Wilcox, but his memory is enshrined on a 23-mile stretch of trail in Montana along a high divide in the Bitterroot Mountains. It runs from the Sapphire Crest to Skalkaho Pass, and north to Sawmill Saddle. The trail was dedicated in his name as the "Easthouse National Recreation Trail." Shortly after his funeral, friends established a memorial fund for the project. The trail along the Sapphire Crest was selected because it was among Don's favorite hikes. It navigates grassy meadows and jagged rock outcroppings as it passes landmarks such as Stony and Burnt Fork lakes. The trail reaches its pinnacle at Dome Mountain, with panoramas of the Bitterroot, Anaconda-Pintler, and the Lincoln Scapegoat mountain ranges. The dedication was well attended by friends and family. At the ceremony, friends shared memories, including those of Mike LaWare and Bob Daniels, who commented, "He was kind of half-legendary in terms of feats of strength…He was the kind of individual who would hike into a high alpine lake, trudging up steep switchbacks for miles, and then exercise when he got there. Returning, he would typically pack out 25 or more pounds of garbage, along with his weighty pack. It was Don against Don…he was always showing someone how to build a better fire, leave a cleaner camp, make better use of an area's resources. He was concerned primarily with preserving existing wilderness, rather than pushing for more of it." Another friend, Mike Wilson, remembered him as "half philosopher." He was referring to Don's appreciation of wilderness and ethics that he instilled in others. His passion for wilderness survives in the Easthouse Trail, but also in his poetry. His wife compiled a book of his poems, and she and her children gave copies to friends and family. Art Seamans was so moved by Don's poem, "Budding, Dying Leaves," that he included a typed copy with every letter of condolence to victims' families.

• • •

As for the remainder of the 1979 season at Moose Creek, few on the District remembered whether or not Guard School ever occurred. It was not as distinctive as years past—it was not a multiday event with a beginning and an end. No customary group photograph was taken on the last day, which had become a Moose Creek tradition. Instead, training sessions were spread out from June 14 to June 28, and only as time permitted between job commitments. Some days neglected training altogether, and others held a single session. Basics were covered, however. On June 14, seasoned Moose Creek employee Gary Miller wrote in his daily government diary, "In an attempt at normality, tool training by Penny, with Dolly & me, Laura Till, Cheshire

Peirce, Mary Gramling (Dave Clarke, Ian Barlow, the new packer, and Carol Mytron irregulars). First things before you go out, basic gear. The ax, the handle. The Pulaski. Sharpening. Saw filing by Warren. We cut and buck a few small logs."

Several reasons account for the irregular or discordant training: First, Emil and Penny, who were the hub of the wheel for these classes, were too busy traveling to the accident site and aiding the search, recovery and salvage efforts. Second, many of the other District employees were helping on the river with their backcountry skills. Third, the ranking District employees were absent. Employees such as Art Seamans, Steve Wright, and Larry Keown were busy answering questions from the media, coordinating the recovery/ salvage efforts, dealing with investigation teams, and corresponding with relatives of those employees/volunteers who were missing or dead. Later, a major cause of leave on the District was employees attending funerals.

Moreover, the management staff had to deal with the labor shortage caused by the accident. People needed to be hired to fill the vacant jobs on the District for the season. Steve Hill and Steve Danielovich were new hires to fill trail-crew positions. Cheshire, originally hired for trail crew, was reassigned to fill in with Warren as an assistant wilderness ranger at the Lost Horse Guard Station. Dave Clarke, a regular seasonal employee who was to inventory fuels across the District in 1979, was asked by Larry Keown to staff the Shissler Peak Lookout for two weeks, until a new hire arrived. As the fire management officer, Larry was in charge of the two wilderness lookouts on the District—Gardiner Peak and Shissler. He hired both applicants over the phone. The Shissler Peak hire backed out, and he then hired Catherine "Tykie" Hodgin.

• • •

"Tykie," as she was known by her family and friends, was the youngest of three children born in Delano, California, in July 1953. After graduating from high school, she attended Cuesta College in San Luis Obispo and then Porterville Junior College, both in California. Tykie married Dan Hodgin; they moved to Flagstaff, Arizona, and then to Eugene, where she attended the University of Oregon in pursuit of a forestry degree. Her marriage lasted but a few years, but she and Dan remained friends, sharing an interest in arts and crafts—Tykie was knitting, weaving, and dyeing her own yarns with natural plants and fibers. While attending university, Tykie spent her summers working as a fire lookout, including a season at Breckenridge Lookout on the Sequoia NF, located 50 miles east of Bakersfield, California. During her years on lookouts, Tykie also became involved in Youth Conservation Corps (YCC) leadership, helping high school volunteers with trail maintenance on BLM land in Oregon. In March 1980, to honor her efforts with the program, a trail along Shotgun Creek near Eugene was named "The Tykie Trail." Forty years later, Timothy Patrick, a colleague with Tykie at the YCC, remembered her as "A wonderful person with a great heart. The kids and her coworkers all loved her, and many gathered at the dedication ceremony when we placed the trail name sign in her honor." The University of Oregon awarded her a posthumous degree. Tykie is buried in Bakersfield at the Greenlawn Cemetery.

As related earlier, although she did not survive the airplane crash, Tykie's K-9 companion Bess, a dog she was bringing along for her summer on Shissler Peak, withstood the accident and was found with a broken leg by Missoula smokejumpers late in the day on June 11. She was flown to Grangeville and treated by a local veterinarian and eventually picked up by Dan, who adopted her. With Tykie dead, Larry scrambled for an alternate Shissler lookout. He finally found one in Eric Wood, who on July 6 relieved Dave Clarke.

• • •

Tim Rich was another person who arrived late for the 1979 season. Beginning in 1975 through 1978, Rich had worked on the District as one of three wilderness rangers and decided he wanted a career in the USFS, which then required the appointment to a permanent position. He obtained that appointment in fire management on a forest in Arizona. However, he was not that pleased with the position and had communicated with Art about returning to Moose Creek. While nothing was entirely agreed upon at the beginning of June, Art was pleased to hear from Tim after the accident and encouraged him to come back. Tim was assigned his previous job on the District as the wilderness ranger based at Selway Falls.

In early July, Tim returned to the District and a gloomy atmosphere, but he was soon back in the fold of the Moose Creek family. People were not only grieving—each felt guilty in their own way. Some of those who missed the flight by unforeseen circumstances or by chance commiserated with each other and shared "survivor's guilt." Others thought that if they had just suggested some different plan, the outcome could have been different. Art was in the vanguard, but he did not share it with his employees. Tim's guilt arose from the fact that he was not there. A year earlier, the assistant ranger/resource assistant approved the organization of an optional hike from Selway Falls to Moose Creek as an alternative to flying in for Guard School. Those who did not want to hike could fly in from Grangeville, as had been done in earlier years. Tim—along with more senior Moose

Creekers, Warren Miller, Gary Miller, Dale Swee, Dick Kuhl—thought hiking in was more in keeping with the wilderness ethics they learned at the training.

• • •

Initially, other than scrapes and bruises, the doctors in Spokane could find nothing wrong with Charlie, and they stitched a cut on his left hand. Julie thought it was odd. He obviously was not okay. She responded, "What do you mean there is nothing wrong? He fell out of the sky…help him." In spite of her argument, on June 12 he was discharged from the hospital. They went to Yvette's parents' house in northwest Spokane. Within 24 hours, Charlie developed excruciating pain in his left knee and saw blood in his urine. Julie took him back to the hospital where doctors concluded his kidneys had gone into traumatic shock, a problem that eventually resolved itself. On June 15, however, he had surgery on his left knee to repair torn ligaments, and his leg was placed in a cast. Charlie returned to Yvette's parent's house for post-op recovery. By the end of the month, he had undergone several more hospital visits, an interview with investigators, and was cleared by doctors and Art to return to Selway Falls.

Because of his leg, however, Charlie could barely hobble. Julie, a volunteer, ended up sharing his job. To accommodate the Dietzes, Tim Rich insisted on switching living quarters with them. He moved into the wall tent, and they into the station cabin. Tim commented, "Charlie was a very quiet and soft-spoken person and had little to say about the accident. I greatly admired their desire to stick it out for the remainder of the season." Once Charlie's cast was removed, he and Julie were more mobile, although still restricted to work around the station. Tim assigned them to re-chinking the cabin. During the season of 1976, Tim started a vegetable garden on the west side of the cabin and improved it each year. By 1979, it had an electric fence and was well fertilized with horse manure from the uphill corrals. Tending and harvesting the garden became a source of enjoyment and a healthy distraction for the Dietzes.

All 1979 Moose Creek employees concurred that Moose Creek was the best place for them to come to terms with what had happened. Not only did their family of coworkers surround them, the strenuous daily labor boosted the healing process. Art noted in a 2014 interview that an event of such magnitude was something one never got over; it is just something one has to live with. The Moose Creek employees of 1979 unanimously agreed they could not have endured the grieving and healing without one another, or without the isolation and time that Moose Creek provided. And they also agreed that the leadership and support of Art Seamans and Steve Wright was critical and indispensable.

STEVE WRIGHT, SELWAY RIVER, 1981. (*B. Farling*)

DON EASTHOUSE, BOB MARSHALL WILDERNESS. (*J. McCarthy*)

Budding, Dying Leaves

We watch the flower and the fading
    of the seasons every year.
Somehow this process is forever
    and the leaves fall without fear.

Our lives on earth are but the striking
    of a match ~ a flash of flame.
Our passing is continuous
    through love we share, but cannot claim.

Sometimes someone among us
    seems to shine more than the rest,
And there is comfort in the feeling
    that through them love glows expressed.

Through their example there is guidance
    to the light that shines above
For those of us who stay revealing
    the flowing movement of this love.

We are all but budding, dying leaves
    upon the tree of life,
At any time a gust of wind may come along
    to free us from our strife.

We do not grieve the change of seasons
    for we see that sun and sky remain.
No use to fear or grieve lives passing,
    you see, therein, lies loves refrain.

DON EASTHOUSE'S POEM. (J. McCarthy)

CATHERINE "TYKIE" HODGIN. *(C. Mason)*

TIM RICH AND CHARLIE DIETZ (L) AT THE SELWAY
FALLS GUARD STATION, 1979. *(Dietz Collection)*

JULIE DIETZ (R) AND SISTER AT SELWAY FALLS
GUARD STATION. *(Dietz Collection)*

CHARLIE DIETZ CHINKING SELWAY FALLS
GUARD STATION CABIN. (*Dietz Collection*)

RICHARD H. HOLM, JR.

CHARLIE DIETZ AND THE 148Z FUSELAGE AT THE END
OF THE SELWAY RIVER ROAD. (*Dietz Collection*)

11

INDEPENDENCE FIRE

"Fortunately we went from that accident [the DC-3] into one of the busiest fire years we had ever had. Being that busy and that involved probably saved our bacon..."
—ART SEAMANS (2008 INTERVIEW)

On July 2, 1979, Ralph Fireoved, a seasonal employee on the Moose Creek Ranger District, reported to Larry Keown at Moose Creek. Ralph came to the District three years earlier in hopes of landing the fire lookout position on Shissler Peak. The position had already been filled; instead, he signed on as a member of a two-person trail crew. Still wanting to be posted to a fire lookout, he persuaded management to assign him to Gardiner Peak for the summer of 1978—the District's most remote active lookout. Painted white and trimmed in green, the 14-foot by 14-foot glass-windowed lookout built in 1953 is a classic 1930's USFS design and sits on 10-foot wooden legs. At an elevation of 6,597 feet, it commands views of the southern end of the District, especially the Selway River drainage, the Bear Creek drainage, and the Bitterroot Divide.

Until Ralph's arrival, the Selway region had experienced seasonally cool temperatures with daytime highs in the 60s. On the day he set out to hike from Moose Creek to Gardiner, however, temperatures reached 90, and the forecast was for more of the same. The increased temperatures meant convective activity in the mountainous region of north central Idaho, with potential lightning storms. In an effort to beat the heat, the 30-year-old Ralph departed Moose Creek early. By late morning, he reached the trail junction and began the 4,000-foot vertical climb toward Gardiner Peak. As he ascended and earned a better view of the surrounding mountains, he saw cumulonimbus clouds building; still he remained intent on reaching his destination.

By late afternoon, he was settling in at the lookout: unpacking his supplies delivered ahead of him, hauling water, and splitting wood. Tired from the long day of travel and chores, he bedded down before the sun fell behind the distant mountains. The next morning dawned warm, and the temperature generated fresh thunderheads. Afternoon clouds swelled skyward, towering thousands of feet, threatening severe fire weather. Heavy winds, rain, and lightning followed.

Ralph turned to fire detection. Atop his glass-footed stool, hunched over the alidade (firefinder) in the center of the room, he was ready to plot the lightning strikes. Rain pelted the lookout windows and hail bounced off the stove pipe and wooden shingles almost in rhythm with one another. The darkened sky yielded the smell of ozone and the strong winds bent the trees over in pulsing arches. The noise and the eagerness of calling in a fire before other lookouts were part of the job. To quickly measure the distance to a strike, Ralph counted the time between a clap of thunder and the flash. The storm was soon upon him...with a deafening BOOOM, and an instantaneous lightning strike off the north side of the mountain. He called in the location—south side of the Bear Creek drainage about seven miles up from the Selway River. Once the storm swept through, he kept his eye on the spot. A thin column of smoke rose, but he could not confirm flames.

Several hours later, the forest dispatched a single-engine fire patrol airplane from Grangeville to scour the Gardiner Peak area to see if the strike had resulted in fire. The pilot flew low recon up and down the Bear Creek drainage—a vast area more like a river with massive topographic relief rising to the east and fading into the Bitterroot Divide. The fire patrol confirmed by radio an active fire in the drainage, but it was in fact on the north side of Bear Creek and not the south as reported. Since the ignition began on July 4, the fire was named "the Independence Fire" and was allowed to burn for three months to just over 16,000 acres mostly unsuppressed by human influence until extinguished by fall rain and snow. Although trivial compared to the DC-3 accident, it kept the Moose Creek Ranger District in the media. Larry Keown, the Moose Creek fire management officer commented, "The press had a heyday with us. A horrific airplane crash and then a huge fire we were letting burn. It was unheard of…people were wondering, 'What the hell is Moose Creek doing?'"

For several reasons the fire became significant to the Moose Creek District and its employees. First, it was the largest fire allowed to burn on the Moose Creek's portion of the Selway-Bitterroot Wilderness, which was part of a new fire management policy drafted by Larry and approved in August 1978. The underlying concept of the plan recognized that in wilderness, fire is a natural occurrence yielding ecological benefits. The plan divided the 560,088-acre District into specific fire management zones. Within each zone the different types of forests were inventoried and identified by one of seven defined Ecological Land Units (ELU) such as shrubfield, ponderosa pine savanna, subalpine, etc. Based on these elements, a specific plan was laid out to manage the prescribed fire if a natural ignition occurred. The plan also outlined exceptions where fire would be suppressed if it threatened specified ranger/guard stations, fire lookouts, bridges, and private inholdings such as Running Creek, North Star, Selway Lodge, and Seminole Ranch. The neighboring Bitterroot NF's portion of the Selway-Bitterroot Wilderness to the south, experimented with two prescription (let-burn) fires on two Selway River tributaries: Bad Luck Fire (1972) and Fritz Creek/White Cap Creek Fire (1973). The Independence Fire exceeded both (the 1972 fire burned less than an acre and the second burned 1,200 acres). The old policy of "fire control" became "fire management." The preparation for prescription fire on the Moose Creek Ranger District, and the resulting 1978 management plan, began with Dick Walker. Dick mapped a prescription plan for the District's 50,000-acre Bear Creek area to mimic similar management set forth by the Bitterroot NF. In 1974, Barry Hicks arrived on the District, and instead of adding 50,000-acre chunks, suggested an all-encompassing plan. It became the 1978 document.

• • •

Through mid-July, temperatures hovered in the high 90s, with little or no precipitation. Coupled with periods of high wind, the fire spread downstream, burning at low intensity on the ground. While managers were satisfied with its progression and behavior, they were not oblivious to the need to protect bridges at Pettibone Creek, Selway Lodge, and Bear Creek, among exceptions in the management plan. To mitigate the potential loss, a fire camp was set up near the confluence of Bear Creek and the Selway at the flat which was once the site of the Bear Creek Ranger Station. By the 1950s the USFS abandoned the site for administrative uses after obtaining ownership of Phil Shearer's homestead upstream (present day USFS Shearer Airstrip). As the DC-3 salvage efforts closed, Emil and Penny had little time to reflect before they were assigned fire detail at Bear Creek.

The establishment of the Bear Creek fire camp added a second significance to the Independence Fire. Emil was to "handle the practical aspects of the operation," and therefore he relied on seasonal Moose Creek District employees to help haul equipment and monitor fire behavior. Alan Carroll noted, "Emil personally scoffed at the very idea of prescribed fire, but he was extremely proud of this effort. He may not have said it, but he showed it. There he was, a former fire control officer back working fire like in the old days. For years he had been teaching fire suppression skills at the annual Guard School, but none of us ever actually used those skills until this fire...after all, we were primarily trained for trail work." Each year at Guard School, as part of the training, Emil set a small, half-acre fire in the vicinity of the Moose Creek Ranger Station—sometimes even two fires, depending on the number of trainees. Once the fire or fires were underway, he and Penny watched the employees put them out, using hand tools, and when they were finished the Kecks gave them pointers for improvements.

Emil was pleased with the application of firefighting skills (equipment set-up and fire lines cleared near the bridges and camp); more consequential was the distraction from the DC-3 accident that had afflicted District morale and the season's agenda. The fire, for many, gave them something positive to focus on for the first time all summer, and an opportunity to work together as a team. There were some members of trail crews, however, who viewed it negatively. "The Independence Fire was just another setback, in addition to the airplane accident. There was barely enough time in a 'normal season' to clear all the necessary trails. It was another ordeal that pulled us away from the work we were hired to do and wanted to do."

For the first few weeks, the fire burned on the south-facing slopes of old-growth ponderosa pine—a healthy, low-intensity ground fire. But on August 1, the fire neared the Selway River, and the wind picked up, causing it to crown. Embers spotted over to the west side of the river. The cinders ignited north-facing slopes with heavy understory and dense stands of fir. Then it raced southward toward the Selway Lodge—private structures identified in the management plan for protection. Suppression efforts commenced.

Everett and Freddie Peirce, the owners of the Selway Lodge, were apprehensive about losing structures on their historic inholding. The Peirces were known on the District to be wilderness advocates who welcomed District employees. They were outspoken about the new fire policy, however. They feared this precise outcome. In their annual year-end letter to relatives, friends, and guests, they wrote, "The Forest Service became really concerned and pulled all stops to hold the fire away from us. First, a team of sixteen smokejumpers was dropped in our pasture to extinguish a flare-up across Bear Creek. Then flights of Twin Otters began ferrying men and equipment into the government airstrip up river from us. Then groups of yellow-helmeted firefighters, some from as far as the Arizona Apache Reservation, began arriving. Big army-type helicopters began slingloading pumps, hose, and other material onto our airstrip. It had all the trappings of a wartime operation—noise, confusion, even to the smoke-filled air. Quite a departure from our normal wilderness!"

A 30-foot wide fire line was cleared around the perimeter of the Lodge property and then a backburn was set. The Peirces continued, "The building of the firelines took about three days. All the time, with dramatic effect at night, we could watch the main fire slowly approaching up the river. On the third evening, when wind and moisture conditions were favorable, the backfires were lit. That's when we learned how the marshmallow feels on the end of the stick, smoke and fire surrounding us, exciting, spectacular, dramatic with smoke billowing off the ridgetops in a bright orange sky. By the next morning, the fire had burned out with just a number of snags and down logs still smoldering. The plan had worked and we were out of whatever danger we might have been in."

Several loads of Region 1 smokejumpers jumped the fire, beginning in late July through mid-August; and others were flown in with Twin Otters to the Shearer Airstrip. At one point, more than 200 people were engaged. Several of the smokejumpers were assigned to the Independence Fire more than once, and a few of the jumpers were veterans of the June 11 DC-3 rescue.

At the height of the Independence Fire, word filtered down to Art Seamans and Larry Keown from the Nez Perce NF Supervisor's Office, advising them to "put a short leash on the fire," since political pressure from Washington and the public, complaining of poor air quality, was mounting. Larry said, "The underlying tone of the conversation was if it gets any worse, you better implement a plan ASAP to put it out. Full suppression." The next day, Larry arranged a flight in order that he and Art could make the necessary observations and implement a plan, but before it materialized, rain pushed into the area and tamped it. The fire was placed on "monitoring status" for the rest of the season. Snows extinguished it.

Fire statistics kept by the District up to 1979 revealed an average of 35 lightning-caused fires annually (1961 had 135 fires). In 1979, more than 70 fires occurred, and all but two were extinguished. In general, 1979 was a considered a big wildland fire year across the West. The largest fire of the season burned in Yellowstone; Idaho's Mortar Creek Fire (human-caused) along the Middle Fork of the Salmon River burned 60,000 acres. The media did not target fires as a whole; rather it aimed at the idea of "natural burns." One editorial from the August 10, 1979 *Wall Street Journal* called it "simple misjudgments by local forest rangers." Others in the field of ecology and wilderness management judged prescribed fires, such as the Independence Fire, a success. Since 1979, multiple naturally-occurring fires have continued to affect the landscape of the Bear Creek drainage.

After July 4, Ralph Fireoved's season atop Gardiner Peak was disrupted by this turmoil and turbulence. As a career school teacher, he planned to return east for another school year, but he was asked to stay on an additional two weeks to August-end to monitor the fire. He agreed. He returned as Gardiner Peak lookout for another five seasons—none as memorable as 1979.

Thirty years later, reflecting on the Independence Fire, the 1979 fire season, and how it joined the DC-3 accident, Art said, "Fortunately, we went from that accident into one of the busiest fire years we had ever had. Being that busy and that involved probably saved our bacon…otherwise we would have been a pretty traumatized bunch of people…as it was, we just had so many things to involve our minds and bodies for the rest of the summer that we got through it. We didn't have things like grief-counselling or that type of thing, it just didn't exist then."

GARDINER PEAK LOOKOUT, 1988. *(T. Van de Water)*

RALPH FIREOVED, GARDINER PEAK LOOKOUT. *(G. Miller)*

THE START OF THE INDEPENDENCE FIRE. (*L. Keown*)

INDEPENDENCE FIRE BURNING THE BEAR CREEK DRAINAGE. (*L. Keown*)

INDEPENDENCE FIRE. (*L. Keown*)

ART SEAMANS AND LARRY KEOWN INFORMING THE MEDIA
ABOUT THE INDEPENDENCE FIRE. (*Seamans Collection*)

EXAMPLE OF INFORMATIONAL SIGNS POSTED ALONG TRAILS
IN THE VICINITY OF THE INDEPENDENCE FIRE. (*L. Keown*)

12

WHAT THE HELL HAPPENED?

"Fly the biggest piece down."
—BOB JOHNSON

From the time the wreckage of 148Z was located in the Selway River, until mid-August when the USFS finalized the official accident report, speculation as to what caused the crash was permeated with misinformation, opinions, and rumors in the pages of local and regional newspapers. Airplanes, and subsequently the crashes of aircraft, tend to capture attention. Although aviation is no longer as novel as it once was, it holds a certain fascination, especially to the non-pilot. Statistically, one is more likely to be in a car crash, because of frequency; airplane and pilot failures persist as sought-after news. Flying, after all, is an action that defies what most people do in their daily lives.

The first six months of 1979 were replete with aviation loss in Idaho, and the media reported it. From January 1 until the Selway accident, 20 aircraft had crashed in the state, and 13 people died.

Most notable was the headline accident of a high-wing single-engine Cessna 172 that crashed in poor weather on May 5 in the White Cloud Mountains near the summit of a remote ridge. The airplane was on a cross-country flight from Canada to the Boise area to pick up a recently purchased puppy. All four people aboard initially survived, but two later died at the scene. Rescuers were unable to locate the wreckage. With little survival gear or food, the two survivors resorted to cannibalism. After two weeks of living in the wreckage, surrounded by deep snow at high altitude, they gambled on hiking out. After days of stumbling through rough terrain, they found a mining camp and help (the story became the subject of a book, in 1980).

The same month, Idaho Senator Gerald Blackbird died in a helicopter he was piloting on the St. Joe NF in northern Idaho, while inspecting a timber sale. These events were not unordinary. In 1977, there were 39 aviation-related crashes and 21 fatalities; in 1978, Idaho had 24 crashes, with nine fatalities. In more recent years, from 2013 to 2019, the statistics have remained essentially the same, ranging from 22 to 33 accidents a year. The number of fatalities is somewhat lower, ranging from 1 to 13 people a year. Perhaps the number of crashes and fatalities may be attributed to Idaho being second only to Alaska in having the highest per capita ownership of aircraft, and having more developed backcountry airstrips than anywhere else in North America.

When the Selway accident occurred, journalists latched onto the story; after all, the disaster was charged with tragedy, loss, and survival. The popularity of aviation in Idaho, and the interest in the subject sold newspapers. Grief-laden content, of course. And in this case, the essence of grief was searching for someone, some group, something, anything, wherein to place blame. From the onset, opinion pieces and letters to the editor regarding the accident flooded regional newspapers. The aircraft itself was a popular theme: was it safe?

Another runway of blame was big government: the USFS. After all, distrust of governmental agencies in the West has long been a favorite whetstone. Scrutiny of the USFS's aviation operations by the public and internally by the Agency itself, arrived with alacrity.

At the public level, blame was directed at the USFS generally, but to those who know the interworkings of a large government agency, the structure is not as simple as it appears, and this accident illustrates such entanglements. The USFS is an agency under the US Department of Agriculture that manages public lands across the US. Under that umbrella, the Agency is divided into regions. The regions are then divided into national forests, which are then further subdivided into ranger districts.

The Selway tragedy occurred on the Moose Creek Ranger District, which is within the Nez Perce NF, which, in turn is part of the Northern Region (Region 1) of the USFS, headquartered in Missoula, Montana. The aircraft, however, was a part of the Intermountain Region (Region 4) headquartered in Ogden, Utah, with national forests encompassing Idaho as far north as the Salmon River, where the river canyon is not only distinctive geographically, but marks the boundary between Region 1 and Region 4—some among the Agency refer to it as the "Mason-Dixon Line" or the "Iron Curtain." Historically, at this demarcation the regions rarely infringe on one another's management of recreation, timber, grazing, firefighting—all part of the same agency. Given interagency differences, questions of blame and acrimony were bound to arise—especially involving a Region 4 airplane and crash, and a Region 1 site, staff, and volunteers.

Compounding complexities, the aircraft, owned and operated by the federal government, fell within the category of "Public Aircraft," meaning it was treated as though it were a military-type aircraft subject to a gray area of aviation regulation, compared with other sectors of the aviation industry in the US regulated by a well-defined Code of Federal Regulations (CFR). The Code covers the Federal Aviation Administration (FAA) applicable to commercial air carriers, such as airlines or air taxies (CFR Part 121 and Part 135) or civil aircraft (CFR Part 91). In the event of an accident under the latter federal codes, it is subject to an investigation by the National Transportation Safety Board (NTSB), which serves as an unbiased third party. However, aircraft operated under Public Aircraft were not then subject to an NTSB investigation, but rather one conducted in-house. The investigation of 148Z was carried out by the Agency's administrators at the Washington Office (WO). This was unusual. Typically, accident investigations and the subsequent report are the responsibility of the region charged with the accident. In this case, the accident, if measured by the number of fatalities, was the USFS's worst in its history. And it was the second-largest fatal airplane accident to occur within the state of Idaho (the most catastrophic accident occurred in 1958 near Payette, when a US Air Force Fairchild C-123 crashed in a farmer's field, killing all 19 people aboard).

The lead Washington Office investigation team was headed by Glenn Haney, and it included two sub-teams—one from Region 1 and the other from Region 4. The Region 1 group consisted of seven persons and the Region 4 group consisted of two. The disproportional number can be attributed to the fact Region 4's Aviation Program was under investigation.

With such overwhelming media and public attention, the USFS's primary investigation team was promptly assembled and at work. The team grew in the days following the accident, and its outcome was an exhaustive 872-page report completed within less than nine weeks. Investigators tracked down and took the statements of eyewitnesses, survivors, rescuers, and anyone else thought to have knowledge of the aircraft, its operations, and the events leading up to and following the accident. Maintenance records were demanded. The crux of the investigation lay in the examination of the recovered Pratt & Whitney engines, eyewitness interviews, and the reconstruction of the events leading up to the flight, such as maintenance and pilot actions before and during the flight.

• • •

By August 24, 1979, the media had obtained copies of the report. The media spotlighted the autopsy for Whitey Hachmeister. It revealed an alcohol level exceeding ten percent by weight in Whitey's organs. Given the seriousness of potential accusations, the USFS appointed a special investigator. As part of his research, he retraced Whitey's steps for the 24-hours leading up to the flight. He interviewed every person Whitey had knowingly come in contact with, searched his trailer where he spent the night of June 10, consulted with four pathologists, and with an attorney who specialized in toxicology litigation. Furthermore, the investigator collected character statements from coworkers and friends regarding Whitey's drinking habits. The investigation revealed that no one observed him drinking the day leading up to the flight; moreover, he was known to be only a casual social drinker. Examination of his trailer in McCall did not discover any bottles or cans containing alcohol. The five experts interviewed "unanimously" stated, "Decomposition through bacterial contamination will produce alcohol in organs." They were all insistent that the autopsy was unreliable with respect to liquor consumption because of the lapse between death and the autopsy (33 days). The investigator then confirmed, together with the undertaker, who was present when the body was recovered from the river, that there was significant decomposition. Whitey's character and reputation were reaffirmed. The media, however, were not assuaged.

• • •

A reconstruction of events and findings determined the plane departed from McCall and arrived in Grangeville at 0900 hours Pacific Daylight Time. 148Z was then loaded with 10 people, their gear, two dogs, and the two-pilot flight crew. All the gear was properly weighed, and corresponding weight and balance for the aircraft was completed, noting 5,058 pounds of cargo and passengers, for a total estimated gross weight of 25,870 pounds (max certified gross weight for 148Z was 26,900 pounds and the certified empty weight was 18,575 pounds). There are no records of fuel orders for the day or how the gross weight was derived, because the load master's report in Grangeville includes only passenger and cargo weights. In discussing the number used by the investigation team with a seasoned, retired Region 4 DC-3/C-47 pilot, who also flew 148Z, the numbers were deemed "accurate." He reasoned, given the mission of the day, it was likely that Whitey had on board about 400 gallons of fuel, split between the plane's four tanks (max holding capacity was 804 gallons—right and left main tanks held 202 gallons each, and the right and left auxiliary tanks held 200 gallons each). The plane departed Grangeville for Moose Creek 28 minutes after arriving from McCall.

At the time of takeoff, there was little-to-no wind on the ground;

the temperature was 75 degrees; the sky was clear, with a thin over-cast layer of clouds reported at 25,000 feet Mean Sea Level (MSL), and there was no limitation on forward visibility. As good as it gets for a June day in the Idaho backcountry. With a report of good weather, and the plane heavy but below max gross weight, the pilots climbed out of Grangeville on a generally easterly heading. The plane performed as it should, and they leveled off at an estimated altitude of 7,000 feet MSL and configured the aircraft for cruise. Until approximately 15 minutes into the trip, all phases of the flight were normal. 148Z slid past the confluence of the Lochsa and Selway rivers, flying gener-ally east up the lower Selway canyon at a distance of 30 miles from Grangeville and approximately 30 miles from the Moose Creek des-tination. Although not on a straight flight path from Grangeville, it is a customary flight path for professional pilots planning for smooth ascents and descents in mountainous terrain. This route also provides for more passenger comfort and for proper engine cooling. The pilots likely aligned the plane to the right side of the river canyon, a standard operation for mountain/canyon flying, since it provides separation from oncoming air traffic and allows pilots to maneuver the plane 180-degrees in the opposite direction in case of a mechanical failure or the need to turn around due to poor weather.

At the 15-minute mark, the pilots likely noticed abnormal engine gauge readings on the left engine—probably a high oil temperature coinciding with a reading of decreasing oil pressure. While reducing the power and feathering and securing the left engine, the pilots then may or may not have increased power on the right engine to maintain altitude. Even in the feathered position, the left propeller continued to slowly rotate, which is normal. It is also imperative to recognize that the DC-3/C-47 is very capable of flying on one engine, and it was certified in the event of an engine failure after obtaining V1 to takeoff on one engine.[8]

· · ·

Much conjecture exists about the sequence of events at this point in the flight, and about what Whitey and John must have been thinking. This stage was principally reconstructed by accident investigators based on interviews with the survivors, Bryant Stringham and Charlie Dietz, as well as on a few ambivalent eyewitnesses who saw the airplane at a distance. The most consistent thread indicates the pilots voluntarily shut down the left engine and, within the same time frame, informed the passengers over the loudspeaker of the situation. But the actions preceding the shutdown and those immediately afterwards are somewhat unclear. What was the aircraft's true altitude before shutting off the engine? Did Whitey and John begin a slow descent to Moose Creek before the engine was shut down? And after the shutdown, had they intended to execute a 180-degree turn back toward Grangeville? The only indication of their contemplating such a turn was from Charlie's statement to investigators, wherein he recalled one of the passengers returning from the cockpit saying, "They're gonna have to turn around."

Although the two survivors and eyewitnesses consistently indicated the aircraft made no noticeable deviations from a relatively direct flight path toward Moose Creek, their performance begs more questions. Pilots consulted noted the safest action Whitey and John could have taken when seeing the irregular engine instrument readings was

---

8   V1: maximum speed during the takeoff roll at which the pilot can take the first action to abandon the takeoff and stop the aircraft.

to execute a 180-degree turn back toward the Grangeville Airport and then address the left-engine concerns. A golden rule of aviation is "aviate, navigate, and communicate," meaning first fly the aircraft. This would have put the airplane flying toward more favorable, flatter, and open terrain for an emergency landing. The pilots then could have left the engine running or at least brought it back to zero thrust (idle), which would keep the generator online (for electrical needs) and potentially preserve the motor, making it available for power if a sudden necessity arose. At idle, with continuous airflow over the engine, it may have cooled off. Additionally, a single-engine landing at Grangeville would be favored over one at Moose Creek. And, Grangeville had resources to repair the aircraft.

· · ·

No turn was made, however, and seconds after the left engine was shut down and secured, additional power likely was added to the right engine, and then the number eight cylinder blew.[9] Then either because of lack of time or altitude, or both, the pilots committed onward toward Moose Creek. For a few moments, the loose cylinder was held in place by the engine cowling. But once its latch bolt failed, the pounding piston hurled itself through the cowling. At the same time, engine gas and oil escaped. The fluids formed a vapor trail noticed by eye eyewitnesses—a fire engulfed the right engine. Within seconds, the flames began sweeping across the right wing. The pilots pulled the firewall shut off-valve control to off, which closed the fuel, engine oil, and hydraulic fluid lines. Reacting to the destruction of

---

9   Secured—an aviation term that applies to the sequence of shutting down an engine which includes throttle to cutoff, propeller to feather, and mixture to off.

the right engine, the airplane shook violently—caused when the cylinder broke loose and began to pound against its aluminum cowling. When it broke through the bottom, the remaining cowling fanned out and produced drag. Within a few revolutions of the engine, the piston and piston pin sheared free. Heat and oscillation twisted the engine out of its mount and it sailed off. Investigators estimated these events occurred in fewer than 30 seconds.

From the time the left engine was secured and the right engine fell off, the pilots were undeniably occupied. Restarting the left engine, which takes one or two minutes, was an unlikely consideration in the stressed cockpit environment. Some experienced DC-3/C-47 pilots say it could have been, however. For the quickest, although not entirely "by-the-book" normal restart, the pilot follows this procedure: "firewall shutoff valves reopened [controlled by one handle actuating fuel, oil and hydraulic fluid], magneto switch on, mixture rich, throttle idle, prop full increase, push and hold the feathering button in until prop is rapidly windmilling, throttle setting as desired once running." The time varies that it takes for the feathering pump to build sufficient pressure to shift the distributor valve in the prop dome to start bringing the propeller out of feather. The windmilling propeller will then achieve a start, and there is no need to even engage the starter. If the firewall shutoff valves were not fully open when the control was pushed back, there will not be enough fluid flow to start and run (visually checking the valves for full open was part of the preflight walk-around). After the propeller is quickly windmilling, the feathering button must be pulled back out (if it has not occurred on its own) to avoid returning to a feathered condition.

Owing to the severity of the situation and the response time, Whitey and John probably chose not to attempt a restart because investigators of the wreckage found the cockpit firewall shutoff valve control handles were pulled closed for the left and right engines. "Both rods were identically bent in a U-shape. They had to have been pulled out before impact with the river in order to permit identical landing [positioning]. This is also a key point in that the left engine could not have been restarted unless the left emergency firewall shutoff valve had been repositioned by pushing the handle back into the original position."

Aviate, navigate, and communicate: the pilots continued to fly on a track and altitude toward the Selway River canyon. Given the steep, forested topography, a water-ditching clearly became Whitey and Johns' only forgiving option.

Complicating their control of the aircraft were atypical flight characteristics: a potential center of gravity (CG) shift caused by the loss of the right engine and propeller, and a yaw or twist about the aircraft's vertical axis introduced by unequal drag. The drag was not the outcome only of the exposed right engine firewall acting like a giant differential speed brake, but also the result of the extension of the main landing gear. The DC-3/C-47 landing gear is held in the up position by hydraulic fluid, not mechanical locks. The design holds the gear in the retracted position by trapping pressure in the up-line, which is connected to both main gear retract cylinders. This was done so that in the event of a failure such as a leak causing hydraulic pressure loss, the gear will still lower. However, since the landing gear up-and-down lines do not penetrate the firewall, it is unclear why this failure occurred (the lines do pass closely behind it, which may explain the failure). The accident report surmised that when the right engine twisted off, extreme vibration from the right engine either broke a hydraulic line or one of the retract cylinders was damaged.

In any event, the lowered gear induced additional drag, infringing on the airplane's ability to glide.

• • •

The plunge of the right engine and propeller caused an increase in drag on the right side of the airplane because of the exposed nacelle (streamlined housing for an engine) firewall. Since the streamlined portion of the nacelle was still behind it, the firewall in this instance was not acting as a true "flat plate." These aerodynamics generated more drag than a smoothly-cowled engine. While not able to precisely quantify the drag produced, one can predict significantly less than that produced by a windmilling propeller, which was one of the conditions originally factored into the determination of single-engine, minimum control speed (Vmc) of 67 knots when the airplane was designed. Knowledgeable DC-3/C-47 pilots indicated a right-yawing moment induced by the increased drag on the right side would have been less than that induced by the left engine operating at nearly any power setting. Since the left engine had been shut down and feathered, no asymmetric thrust condition likely existed—only a bit of asymmetric drag. In conclusion, the drag asymmetry was probably a nominal control factor for the pilots; then again, it was a remarkable anomaly, not replicated in training.

• • •

As for pitch authority, the loss of the right engine and propeller would have resulted in an immediate shift of the airplane's CG to a more aft position. The position of the new CG location is less clear, because several related factors are largely unknown. Weight and balance and CG calculations were not addressed in the accident report. Region

4 DC-3/C-47 pilots who were consulted said typical loads, using the seating and cargo area configurations in or similar to 148Z, made it hard to load a DC-3/C-47 outside of its permissible operating CG range. To illustrate this point, one of the pilots commented "One would almost have to stack all the anvils one could find against the rear bulkhead, and all the feather pillows one could find against the forward bulkhead, to get the CG behind the aft limit. In this regard, it was a very forgiving design. The forced distribution of most loads within the interior of the cargo/passenger area almost guaranteed that the CG would fall within the permissible range." Although the weight of the people and gear loaded in Grangeville was determined (1,956 pounds and 3,102 pounds), the distribution of the 5,058-pound load was not examined beyond the fact that all the passengers were sitting on the left side, and all the cargo was stacked on the right side. The accident report estimated the gross weight of the airplane leaving Grangeville was 25,870 pounds. No explanation was given about to how the figure was derived, or what the CG position was. It is a fair assumption that the CG was likely near the midpoint of its permissible range, and shifted somewhat aft when the right engine and propeller twisted off. Whitey and John presumably had to apply forward pressure on the control yoke, which moved the elevator to counteract the shift.

A conventional airplane, such as the DC-3/C-47 design, will normally experience a tail download produced by the horizontal stabilizer. As the CG may shift rearward, the magnitude of this download will steadily decrease. It will be accompanied by more control sensitivity, along with a decrease in pitch stability. At the aft CG limit, the horizontal stabilizer down-force will generally have reduced to or near zero, and if beyond the aft limit, keeping level flight will require some additional input from the horizontal stabilizer as positive lift. The more aft the CG, the more lift required. The amount of lift that can be generated by the horizontal stabilizer is a derivative of three factors: total horizontal stabilizer and elevator area, the degree of elevator deflection, and airspeed. The area is fixed and thus invariant, and the contribution of the elevator is limited by its built-in downward travel limit. Thus, if the elevator has reached its most downward travel limit, the only remaining control variable is the airspeed. If airspeed is allowed to decay beyond a certain level, the result will likely be an unintentional pitch up attitude, shortly followed by a stall/spin with unlikely recovery.

In conclusion, Whitey and John were highly skilled airman and must have instinctively made the necessary control inputs. In concert with the elevator in pitch authority, is the use of power to control pitch. In this situation, however, the pilots had no power, and based on the angle of the reconstructed flight, following the loss of the right engine, they controlled airspeed by pitching the airplane downward, probably about 15 to 20 degrees, thus preventing a stall/spin. While the aft location of the CG following engine and propeller loss would have been near the aft CG limit, the resulting pitch authority was clearly not significant enough to deny the pilots sufficient control to maintain a stable glide.

• • •

From the moment the right engine tore away from the airframe, 148Z struggled in flight without mechanized power and glided another three miles to the vicinity of Wolf Creek Rapid. Looking upriver and above these rapids, Whitey and John may have thought they had a chance of getting the plane to the water under directional control.

By this point, to maintain airspeed the pilots had the plane's nose pitched down at about 15 to 20 degrees. Then at about 200 feet or 300 feet AGL, as they attempted to maneuver to the left side of the canyon over Dry Bar to line up to a straight stretch of relatively smooth water, the left wing struck a large Douglas fir about 15 feet inward from the wingtip. The plane hit the water nose first with the left wing low. It broke apart on impact.

From the time the left engine was shut down, until hitting the river, Whitey and John battled to save the lives of their passengers and themselves. They had three or four minutes. They never stopped flying the airplane. Legendary Idaho and Montana pilot Bob Johnson, who owned the largest commercial backcountry flying operation in the US, advised more than 400 pilots from the 1930s through the mid-1970s: In the worst situation, keep flying the airplane, "Fly the biggest piece down." Aviation Safety Officer Tex Wright wrote in the final report, "The fact that these pilots were able to maintain control of the aircraft, considering the magnitude of the problems being encountered, speaks highly of their skill. Any survivors of an accident like this is considered somewhat miraculous." While decisions made by Whitey and John will never be clarified, clearly they flew the airplane all the way to the ground.

A PILOT'S PERSPECTIVE OF THE SELWAY RIVER CANYON
IN THE VICINITY OF THE CRASH SITE LOOKING
UPSTREAM TOWARD DRY BAR, 2018. (*R. Holm, Jr.*)

13

THE WHY

*Near the end of many tragedies it seems right that there should
be moments when the story stops and looks back for something
it left behind and finds it and finds it because of things it
learned, as it were, by having lived through the story.*
—NORMAN MACLEAN, *YOUNG MEN AND FIRE*

On June 22, eleven days after the accident, the engines were off-
loaded from an Aero-Dyne Aviation DC-3 at the Long Beach
Airport in southern California. They were then transported a short
distance by truck to the west side of the airport to a nondescript
industrial building nestled between Runway 8, Cherry Avenue, and
the 405 San Diego Freeway. The building at 3200 Cherry Avenue
housed Steward-Davis, Inc., an engine overhaul and machine shop
that specialized in Pratt & Whitney radial-engines. Chub Riggleman
and Tex Wright of the investigation team accompanied the engines.
They stayed for four days to oversee, photograph, and document the
findings. In the days leading up to and following the engine analyses,

other members of the investigation team were probing Region 4 for maintenance records, logs, and general data regarding the history of 148Z, which proved to be appalling. Uniting the engine teardown analysis and aircraft records, or lack thereof, revealed why the airplane went down.

· · ·

To better comprehend the findings of the engine teardowns it is important to understand how the Region 4 Aviation Program evolved through 1979. The Program originated in the late 1920s, when many USFS regions began their own experimental cargo-dropping tests by hiring local pilots. By the mid-1930s, the USFS began developing an aerial surveillance program, and Region 5 purchased a five-seat Stinson Reliant based in California.

In 1939, David Godwin, assistant chief of fire control in the Washington, D.C., office of the USFS, and the head of the new Aerial Fire Control Experimental Project, began using the Stinson. Several fire-suppression experiments were performed. By October of the same year, the preliminary smokejumping experiments began with Captain Harold King at the controls of the plane. The Eagle Parachute Company successfully bid to design the chute that turned the smoke-chaser into a smokejumper.

Following some success, experiments began as soon as possible the following year, not only in Washington State, but also in Region 1. Johnson Flying Service of Missoula contracted to fly the smokejumpers, and it became a critical part of the Program's development. The first activity for Johnson started in June at Winthrop, Washington, using a Travel Air 6000. After training in Winthrop ended, the company began flying the new Region 1 jumpers at Seeley Lake, Montana, in the same airplane. By the first part of the summer, a crude operation was established for the Region 1 smokejumpers at the Moose Creek Ranger Station. On July 12, the first jump on a wildland fire was made from the Moose Creek base. Many improvements were made to the Program, and in 1943, by establishing a base in McCall, it was extended into Region 4 (these jumpers were trained in Region 1 until their own base was completed the following year).

The US military's Major William Carey Lee, was keeping an eye on the smokejumper program from its inception and became known as "Father of the United States Army Airborne." He visited Region 1 and later incorporated many of the USFS techniques into the first paratrooper training facility at Fort Benning, Georgia. The military made one significant change: the utilization of the more modern Douglas C-47.

The C-47 was the military version of Douglas's DC-3 "Douglas Commercial" airliner that revolutionized air travel in the 1930s. Capable of carrying up to 6,000 pounds of cargo or 21 to 32 passengers, depending on configuration, it had remarkable characteristics that were new to air travel—speed, long range, inclement weather capabilities, and was relatively comfortable. It pioneered airline routes, and was the first airplane that financially supported itself by carrying passengers, rather than relying on subsidized mail or freight. It came to be known as "the plane that changed the world."

With the onset of World War II, Douglas began production of a military version, C-47, often called the "Skytrain," or informally, as the "Gooney Bird." Over the course of the production run, several variations were produced, but they were distinguished from the civilian DC-3 version by a large rear cargo door, a stronger reinforced floor, a shortened tail cone, and an astrodome on the front of the fuselage.

The C-47 played crucial roles during the war transporting troops, cargo, and supplies from Europe to the Pacific and the India Burma-China supply route. The number of C-47s/DC-3s manufactured by McDonnell Douglas is imprecise, but sources add up to 11,000. Of these, only a few hundred were true DC-3s. Time has merged both aircraft as generically a "DC-3." All variants of the DC-3/C-47 aircraft were powered with variations of the Pratt & Whitney radial-engine. When the C-47 was introduced, most were equipped with the higher horsepower, 14-cyclinder, R-1830 models—a powerplant considered as a reliable and as safe as the airplane itself. So much so that author Ernest K. Gann, who immortalized the DC-3/C-47 in *Fate is the Hunter,* wrote that the maxim of pilots and crews flying the Doug across the North Atlantic was, "Put your trust in God and Pratt and Whitney."

Johnson Flying Service noted the military's success with the design, and after the war purchased a pair of military surplus C-47s, along with its lesser known predecessor, a DC-2. Johnson then modified the C-47s to meet the requirements of civilian-type certification to carry passengers, yet retained the larger military rear cargo doors. These planes dominated the skies of Region 1. They were not used on Region 4 smokejumper contracts until the summer of 1949, however.

The DC-3/C-47 was not only a good smokejumper platform; it was also a versatile mountain and canyon airplane owing to its performance characteristics. It was capable of short-field takeoff and landings and of carrying heavy loads. The plane had already proven itself globally during the war—hauling for example fuel across the English Channel and landing on dirt runways less than 3,000 feet long.

The Idaho and Montana backcountry was perhaps even more challenging, with narrow canyon and high elevation airstrips—the plane

quickly earned a reputation for hauling heavy machinery—bulldoz-
ers, generators, and well-drilling equipment—to remote ranches and
USFS administrative sites. In fact, the USFS was so impressed with
the capability of Johnson's DC-3/C-47s that from the late 1940s into
the late 1950s they lengthened and widened airstrips at the remote
outposts of Chamberlain, Cold Meadows, Indian Creek, Big Creek,
and Moose Creek solely for the aircraft. Johnson developed unwritten
performance perimeters for the aircraft, and it was not uncommon
for their top pilots to operate a DC-3/C-47 in mountainous flying at
gross weight on airstrips well under 2,500 feet in length and a consistent takeoff distance of 1,900 feet. The by-the-book numbers of
the manufacturer's operation manual, mainly airspeed standards,
were thrown out the window, and rotation was made before the V1
indicated airspeed (maximum speed during the takeoff roll at which
the pilot can take the first action to abandon the takeoff and stop the
aircraft). One Johnson pilot commented, "Flown by the right person,
it was one hell of a good airplane for big loads and short field work."

The plane was even enlisted for winter missions such as the
paracarago-dropping of building materials for the Bear Wallow
Fire Lookout (1955) and Bailey Mountain (1960) in the Bitterroot
Mountains. The plane was used for other low-level flight operations
as well, including the dropping of hay bales. For many years, the
planes were rigged seasonally with wing-mounted spray bars and
internal tanks for the aerial application of pesticides in the fight
against spruce budworm infestations.

In 1948, Region 4 added a smokejumper base in Idaho City, Idaho.
Flying from this base was not covered in the Johnson contract, and
the USFS obtained a surplus Noordyn Norseman flown by Region 4
Chief Pilot Clare Hartnett. He was stationed at the Regional Office,

and during fire season was detailed to the Boise NF, or elsewhere as needed. Clare is regarded as the first Region 4 fixed-wing pilot, and in 1946 he was hired to fly the Region's Stinson Voyager—primarily for light administrative work and fire patrol. This was the seed of the Region 4 Aviation Program.

The next major change occurred in 1953, when Clare retired and J. Karl Bryning, an airport operator in Pocatello, Idaho, was hired. He elevated the job within the meager Aviation Program in order to become the official Region 4 Air Operations pilot and manager. During his tenure, the Program embraced the use of a Cessna 180 and C-45 Twin Beechcraft. With the adoption of the Twin Beechcraft E-18, the latter was phased out. In 1958, Karl moved to Ogden, where he assumed the new position of Regional Air Officer. A new employee, Jim Larkin, was hired as the main line pilot. Jim, having grown up in Donnelly, just south of McCall, lived for aviation—he served in the Army Air Force (AAF) Ferry Command and flew C-47s on the India Burma-China route in World War II. He returned home and went to work for Johnson Flying Service, flying everything in their fleet from small single-engine Cessnas to Douglas DC-3/C-47s. He wearied of Johnson, and in 1956 started his own single-pilot company, flying a Cunningham-Hall; he was awarded the Region 4 contract to haul jumpers from Idaho City. In 1958, he took a permanent job with the Agency.

In the meantime, Johnson's grip on the Region 1 and 4 contracts remained exclusionary, but competitors with more modern equipment slowly edged them out of Region 4. Intermountain Aviation of Marana, Arizona, for example, was employing new STOL turbine-powered equipment, such as PC-6 Pilatus Porters and de Havilland Twin

Otters.[10] In 1965, Johnson lost the Region 4 smokejumper contract.

Other changes were in the air. The Civil Aeronautics Board's (CAB, now FAA) regulations affecting non-scheduled air carriers were introduced. With the glut of military surplus aircraft and well-trained pilots following World War II, combined with higher demand, small air freight and charter airline companies arose all over the US. A DC-3/C-47, for example, cost as little as $5,000. However, by 1962 the CAB established new regulations governing all aircraft in excess of 12,500 pounds takeoff weight as Transport Category Aircraft, and required they meet supplemental air carrier standards (formally designated as irregular carriers). The new rule gutted this sector of aviation, leaving only 15 nonscheduled carriers (non-skeds) nation-wide still in compliance. In the sparsely populated West, only four survived the new regulations—one being Johnson Flying Service. As aviation became more essential for USFS fire suppression, it found the new regulations hampered its ability to hire non-sked operators. Region 5 of the USFS tired of the shortages, and it decided to enter the Public Aircraft arena by acquiring a surplus Lockheed Lodestar, followed by two C-47s and two C-46s.

Since they, too, were limited in access to the non-sked carriers, Jim and Karl contended Region 4 should follow Region 5's lead. They argued that in times of high demand, Johnson's fleet of large aircraft was tied up servicing Region 1. Frustrated and having flown his share of big multi-engine aircraft in the military and for Johnson, Jim, along with Karl, coaxed the Agency to procure two of Region 5's C-46s for the 1963 fire season. Simultaneously, Jim urged the Regional Office

---

10 STOL refers to conventional fixed-wing aircraft with "short takeoff and landing" capabilities.

in Ogden to secure a permanent DC-3/C-47 for the 1964 fire season.

Their views were persuasive, and in November 1963, Region 4 obtained its first DC-3/C-47 from the Utah Air National Guard. It was flown to Boise, where an airframe inspection revealed several major issues. Another C-47 was acquired at Davis-Monthan AFB in Tucson, Arizona, for parts. Upon inspection this C-47 proved to be a better overall aircraft. The Utah ship and the Arizona ship switched places. The finished airplane became 146Z and served Region 4 for decades. Eventually, in 1991, it was retrofitted with the Basler Turbo Conversion and was officially certified as a DC-3. Before the contract for the conversion was completed, the plane was transferred to Region 1 and re-registered as 115Z. From 1964 on, the Region's aviation program grew rapidly, and by 1979 its fleet included two operating C-47s, two DC-3s, one Beech 99, and multiple smaller aircraft.

Although the fleet was growing, in 1979 the Program had limited resources. The office on the Ogden Airport was in a small leased building just north of the control tower. There were two rooms: a small front office containing three desks with three phones, and a larger backroom jammed floor to ceiling with piles of un-binned, untagged, and uncatalogued aviation parts. The parts were mainly acquired from government surplus lists, and the majority of the inventory originated from the Point Barrow, Alaska, Naval Research Station. In the mid-1970s, a bulk of the parts was delivered to Ogden by three semi-truck flatbed trailers. This minimal facility—with the exception of the Regional Aviation Officer and the Safety Officer, who held offices downtown in the Federal Building—housed the entire regional aviation force. There were also two leased hangar spaces sufficient to house two Region 4-owned Aero Commander 500Bs. There was no hangar space for the DC-3/C-47 fleet in Ogden or Boise. The only time they were inside a hangar was when they were in a shop (usually at Morrison-Knudsen in Boise) for maintenance. Otherwise, when not on a mission they sat out at the Boise Interagency Fire Center on the north side of the Boise Airport, and on occasion on the ramp at the office in Ogden.

In December 1967, Region 4 procured the C-47 that was to become registered as N148Z from the US Department of Justice—Immigration and Naturalization Service's Southwest Regional Office located in San Pedro (Terminal Island), California. The plane was surplus, along with a Department of Justice Douglas DC-4 (N18660—serial number 42-72711), which was obtained for parts, and then junked. In the spring of 1944, the C-47, serial number 20422 (also: 43-15956) was delivered to the AAF. Eight years later, the plane was transferred to the USAF Aero Medical Lab Engineering Psychological Research division, and then in December 1959 obtained by Immigration from the 2704th Air Force Aircraft Storage and Disposition Group, Davis Monthan AFB, Arizona. Under their ownership the plane was registered as N3630G and converted from a C-47-A to a DC-3C S1C3G by the processes outlined under note 8 of aircraft specification A-669.[11] The plane's engines were also upgraded from Pratt & Whitney R-1830-92s (1,200 hp) to R-1830-94s (1,350 hp). In the ownership transfer to the US Department of Agriculture, USFS, it was to be registered as

---

11 FAA documents pertaining to 148Z indicate the conversion from a C-47-A to a DC-3C S1C3G; however, it appears that the original data plate was never altered, or an additional data plate not added indicating the change as required by note 8 of aircraft specification A-669. The latter observation is supported by aircraft wreckage recovered from the Selway River containing the manufacture's data plate and the military data plate. The wreckage artifact is held at the National Museum of Forest Service History in Missoula.

N145Z, but by the time the transfer was recorded in March the following year at the request of Karl Bryning, the plane was assigned
N148Z from a reserved block of numbers held by the Agency.

Inspection by Karl and Jim revealed the aircraft had been wrecked
once, but it was ferried to Boise for repairs, and the nose section of
the Utah Air National Guard C-47 was grafted onto to the airframe
of 148Z. The plane was on line for part of the 1968 fire season; however, it developed engine problems after 66 hours and was grounded
for the year. In 1970, a third Douglas was obtained from the FAA
in Alaska. Built as a C-47, it then had been re-certified as a DC-3.
This aircraft was assigned the registration number of 100Z, and in
1991 was converted to a Basler and renumbered 142Z. In February
1975, Region 4 acquired a fourth Doug from the Military Storage
and Disposition Center at Davis-Monthan and kept it in the fleet as
143Z until 1984, when it was transferred to the Hill Air Force Base
Museum. This aircraft was unique because it was built as a VC-47,
which meant it was equipped from the factory as a VIP transport
plane. One last C-47 was obtained c.1977 as a parts source—primarily
for instrumentation and avionics and it ultimately was turned into
a static smokejumper training aid in McCall and never flew again.

In 1979, nearly 40 years post-production, it was estimated that
approximately 3,000 C-47s/DC-3s were flying worldwide in passenger and cargo operations, as well as privately. Although decades old
by then, the versatility of the aircraft had not changed, and the used
market price ranged from $40,000 to $150,000, depending on condition. The average life of an airframe was 50,000 hours, with outliers
known to have safely flown more than 90,000 hours. Authors Carroll
Glines and Wendell Moseley in their 1959 book, *Grand Old Lady: Story
of the DC-3*, wrote "In spite of the common belief that an airplane

has only about ten years of useful life, there seems to be one airplane that squats gracefully on the ramps all over the world and refuses to grow old. With face-liftings, new clothes, and slimmer lines, the faithful DC-3 becomes more valuable, faster, and more cherished as the years pass. The airplane that Douglas built is now the 'Methuselah of the Skies.'"

These airplanes also had relatively inexpensive operating costs, averaging out to be about $150–$180 per hour. Coincidentally, in 1979 Region 4 charged $230 per hour within the Agency, which was a competitive rate when compared to non-scheduled, on-demand air carriers it contracted with, such as Johnson Flying Service. Before being bought by Evergreen Aviation in 1976, Johnson charged $225 per hour or $1.25 per mile for DC-3/C-47 flight time. Region 4's in-house flight department out-competed the contractors in the cost of operation, which was about $70 per hour, compared to a contractor like Johnson that had an operation cost of $150 per hour. The Region 4 Aviation Program was able to reduce this cost by operating under the umbrella of "Public Aircraft," where the regulations of engine inspection times, time controls, pilot training, and pilot qualifications were absent. Compared to other heavily regulated sectors of private or commercial civil aircraft operations administered by the FAA, the Program had certain financial advantages: self-insured airplanes; airplanes were government surplus to the Agency and not purchased; fuel provided at military prices; pilots were usually government employees. Whereas an air carrier had to account for the purchase price of the airplane, aircraft insurance, market price for fuel, and pilots hired year-round to fly the airplane, whether it generated revenue or not.

In spite of these advantages, the Region 4 fleet of large, complex, radial-powered aircraft was expensive, and there was always an underlying concern of trying to be within budget. It became clear that staying within budget on a meager stipend for what the Department had become was very challenging. Evaluation of safety regarding the age and reliability of the C-47s/DC-3s was another hurdle. Ironically, as Region 4 acquired more and more C-47s/DC-3s, there were rumblings as early as 1970 from non-aviators in the high ranks of the Agency asking whether the C-47s/DC-3s needed to be replaced with more modern aircraft. The *Region 4 Air Operations Study* the same year stated, "Replace present DC-3 fleet no later than July 1973, and sooner if possible. Replacement aircraft should have STOL characteristics, aft-loading cargo ramp, speed in excess of 200 knots, and passenger/cargo capacity of no less than 10 tons and 35 to 50 passengers. Since this aircraft will be utilized for utility missions, it is recommended that it should be purchased new, as surplus machines are not available to suitably replace the DC-3." Then the following year, in the *R-4 Airops Action Plan* dated June 11, the report again targeted the liquidation of the DC-3: "Phase out Forest Service use of all aircraft over 25 years old by 1976 and establish a service life for all aircraft utilized." No action was taken and until the aftereffects of the 148Z crash the reports were ignored.

Howard Koskella was a staunch advocate for disposal of the C-47s/DC-3s. A career USFS employee, he grew up in the McCall area. In 1965, he became the fire and aviation staff officer for the Payette NF. Under his direction, he strongly advocated for the elimination of piston-powered aircraft in exchange for turbine-propelled aircraft, and he was instrumental in forging contract relationships with Intermountain Aviation for the use of their Twin Otters and Turbo Porters for missions on the Payette NF (a sizable portion of Region 4).

He left the Payette in 1971 for a position in the Washington Office, and a few years later relocated to Region 5. In 1973, during his tenure in Region 5, he successfully banned the use of C-47s/DC-3s for USFS air operations. He retired in 1978, and when 148Z crashed, he spoke to several regional newspapers regarding his safety concerns about the aircraft: "Age is catching up with these planes. They're very, very old and are subject to metal fatigue and cable breaks. It's like driving a used car. No matter how well maintained it is, it's more likely to break down than a new car." But each time he pushed for USFS replacement of the airplane, economics prevailed. "We [the USFS] could get them surplus for just a few thousand dollars each. Spare parts cost next to nothing when they came from the government. It was the only aircraft we could afford to own and paint our own colors on."[12] The pilots who flew them were just as resistant to change. According to Howard, "These guys [the USFS pilots] had a nostalgic attachment to the DC-3. Some of them had learned to fly on them." Refuting Howard's public comments to a local newspaper, Dale Matlack, the head of the Region 4 Aviation Program, stated, "That plane [148Z] was the lightest DC-3 we had. It had fewer than 18,000 hours on it. It was a cream puff."[13] However, he did agree that the Agency ultimately needed to come up with an alternative, "[The USFS] recognizes the need to replace the DC-3. I don't think it's any

---

12 Technically aircraft are not "purchased" within government entities they are surplus or excessed.

13 Matlack is incorrect about N148Z being the lightest DC-3/C-47 in the Region 4 fleet as 148Z had an empty weight of 18,575 pounds and N146Z had an empty weight of 17,764.4 pounds. His statement of the airframe having less than 18,000 hours is correct, but to be more exact, 148Z, for its age, had a relatively low-time airframe. At the time of the crash, total airframe hours were 12,428.8 hours.

big secret that we'd like to replace them all eventually. But money is a constraint. We feel it will service our purposes for another five years."

Jim Larkin also came to the defense of the Region 4 C-47s/DC-3s. He, like Howard retired one year before the accident. He wrote a poignant letter to the editor of the *Idaho Statesman*, dispelling many of the inaccuracies circulating about the aircraft and accident conjecture. "The papers have been full of fact and fancy, claim and counterclaim, concerning the airworthiness and capability of the Douglas DC-3." Jim's explanation and clarification about the plane's performance and flight characteristics were accurate. However, his bias about the airplane and the Program he spent two decades building showed. "The civilian facility responsible for maintenance of these aircraft is internationally known." This statement is misleading. First, the company was known; however, "internationally known;" the aircraft maintenance was not. Second, the findings at Steward-Davis, Inc., as well as those by the investigators of the maintenance program within the Region 4 Aviation Department, do not support his statement. It is important to emphasize that 148Z as a DC-3 aircraft did not fail, the engines failed owing to improper maintenance. 148Z as it existed on June 11, 1979, was mechanically no "cream puff."

• • •

At Steward-Davis, the left engine was torn down first. The technicians began by pulling the left engine oil pump, and they were alarmed that it would not turn by hand. With more effort, the pump turned and sand from the river imbedded in the gears was found to be the cause of the difficulty. The scavenger side of the pump was then inspected, along with the plugs and screens. Small amounts of metal "fuzz" and slivers were present, but were not considered a part of the internal engine and were noted as "normal" for an engine that had nearly zero hours of run time. Next, the propeller shaft was turned with a prop wrench and the engine turned freely, indicating it had not seized up due to lack of oil.

The main power section was completely disassembled and represented a healthy low-time engine. Referring to this section, Chub Riggleman wrote in his report, "Everything looked good, shiny new, and the cylinders looked good on the inside, and they still had the hone markings from the overhaul. In fact, the rings had not even seated at this time. The front and rear cams and cam followers were checked. They looked good. The rod bearings, the rods looked good. The pistons looked good. The rings were in top shape. We did find one rod, number 4 rod at the crank end, it was loose, but it was within limits. The rear crankshaft and rods were okay."

Then the front nose section was removed from the power section. Disbelief. The technicians immediately observed that the crankshaft to propeller shaft oil-transfer pipe had been left out upon assembly of engine and nose case—not an insignificant part to have overlooked: it measures about three-eighths-inch in diameter and eight to ten inches long. Logbooks later documented that the nose section had been installed by Trans-West of Salt Lake City. The oil-transfer pipe lubricates a series of reduction gears and bearings, and these had evidence of bluing and discoloration. The entire reduction seat assembly had been deprived of proper lubrication. Tex Wright surmised, "[T]he heat was transmitted into the oil which would have been puddled in the lower portion of the nose case. The oil cooler could not cool the oil sufficiently before reentry into the engine. Oil pressure would lower and oil temperature would increase dramatically. These changes would have been indicated in the cockpit on oil temperature and pressure gauge[s]." A series of experts on Pratt & Whitney 1834-94s were consulted; all agreed with the team's conclusion. These experts also discussed whether or not the propeller would have functioned properly with the missing oil-transfer tube. Yes. It would have performed as usual until excessive heat buildup, and also would have feathered and un-feathered properly.

Investigators confirmed beyond a doubt that the pilots shut the left engine down owing to overheating indications on the cockpit gauges.

Steward-Davis discovered two other odd findings during the left engine inspection. One was an undamaged quarter-inch iron nut lying loose inside the rear accessory section of the case. The nut appeared to have caused no internal damage and was thought to have fallen in at the time the nose section was off the engine. Very little discussion or concern was aimed at this finding. In fact, all Tex wrote in his report was, "It [the nut] showed no damage and was of a type nut not used on this type engine. Origin is unknown. There didn't appear to be any way that the nut could have caused a problem." The second incidental finding occurred when Steward-Davis removed the cylinders from the power section and discovered improperly torqued cylinder base nuts—two each at the rear of the number two cylinder, one each at the rear of the number four cylinder, and two each at the rear of the number six cylinder. No elaboration was given for this finding either, but it reveals a compounded lack of quality maintenance.

The left engine inspection was completed, and all of the removed parts and components were placed on a storage stand to avoid confusion with the right engine inspection.

The nose section and propeller of the right engine were torn off from impact. The power section, although intact, had severe fire scars and overall damage from impact. Several components for this engine were recovered from the river and pieced back together for inspection.

The most significant missing pieces were of the number eight cylinder and its related piston and piston pin. The rod was intact, yet badly damaged from flailing in the crankcase as the crankshaft turned freely. Technicians determined the number eight cylinder had parted at the lower skirt or flange from a pre-existing crack that was overlooked during prior engine inspections. The remnants of the lower skirt still attached to the power section of the engine were removed and sent off for metallurgical analysis. The results confirmed metal fatigue failure. Furthermore, they learned that four of the hold-down studs for the number eight cylinder were broken and missing—one stud had a missing nut and two studs had loose nuts. Combinations of bronze and steel washers were found on the intact studs. All bronze washers should have been replaced with steel washers, as recommended in the Pratt & Whitney Service Bulletin #20-2E-4A dated April 22, 1946. The combination of different metals on the studs caused cold-flowing or unequal tension over time reacting to the heating and cooling of the engine. The Steward-Davis report elaborated, "The bronze washers were abandoned for use on higher power engines such as the 1830-94 [as on 148Z] and R2000 models because they tended to cold-flow slightly during service, resulting in loss of tension and uniformity of tension on the cylinder hold-down studs." Moreover, "Mixing steel washers with bronze washers indiscriminately on each cylinder could cause a situation in which: 1. The 16 studs which hold a cylinder down on the crankcase equally share the load when the cylinder is the first installed, and all of the hold-down nuts are carefully torqued, tensioning each stud uniformly, let us say, a load of 1,000 pounds each. 2. Under such an initial load, and subsequent operational loads, the bronze washers could cold-flow into small spaces or imperfections in the cylinder flange and relieve the load on the affected stud. If the adjacent studs on each side of the bronze washer are fitted with steel washers, they must now share all loads previously taken by the stud with the bronze washer."

With the engine teardown completed, the investigation team scrutinized the origin and history of the components of 148Z as they existed the day of the accident. Individual logbooks are typically kept for C-47s/DC-3s, detailing the maintenance history of the airframe, each engine, and each propeller. As of June 1979, Region 4 had one in-house person whose primary duties were maintenance related—Jack Vandehei, whose title was director of maintenance. He was more of a front man than a mechanic. Although several of the Region's pilots did hold Airframe and Powerplant (A&P) certificates (Chris Hayne, Stan McGrew, Whitey Hachmeister, Bob Black), the only maintenance they ever did on the Region's aircraft is best described as "on-demand" field repairs. For major work and inspections, Region 4 contracted with approved vendors, and in 1979 the Agency contracted with Morrison-Knudsen (MK) Aviation Center located on the south side of the Boise Airport. The facility was the aviation venture of the once well-known Morrison-Knudsen Corporation, which built its empire and success on substantial engineering and construction projects around the world. The aviation side of the company was founded in the late-1950s as an FAA Certified Repair Station. By the early 1980s, the company became Western Aircraft, Inc. Retired Region 4 aviation managers of the 1970s recalled the paperwork on each aircraft was pretty "slack." When big jobs, such as an engine replacement, were done, a work order might be filed and kept. Minor maintenance was often unrecorded. The USFS was responsible for the paperwork and the keeping of logbooks. The available 148Z logbooks state the airframe and the right engine underwent a 100-hour inspection on September 19, 1978, with a total time on the right engine of 1,049 hours. Since the left engine was scheduled to be replaced soon, its inspection was deferred. Then on May 15, 1979, Region 4 delivered 148Z back to MK Aviation Center for its routine "preseason inspection." With another 20.6 hours logged since the 100-hour inspection, the airframe and right engine were inspected again, and an overhauled engine was scheduled to be installed on the left side. From the time the USFS took final possession of the airplane on May 30, to the time of the accident, the plane only flew another 6.2 hours. The right engine at the accident scene had 1,074.8 hours since major overhaul.

Events between May 15, 1979 and June 11, 1979 are entangled—muddled by missing paperwork and after-the-fact recollections. Searching for answers, the investigation team found itself confused by he-said, she-said comments, and frustrated by missing logbooks. The logbooks that were found, confirmed that the right engine was signed off for inspection with 1,069.6 hours. A somewhat odd time, as experienced pilots who have flown tens of thousands of hours with Pratt & Whitney 1830s assert the engine will predictably lose the master rod bearing at 1,200 hours. In fact, contractors for the USFS in 1979, operating identical C-47s/DC-3s with Pratt & Whitney 1830 radials, were held to higher maintenance standards than was their own fleet. For example, to operate for the USFS at the preseason inspection, the contractors' 1830 engines could not exceed 1,000 hours.

At the time of the accident, the airplane had an airframe time of approximately 12,428.8 hours, with 6.2 hours on the left engine and 1,074.8 hours on the right engine. An exact date correlating the time of the right engine installation was not available, but it was documented to have been overhauled by the Gary Aircraft Corporation of

San Antonio, Texas, on February 6, 1973. On average, 148Z flew about 200 to 300 hours per year, which fixes the engine installation in 1973 or 1974. The records from Gary Aircraft indicated it was rebuilt as a zero-time engine from a core that had approximately 8,000 hours of total time. Again, it was signed off for a preseason inspection by MK Aviation Center and accepted by Region 4.

On May 15, MK Aviation Center began the installation of the left engine, and completed it on May 25. The plane was released on May 24 to the USFS for a test flight and problems were apparent. On May 25, follow-up work was completed by MK. The power section of the engine was originally received by Region 4 from Point Barrow, Alaska, Naval Research Station, and had been overhauled by Cooper Airmotive of Dallas, Texas. The nose case had the same origin and also was assembled by Cooper at the same time. The USFS then had Trans-West Air Services, Inc., of Salt Lake City, assemble the units into a "quick engine change" or a QEC, which is where the bare power section and nose case are fitted with components such as exhaust, starter, generator, carburation, etc. The USFS brought the QEC to the MK Aviation Center for installation. According to personnel interviewed by the investigation team, no serviceable tags or certifications for the engine were provided, which owing to the Public Aircraft status of 148Z, were not required. Although MK was an FAA-certified repair station, it was performing work for a government agency that could legally operate aircraft without airworthiness certificates and did not require certified parts. MK was merely directed by the client (the USFS) to carry out work, which in this case was to install government-owned aircraft parts on a government-owned aircraft. Before the airplane was released for service, in situations such as an engine installation, a supervisory pilot or director of maintenance from Region 4 would oversee certain contract work and be present during engine run-ups and tests.

Areas of concern by the investigators stemmed from the engine teardowns and logbooks. Further disarray was discovered during interviews with Region 4 pilots and maintenance staff. On June 14, 1979, Chris Hayne, one of two Region 4 supervisory pilots, was deposed in Grangeville at the Nez Perce NF's Supervisor's Office. Chris's job entailed management of smokejumper force account aircraft—specifically C-47s/DC-3s, throughout the year, and the Beech 99 during the fire season. He was also a pilot in rotation on the C-47s/DC-3s, the supervisor of pilots, served as the coordinator of maintenance, and made decisions concerning crews and maintenance. Thus he was responsible for 148Z's airworthiness. Before starting with the USFS, he had a well-rounded aviation career because he owned his own flying business, offering air charters, maintenance, aircraft brokerage, and general aviation services. For a number of years, he was the contract mechanic for Texas International, where he was involved with an operation running 25 DC-3s, and later switched to a fleet of turbine-powered Convair 600s. In 1968, Chris began working for the USFS in Alexandria, Louisiana, and in 1974 moved to his position within Region 4 in Boise.

Interviewers asked Chris to walk them through the days leading up to the June 11 flight of 148Z. Chris confirmed that he oversaw the maintenance of the aircraft to get it ready for the fire season, including the work at MK's facility, and the final test flight on May 29. From the beginning, it was a scramble to get a DC-3/C-47 on the flight line for McCall smokejumper training missions scheduled to begin in early June. Of the fleet, 148Z was chosen as the airplane to ready. A new engine overhauled by California Engine Service was lined up for the left wing and hung. During the initial ground run-up of the new engine, it failed several tests. The oil screens were checked and revealed metal filings.

The first left engine was removed and a second one was hung. Again, trouble. Within the first five minutes, before the engine was run up more than 1,000 rpms, the oil temperature exceeded normal range and the engine was shut down to prevent damage. They discovered the oil lines had been attached to the oil cooler in reverse order. Transposing the correct attach points solved the problem. The next test run-up developed a severe vibration between 1,500 rpm and 1,900 rpm. Two different props were tried with the same result. Another Region 4 DC-3/C-47 was in the shop getting an engine change as well. They pulled a prop off it, because it had been on the plane 1,300 hours, and was considered "sorted." Problem solved. On May 25, the plane was test flown 0.5 hours locally in Boise by Stan McGrew and Dave Holley. A post-flight inspection revealed a major oil leak. They tried fixes to the oil sump and exhaust stack. They re-ran the engine and it ran smoothly. No spark plugs were fouling. They observed that the oil leak was only excessive after it sat for an extended time; thereafter it was normal. Chris explained, "On a new engine, we made this assumption that we would live with this for up to 25 hours as long as the engine ran good...We felt that it was probably rings that had not seated properly, and this oil would leak past the rings, out through the open exhaust valve into the exhaust stack...So, that was about where we were with the oil leak." On May 29, Chris then flew the plane another 2.0 hours locally around Boise and decided the new left engine was okay. All radial-engines leak some oil and consume some oil during operation, so a leak is not unusual. Oil loss on a well-running Pratt & Whitney R-1830-94 averages about one gallon per hour, most of which is consumed internally, but some is lost through external leaks after shutting the engine down owing to the inverted lower cylinders. Chris told the investigation team that Whitey was made aware of the oil leak. "Whitey is a mechanic, and he was warned of this particular problem to guard it, and if it got anything but better, to advise me and we would take immediate action."

Beyond detailed questions on both the right and left engines, the investigators had a plethora of other questions for Chris. At some point, they realized on March 14, 1979 that the spherical, dry-powder fire-extinguisher bottles had been removed from 148Z for hydrostatic testing at Hill AFB and were not present on the ship at the time of the accident. There are two fire-extinguisher bottles on DC-3/C-47s, one for each engine. The bottles are located inside the wheel well and are mounted to the sidewall of the nacelle, the outer casing. Each bottle is activated by its guarded electrical switch in the cockpit. In the event of an engine fire, the switch can be actuated, which then expels a fire retardant chemical (Bromochloromethane) from the bottle inside the cowling between the back of the engine and the firewall. There was no Minimum Equipment List (MEL) for 148Z, the document used in aviation to provide direction to operators about specific items installed on the aircraft which could be inoperative at the time of flight. While the fire-extinguisher bottles would likely be considered a critical airworthiness item, they were not required under Public Aircraft use. The investigation revealed that the director of maintenance for the Region 4 Aviation Program in Ogden at the time of the crash had received the bottles and overlooked getting them to Hill AFB before it was too late for the June 1979 flying.

According to Chris, the problem with the fire-extinguisher bottles was discussed during the two-day ground training for the DC-3/C-47

pilots when aircraft systems were reviewed. He also stated his immediate boss, Dale Matlack, was aware of the issue. One of the investigators in the interview asked, "Was your decision to go ahead without
them based on a time period, or just, 'we are going to operate until
they come in?'" He responded, "I was pressuring very hard to get them
back. It was not something I took lightly, 'Oh what the hell;' it was a
major concern. I didn't like to do it, but I was having problems getting airplanes on the line. I had 43 down. I had robbed 43's propeller,
and it was held up. I had 46 due [for] a 50-hour inspection, and I was
trying to get 48 back on the line before I put 46 in. All of these pres-
sures in retrospect, you look back at your sins and don't know how you
committed them, but nevertheless, for whatever reason I did let this
happen."[14] The interviewers then asked, "Did anyone disagree with
the idea of flying without the bottles?" Chris: "No, nobody voiced a
disagreement, nor did they voice agreement. There was just no debate
on it. The primary debate was between Whitey and me, because I
wanted Whitey to know, since he was going to be flying the aircraft,
and I would be his relief pilot, that we would be the two people to
operate this airplane. I said, 'Whitey, it does not have fire bottles in it,
now if you don't want to take it that way, don't.' And that's about the
way the conversation went and, 'Oh,' Whitey says, you know, probably some casual comment or something, but 'sure I'll go ahead and
use it until you get the bottles back here in a day or two or whatever.'
I said, 'We are pushing it just as hard as we can push it, Whitey. We
are going to have those bottles here as quick as we can.' And that
was about the agreement that we had about the fire bottles." Chris

---

14 For clarification Chris, abbreviated the Region 4 Aviation Program's fleet of C-47s/DC-
3s: N100Z, N143Z, N146Z, and N148Z.

assumed full responsibility for the lack of the emergency fire equipment, and this was as of June 14, well before Steward-Davis released its report, and before the USFS investigation team released its findings. In the end, the absence of the fire bottles was determined by both Steward-Davis and the USFS to be of negligible concern, since they would have done nothing to prevent or combat the onboard fire or the ensuing accident.

• • •

Stewart-Davis's report to the investigation team concerning why the left engine went out when it did noted that a Pratt & Whitney 1830-94 engine would pass a flight test with an omitted oil-transfer tube: First, if the engine was equipped with a high capacity oil pump—which it was. Second, the clearances of parts in the engine were extremely tight "so that oil flow through those parts would be at minimum. This minimum oil flow through the engine in all other areas would conceal the abnormal flow of oil leaking from the area flooded because of the missing transfer tube, and the engine would still be able to maintain the required oil pressure during acceptance ground runs and test flights." This was hypothetical on the part of Steward-Davis because it would have taken reassembly to confirm, which was impossible. Third, the oil temperature indications in the cockpit during ground run-ups and test flights were acceptable. With these assumptions in place, Steward-Davis concluded, "To continue this line of reasoning, it is believed that an engine with the transfer tube omitted and otherwise fitting the above conditions would be susceptible to a chain reaction of symptoms which could cause a pilot to perceive a cycle of rising oil temperature and dropping oil pressure, which he would interpret as an incipient master rod bearing failure."

June 6 was the last flight log obtained by the investigation team. The record of flights occurring in McCall on June 8 and June 11 most likely went missing in the accident. However, with the help of Neil Davis, the former McCall Smokejumper Base manager, the training jump records were retrieved from the archives and confirm the take-off times and flight times for June 6, as well as the June 8 flights of 148Z. The June 11 takeoff and flight times were confirmed using the dispatch logs retrieved by the investigation team.[15] Utilizing these primary documents, and comparing them to weather history, the takeoff temperature in Boise on June 6 at 0540 hours was 49 degrees. Then the two takeoff air temperatures later the same morning were again 49 degrees at 0655 hours and 51 degrees at 0755 hours. On June 8, the air temperatures were at 50 degrees at 0835 hours and 56 degrees at 0941 hours. The takeoff air temperature in McCall on the morning of June 11 was 60 degrees at 0800 hours. Then the take-off air temperature in Grangeville at 0928 hours on June 11 was 75 degrees—a significantly higher air temperature than had occurred at any other takeoff since the left engine was hung. The warmer air temperature, combined with several other factors, including a short turnaround of fewer than 40 minutes (earlier turnaround times were one hour), prevented the oil from cooling as much as it had following the previous flights. Additionally, where back-to-back flights were made earlier, they were for training jumps. In that era, training jumps from DC-3/C-47s were typically executed at 2,000 feet AGL with low power settings. Ideally, jumpers exited the plane at the lumbering speed of 90 knots (103 mph). From this configuration, and given

---

15 It is interesting to note that the training jump records indicate Neil Davis was the last smokejumper to jump from 148Z on June 8, 1979.

the close proximity to the McCall Airport of the two practice-drop locations, the aircraft would have been set up for a descent back to the airport without any increase in power.

As for the overall aircraft weight—none of the previous flights would have had as much weight as the airplane leaving Grangeville did. The earlier climb-outs from Boise to McCall and McCall to Grangeville would have good climbs of several thousand feet, but, other than fuel, the airplane would have been nearly empty. Based on terrain, the most direct routing to Moose Creek at the top of the climb or cruise attitude would have been an estimated 7,000 feet MSL, for a total climb of roughly 3,600 feet. So for the first time since installation, the left engine and oil were warmer at the time of restart, the air temperatures were 15 degrees higher, and with a heavier load more demand than ever before was placed on it. The flight, there-fore, required the standard climb power setting for a longer period of time than had been previously asked of the engine. Consequently, the engine temperatures and oil temperatures would have been higher. The Steward-Davis report surmised, based on these assumptions, that "[t]he higher the oil temperature, the lower the oil viscosity and the thinner oil would leak more freely from the compartment contain-ing the oil normally contained by the transfer tube...As this would increase, the tail shaft bearing and reduction gearing, normally lubri-cated by a very light flow of oil, would be increasingly loaded by the flood of oil and would generate a great amount of heat. As leakage increased, area E [the propeller reduction-driving-gear face where it meshes with the reduction-drive pinion gears] would be very heav-ily and uniformly flooded by the centrifugally distributed oil, gen-erating extreme pressure and heat on the complete reduction-gear trains. Heat discoloration was noted on the reduction gear support bearings and the inner tips of the fixed reduction gear teeth during disassembly."

While Steward-Davis reported no physical distress to the gears, and only thermal-related discoloration or bluing, another expert suggested the overheating of these gears due to the lack of lubrication from the day the left engine was hung would cause continual distress to the gears, which could also exacerbate the oil temperature. The combined effect of all of these factors clearly led to a red-lining oil temperature indication, alarming enough for the pilots to shut the engine down.

• • •

The right engine was a high-time engine, and the part that failed was not caught during the preseason inspection, and therefore the most likely reason why it failed when it did. Did Whitey or John "bust the power to it?" After the accident, there was speculation that the right engine failed because Whitey or John "over-revved it," following shut down of the left engine. In conversations with highly experienced DC-3/C-47 pilots, they all agreed it was unlikely because the engine was governor-regulated to a fixed maximum 2,800 rpm. What the non-experts with the "over-revved" view likely meant was over-boosted. Was that probable or even possible? If manifold pressure and rpm adjustments were made in the correct order, it would not be possible. The Pratt & Whitney 1830-94 engine was rated for 52 inches of manifold pressure and 2,800 rpm for two minutes, which is called max takeoff power, or in DC-3/C-47 manuals "METO" (the highest power setting that can be maintained continuously). While that rpm could have been achieved, 52 inches of manifold pressure could not have been achieved at the 7,000 feet MSL altitude at which

148Z was estimated to be flying. A pilot of a DC-3/C-47 could try to demand that level of power—without succeeding, assuming that the adjustments were made in the correct order. The correct order would have been: increase the rpm and then increase manifold pressure. But what if this were done in the reverse order? In that case, over-boost in terms of excessive Brake Mean Effective Pressure (BMEB) generated within the cylinders could well have occurred. How likely would that have been? Under normal flight conditions, the experts all agreed not very likely: Whitey was reputed to be one of the most "by the book" pilots among his peers in the Region 4 Aviation Program. Furthermore, Whitey was described by one pilot who flew with him as "not a natural pilot," but a "textbook pilot who was methodical and calculating—he was not one to get tripped up even in simu-lated emergencies during training." Whitey, moreover, was an A&P mechanic, and since 1972 had been flying the Region 4 Dougs 200 to 250 hours each season. These credentials make it difficult to imagine him "busting the power" to the right engine.

One expert pointed out an alternative: What if Whitey had asked John to make the necessary power adjustments? Not an uncommon request by the captain to the co-pilot/first officer/second in command. All indications are that John was a very experienced and highly com-petent pilot with more than 10,000 hours of flight time, but the record reveals that his previous experience in DC-3/C-47s may have been 30 or 40 years earlier. Additionally, 148Z, along with all DC-3/C-47s, had a nonconventional arrangement of engine controls on the cockpit pedestal. In the conventional arrangement, control levers on multi-engine airplanes have from left to right: throttles, props, and mixtures. On DC-3/C-47s, the arrangement of those levers is *props, throttles, mixtures*. A Region 4 check pilot from this era noted that he observed confusion with this unconventional arrangement, usually during a stressful situation, such as an instrument-check ride or a simulated emergency, where he witnessed the application of advanced-power settings attempted in an incorrect order. According to John's flight history, he had logged 70.2 hours as a co-pilot in the USFS DC-3/C-47s during the 1978 season. However, he had logged, at some point in his military career, a combined 435 Pilot in Command (PIC) hours and 100 Second in Command (SIC) hours in R4Ds (the Navy version of the DC-3/C-47) and C-46s. Both aircraft utilize the unconventional sequence on the cockpit pedestal.

It is also unlikely Whitey and John would have wanted "all the power they could get" out of the right engine, as the normal routine procedure following an in-flight engine shutdown would have been (at least initially) to go to the next-higher power setting. At the time of the left engine failure, the pilots were likely operating with cruise power settings; the higher power setting wanted and called for would likely have been climb power, and not METO. There will always be some mystery here. If the engine survived takeoff power (essentially, max power obtainable - METO) upon departure from Grangeville at 3,314 feet MSL, why could it not then survive what could only have been somewhat lesser max power values obtainable at 7,000 feet MSL?

No one will ever know with certainty. Some speculation lies in not knowing the urgency in shutting down the left engine…was it perhaps a slower precautionary shutdown? The findings indicate that it was. In this event, however, it seems Whitey would have given his passengers some comforting information, such as, "Don't be alarmed, but we are going to shut down the left engine." Based on the 1979 interviews with the two survivors, this never occurred, suggesting that the shutdown might have been made more quickly. Since the aircraft did not have cockpit voice recorders, no one will really know *exactly* what went on in the cockpit of 148Z in its last few minutes.

REGION 4DC-3/C-47S ON THE USFS RAMP IN MCCALL, 1980S. *(S. McGrew)*

MID-1970S REGION 4 DC-3/C-47 FORMATION FLIGHT. L TO R: 143Z (FLOWN BY WHITEY HACHMEISTER AND ED KRAL), 148Z (FLOWN BY CHRIS HAYNE AND DAVE HOLLEY), 146Z (FLOWN BY JIM LARKIN AND MILT OLSEN), AND 100Z (FLOWN BY RUDY HARTMAN AND JOHN PIEKARSKI). *(USFS Region 4 Smokejumper Archives)*

MID-1970S REGION 4 PILOTS AND ASSOCIATED STAFF.
STANDING (L TO R): WHITEY HACHMEISTER, JOHN PIEKARSKI,
MILT OLSEN, HERB CORN, JIM LARKIN, RUDY HARTMAN,
ED KRAL, AND BUD MUNDAY.

KNEELING (L TO R): CHRIS HAYNE, DALE MATLACK,
BOB BLACK, AND DAVE HOLLEY.
(USFS Region 4 Smokejumper Archives)

INSPECTION OF ENGINE AT STEWARD-DAVIS.
(*USFS Collection/Accident Report*)

CHUB RIGGLEMAN INSPECTING THE LEFT ENGINE
AT STEWARD-DAVIS. (*USFS Collection/Accident Report*)

THE AFT END OF THE LEFT ENGINE'S PROPELLER SHAFT AS
PHOTOGRAPHED AT STEWARD-DAVIS. HOLE AT CENTER IS
WHERE THE MISSING OIL TRANSFER TUBE SHOULD HAVE
BEEN FITTED. A SAMPLE OIL TRANSFER TUBE IS VISIBLE
IN THE FOREGROUND. (USFS Collection/Accident Report)

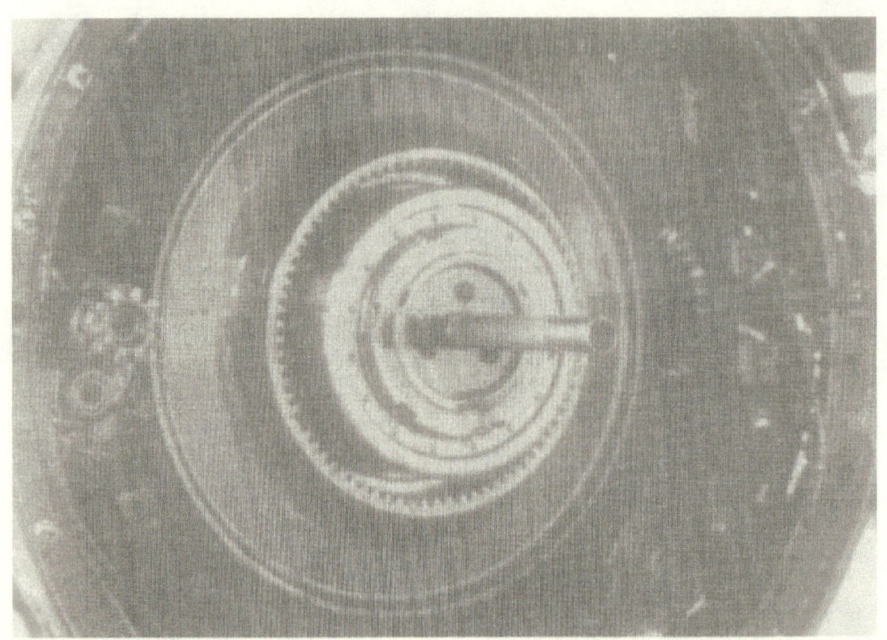

THE AFT END OF THE LEFT ENGINE'S PROPELLER SHAFT
SHOWING THE PROPER INSTALLATION OF THE OIL
TRANSFER TUBE. (*USFS Collection/Accident Report*)

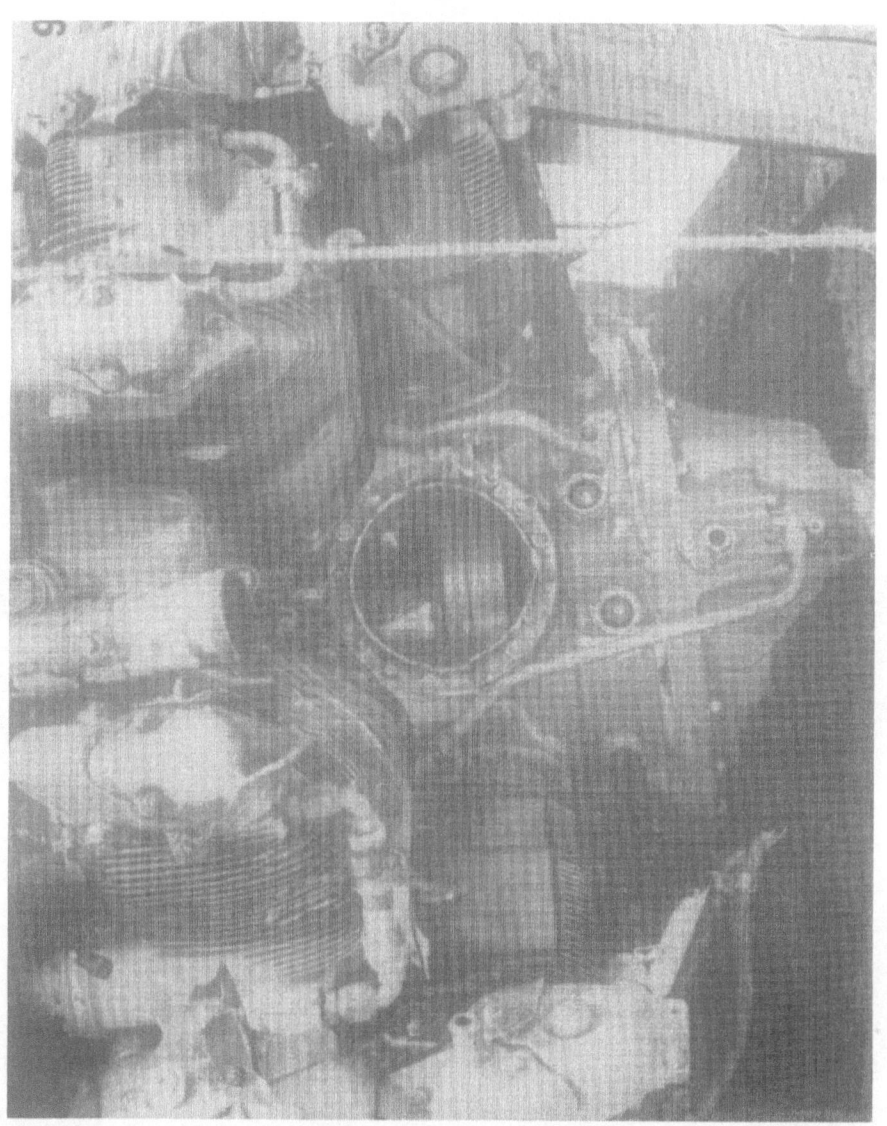

RIGHT ENGINE SHOWING LOCATION OF MISSING NUMBER
EIGHT CYLINDER. (*USFS Collection/Accident Report*)

14

WHAT WAS MISSING?

Accident investigation demands attention to the slightest detail. One must give the benefit of doubt whenever possible, with a nod toward the unknown.
—DICK WILLIAMS, LETTER TO RICHARD H. HOLM, JR. (2024)

The investigation was done in an astonishingly short time—nine weeks. Some parts of the final 872-page report are minutely thorough: events and findings are supported by a redundancy of interviews, primary documents, and fact-checking. Other parts of the report gloss over areas where one might expect more immersion. The report is loaded with the immaterial: 30 pages of excerpts from the *USFS Aviation Manual* (5700), 180 pages of communication logs (none of which are referenced in the report), 300 pages of maintenance reports (no actual logbooks for the aircraft), and a haphazard mix of newspaper clippings and press releases.

Among the fluff, the authors of the report hone in on two areas: the incorrectly-assembled engines and their related maintenance.

Even where the report displays professional investigation, the findings lack quality analysis. So, what was missing?

• • •

It was clear the cause of the left engine problems was the missing oil-transfer tube—a part that could not have been detected by any subsequent external inspection method following re-installation of the nose case. However, not answered was whether the USFS should have more closely monitored the re-installation of the nose case? Since this operation was performed in a properly licensed facility fully capable of the job, a persuasive rebuttal exists.

Some of the findings about the engine maintenance are misleading. For example, Finding 25, which states, "The coincidence of the 2 engines failing within less than one minute in flight is extraordinary, probably greater than 1 million to 1." A startling statement. Erroneous in that investigators concluded that the left engine never failed; rather it had been voluntarily shut down.

As for the right engine, the failure was indisputably caused by the random mix of phosphor-bronze and steel washers installed under the cylinder base hold-down nuts during an earlier overhaul process—an action which occurred while the engine was in the hands of other outside vendors.

Who then was responsible? The report insinuates, but it does not fully answer the question. Reading between the lines, it is reasonable to contend that during the right engine inspection, Morrison-Knudsen should have detected the incipient failure of the number eight cylinder had the preseason inspection checklist been scrupulously followed. Item number 5 on Region 4's "Preseason Inspection" checklist specifically notes, "Inspect cylinders for cracks and security of attachment." The post-incident teardown of this engine suggests that the ultimate failure did not happen "all at once," rather, it had been progressive. Thus, had hold-down nut torque values been checked during the inspection, under-torqued or missing nuts likely would have been detected, and the subsequent failure prevented. Based on the findings in the accident report, Morrison-Knudsen did not perform this check. Morrison-Knudsen in the end dodged legal accountability for the accident by pointing at Gary Aircraft Corporation, the company that rebuilt the engine. It also apportions responsibility to the Region 4 Aviation Program because it had a duty to oversee the actions of the maintenance contractor, Morrison-Knudsen.

Would better oversight of the inspection process by the Region 4 Aviation Department have prevented Morrison-Knudsen's error? If so, then the managers contributed to the cause of the accident. Consider the circumstances: the single individual on the Region 4 payroll at that time with job-specific maintenance responsibilities was Jack Vandehei, the director of maintenance who was based in Ogden, rather than in Boise, where DC-3/C-47 maintenance routines were generally performed. So whether by default or decision, this left such oversight responsibilities to Chris Hayne, whose role and title was supervisory pilot. Based on Chris's testimony, he was taking on responsibilities well beyond his job description, especially during the fire season because he lived in Boise. Both of these men reported to Dale Matlack, the regional aviation officer. Dale Matlack's testimony concerning questions of job-related roles and responsibilities within the Region 4 Aviation Program were in a state of transition. Essentially, responsibility for certain tasks could best be described as muddled.

Chris admitted to being under substantial pressure from his superiors and the entire Region 4 Aviation Program. One of his contempo-
raries, also a pilot, noted, "Chris's span of responsibility and control
covered several pretty large and diverse areas, and required a lot of
time and attention to keep all the balls in the air at once, probably
more so than one would ever have when compared to a similar corporate aviation department. Then, the management of that fleet only
represented the 'tip of the iceberg' regarding the overall demands of
the job. But what was so great about Chris is that 'he gave a shit.'"
The pilots and the staff were all well qualified professionals who for
the most part worked well together, but it was clear that it was a program that was always under scrutiny to prove its own legitimacy as
a cost-effective, in-house aviation program compared to the contract
alternative, and its budget reflected this. During the late-1970s, it was
the understanding of many in the Region 4 Program that Region 6
once had the largest in-house or force-account aviation structure in
the USFS. That is, more owned/operated airplanes, and more pilots
and mechanics than any other region. A Region 4 pilot from this
era stated, "But then, the Region 6 pilots started fouling their own
nest by stridently beating the drum for more modern, turbo-prop
airplanes. Management got so tired of hearing this that it decided to
go the contract route for aviation services, and that a very large part
of the in-house aviation program [airplanes and maintenance facili-
ties] then pretty much faded away. And Region 4 did not want to go
down this same path."

This insistent pressure to prove the Region 4 Aviation Program
was cost-effective resulted in a "get the job done" culture. Not at the
cost of safety, often, however, at the cost of demarcated responsibilities. Discussion of this culture came up in several of the interviews

with Region 4 pilots by the accident-investigation team. The selection of pilots interviewed was not all-inclusive; some pilots who may have offered critical insights were overlooked; others included had only been on the job a short time.

An authorized FAA DC-3/C-47 check pilot with the Region 4 Aviation Program pointed out issues with extended duty times, pilot qualifications, and inadequate flight proficiency checks, and told investigators, "Pilots often exceeded their duty limitations, and that there was continual pressure on the part of management to get the job done even if it meant exceeding duty limitations…the biggest offender in exceeding duty limitation was Chris Hayne…there was pressure from Dale Matlack to get the job done, and there was always the threat that if they [pilots] did not produce, contract operations would take the place of present force-account operations." In Chris's own deposition with the investigation team, he agreed with the determination of excessive duty hours. For him, it was the only way to get the work done, work noticeably more than that encompassed by his title.

Chris and Whitey got along well. They were friends outside of work, and even owned a Cessna 172 together that they used for pleasure. One will never know how much Chris did or did not lean on Whitey to agree 148Z was ready to be released for flying missions. Or how nonchalantly Whitey may or may not have agreed to flying 148Z without the fire-extinguisher bottles. According to Chris, Whitey knew the left engine had an excessive oil leak, and he knew the fire-extinguisher bottles were absent—factors that in the end were determined not to have contributed to the cause of the accident. Whitey was a very experienced pilot who knew that "the pilot in command of an aircraft is directly responsible for, and is the final authority as to the operation of that aircraft," not one's superior. Whether or not

311

Whitey flew the airplane anyway, because he wanted to get the job done, will remain unknown.

The question of fiscal parsimony to help the Program leads to conjecture about whether Whitey and John were trying to save the left engine at the expense of their own safety and their passengers. Present-day pilots are taught to leave alone an engine that is developing power, even in the event of an abnormal instrument reading; the thinking is that if an engine is producing power, it may run long enough, especially when flying over rugged terrain with no ideal emergency landing areas, to put the aircraft in a safe position, either by getting directly to a landing site or by gaining altitude to get to a landing site. In the process of maneuvering to a place of safety, the pilot can assess (trouble shoot), as time allows, if the engine instrument gauges are accurately depicting the potential engine problem. Whitey and John, however, elected to make a precautionary left engine shutdown, having likely observed rising oil temperature and dropping oil pressure. A Region 4 pilot of the 1970s–80s observed, "Would I have made the same precautionary engine shutdown as Whitey and John? Back in that same time, I probably would have done the same thing. The Forest Service was running a somewhat 'watch the pennies' aviation program, mainly then concerned about saving whatever is left of the engine prior to its total self-destruction. Today? Today, I would never shutdown an engine that is still producing any useful power, and particularly if over a wilderness area with a bunch of passengers on board. No!"

The frugal attitude and culture also seeped into the pilot training of the Region 4 Aviation Program. Pilot training in an effort to keep up with industry standard recurrent or proficiency requirements was limited. Based on interviews with pilots of the era in the Program, little training was done in the aircraft, and no training was done in flight simulators. The Department argued that the lack of training was offset by hiring only highly qualified pilots with extensive military backgrounds and flight time in the same category, class, and type of aircraft to be flown. Aircraft being operated as Public Aircraft, such as 148Z, have no specified training requirements. In fact, under the literal interpretation of Public Aircraft a pilot does not even need an FAA-issued license. While the Pubic Aircraft card could be played by the Region 4 Aviation Program, all aviation departments under the USFS were to comply with standards set forth by the Washington Office in the Agency's *Aviation Manual*, also known as the *5700 Manual*. When Region 4 pilots were asked about the application of the *5700 Manual*, they said it was never referred to. Pilots regarded the manual as "impractical regulations written by non-aviators, 'tree growers,' flying desks in Washington with little to no applicability in the field out West." But in his deposition with accident investigators, Chris Hayne stated that the Region 4 Program aimed to be in compliance with similar sectors of the aviation industry, such as 135 and 121 Air Carriers. In truth, the Region 4 Aviation Program was not even complying with private pilot provisions under Part 91 (General Operations), the lowest level of aviation standards. For example, under Part 91, for a private pilot to act as the pilot-in-command [PIC] of an aircraft carrying passengers, "a pilot must have conducted at least three takeoffs and landings in the same category, class, and type of aircraft they intend to operate as the sole manipulator of the flight, within the preceding 90 days." In an attempt to meet basic requirements but stay within the limited budget, Region 4 pilots would commonly return to the flight line at the beginning of the season and be seated in an Aero Commander for some recurrent training and proficiency checks, but that is not in the "same category, class, and type" of aircraft as the more costly operation of DC-3/C-47s. It was not unusual for a returning pilot to just strap into a Doug without any recurrent training and without the minimum standard takeoffs and landings. In this case, it could be as many as six months before a Region 4 pilot, such as Whitey or John, had been in the cockpit of a DC-3/C-47.

Owing to the high operating costs of aircraft like the DC-3/C-47 and the general structure of the Program, first-year hires were assigned to fly the season in the right (co-pilot) seat. Management assumed the new hires already had the extensive background to fly the plane, but needed to learn the task of flying smokejumpers, cargo drops, and so on. One pilot remembered, "I did not get out of the right seat the whole first season. The only training consisted of a two-day ground school, which included flight operations and review of aircraft systems and emergency procedures specific to airplanes in the fleet. I was never introduced to the *5700 Manual* or questioned about currency requirements…nor was I surprised, coming from the military. The only manual—other than one associated with a specific aircraft—put in front of us was the *Civil Service Manual*, which had nothing to do with aviation." Returning pilots also attended two days of ground school—that was it.

Region 4 management did require all pilots to pass an annual checkride in aircraft where they acted as PIC. To save costs, this checkride was typically done sometime during the fire season when an airplane was empty on a return leg, or on a reposition flight without passengers, to another location for an assignment. Annual checkrides in DC-3/C-47s did often cover more in-depth training, such as simulated engine outs, but was not required. As of June 1979, records pertaining to a specific pilot's training activity were just as poorly kept as the Region 4 aircraft maintenance logbooks. One Region 4 pilot commented, "The Program was run like a big aero club more concerned with flying, rather than a corporate aviation flight department focused on record keeping and keeping in tune with book requirements."

In the accident investigation the lackadaisical training standards and corresponding record-keeping surfaced. Region 4 provided investigators all of the training records on file for Whitey and John and they were included in the final report. The accident investigators made no written comment on the deficiencies of the records and the noncompliance of the pilots with their own 5700 standards. USFS 5710, as of 1979, specified pilots must have a checkride every 12 months with no grace period. Whitey's records indicate his last qualification checkride was completed on May 16, 1978, which made him overdue. More alarming, the prior currency check for Whitey in his file was May 28, 1974, with an expiration of June 30, 1975, indicating a 30-day grace period was exercised. His flight duty records for 1978 were complete and showed he flew 251 hours, but there were no records for 1979. As for John, there were no USFS records at all. In fact, his last currency was from a 135 checkride performed by an unrelated flight operator in a Cessna 185 on May 30, 1978. These deficient records were ignored by investigators. Finding 17 in the accident report states, "Pilot and co-pilot were well qualified and certified to pilot a DC-3." Qualified based on experience, yes. But the flight records on file reveal they were not current. The incomplete record-keeping and the absence of routine flight training should have made investigators question whether they contributed to the accident. So: could better training have altered the outcome of June 11, 1979?

While all of these issues surfaced during the investigations, they were not analyzed or considered as contributing causes in the report. In truth, when they did surface during an accident investigation interview with a Region 4 pilot, investigator James Torrence wrote, "I could have pursued the interview with [pilot name removed] further, but felt that we were rapidly moving into areas outside of the role of an investigation team, and felt that the matter could best be dealt with through another vehicle."

An additional area neglected in the report regarded the most common cause of death in the accident. The autopsy reports state that a consistent cause of death for passengers killed on initial impact was "fractured cervical spine" or "basal skull fracture." This was because the passengers were sitting side by side along the port side of the aircraft in military canvas seats known as, "troop seats." The side-facing seats placed the passengers perpendicular to the direction of flight, and thus to its point of impact. The human body can better endure impact straight-on, and even more so when facing rearward, because a person's neck and organs are better protected. At the time of the accident, Region 4 did have a set of forward-facing, airline-style seats for the DC-3/C-47s that had been procured as non-tagged parts from Boeing in Seattle. In keeping with the frugality of the Program, during the winter of 1978–1979 the seats where then cut down and modified to fit into the fleet of DC-3/C-47. The intention was to use the seats while hauling non-required crew members (any passenger other than smokejumpers or pilots). According to pilots interviewed from this era of the Region 4 Program, usage of forward-facing seats was at the discretion of the PIC.

• • •

The cause of the 148Z accident and its resulting deaths can be attributed to a storm of compounding factors far beyond the investigators' basic conclusions of improperly assembled engines and unsatisfactory maintenance. From an operations standpoint, the Region 4 Flight Department was inappropriately structured and inadequately funded to support such a complex aviation program. The issues, particularly in the area of safety and "get the job done," were evident during the investigation, yet never addressed. Aircraft training information for the pilots of 148Z was presented, and although outdated and incomplete, was not analyzed. The link between cause of death in autopsy reports and the aircraft's side-seating configuration also went undiscussed.

15

CURRENTS OF CHANGE

In cockpits very few things are done without reason.
—ERNEST K. GANN, *FATE IS THE HUNTER*

B ased on the review of available court records, no individual employee, region, or the USFS as an agency is known to have been held responsible for the accident of 148Z. However, it would have been difficult to find an individual in the Region 4 Aviation Department who was not affected by it or experienced guilt regarding the crash. No one probably bore the weight of responsibility more so than Chris Hayne, and it was unfortunate for someone who cared so much that he was the only one to leave the Department because of the accident; he did so of his own choice. In July 1979, Chris and his superior Dale Matlack, along with line pilot Stan McGrew, were standing on the Region 4's ramp at the Boise Airport and Dale remonstrated with Chris about needing to take his respective scheduled days off. Stan recalled, "Chris looked at Dale and said, 'Dale, you don't understand. I simply cannot take days off during the fire season and

RICHARD H. HOLM, JR.

stay on top of things.'" Dale responded that he had to because the entire Program was under a microscope owing to the accident and the on-going investigation. "Chris then turned to me and handed me his badge of authority (handheld radio) and said, 'Stan, as far as I am concerned, you got it because I quit.' And then he walked off the ramp for the last time."

Chris, who had been with the Department for six years, left Boise and returned home to the South where he pursued his retirement in Foley, Alabama. He flew for pleasure well into his eighties, and he was awarded the FAA's Wright Brothers Master Pilot Award and the Charles Taylor Master Mechanic Award. He died in July 2022 at the age of ninety. After walking off the Boise ramp that day, his job of supervisory pilot was filled temporarily by Milt Olsen until Stan McGrew was appointed to the position in 1981, a post he held until 1992.

• • •

The accident report is not where one would find the appropriate corrective actions for prevention of future accidents by the USFS. Rather, three more steps in the process follow. One, the designation and seating of a review board (or panel) to scrutinize the accident report produced by the investigation team and to formulate corrective actions. Two, based on the discussion of the review board, an "action plan" is formulated. Three, implementation of the plan. Much research was conducted in searching and reviewing primary documents related to the 148Z accident, and in all the efforts no documents were discovered regarding the individuals on the review board or the specific corrective actions. While these documents could not be located, if they do in fact exist, it is known, based on interviews with retired

320

Region 4 aviation employees, that changes to the Program occurred over the years as a result of the Selway accident, direct and indirect.

In 1982, a new hangar facility was constructed in Ogden to consolidate the storage of the Region 4 aircraft fleet. Additionally, the facility allowed for the improvement of aircraft parts storage and office space for personnel. Following the 148Z accident, the USFS severed the maintenance contract with Morrison-Knudsen; at the same time, all aviation management positions were relocated to the Ogden office. Those previously based in Boise were eliminated. This change allowed numerous improvements: closer supervision of contracted maintenance personnel as work was performed on USFS aircraft; an aircraft records and filing system was developed and housed onsite; aircraft parts were organized and tagged in accord with government requirements.

The Region's DC-3/C-47 aircraft were scrupulously checked for cylinder base hold-down nut torque values at each inspection. Also, an improved cargo restraint system was developed by Supervisory Pilot Stan McGrew. While not explicitly noted in the accident report or supported by autopsy reports, there were some Region 4 aviation managers who were persuaded that there might have been more survivors in the Selway crash had the cargo been better restrained. As a result, a standardized system of netting and hold-downs was developed and implemented.

The continuous budget limitations that hung over the Region 4 Aviation Department in the 1960s and 1970s eased somewhat in the 1980s. This is evident not only in the construction of the Ogden hangar facility, but in the effort to phase out piston-powered aircraft, specifically the radial powered DC-3/C-47s. While there was some impetus for this change because of the accident, the fact that parts and expertise to keep the Pratt & Whitney radials operational were becoming more difficult to locate, added to the shift. These issues were exacerbated by a number of inflight radial-engine failures. The first effort to phase out the radials was in 1984, when the Region bought its first de Havilland Twin Otter. At this time, one of the three remaining DC-3s/C-47s (143Z) was surplused to the Hill AFB museum. The following year, Doug Bird, the Region 4 director of aviation and fire management, commissioned a five-person group to find viable replacements for the DC-3/C-47s. In 1986, one alternative submitted by the group was conversion of one of the Region's DC-3/C-47s to turbine engines. By 1990, the contract for such a conversion was announced and it was awarded to Basler Turbo Conversions of Oshkosh, Wisconsin. Between the time the bid was awarded and work began, the USFS decided to convert both aircraft to turbine engines. It decided that one of the finished airplanes would be transferred to Region 1 for use as a smokejumper aircraft. The conversions were completed in 1991 and left Bassler under new designations as DC-3-TP67s. In October 2012, Region 4 retired its Basler converted DC-3 (142Z) and 40 years after the Selway accident, Region 1 retired its in December 2019. The decision to dispose of these aircraft had nothing to do with their flight record. It was simply a management decision by individuals with no background in aviation or by supporters of rotary-wing aircraft, or both.

Although many changes were made as a result of the accident, some, surprisingly, were not. Immediately following Steward-Davis's teardown of each engine and its preliminary findings, it notified the USFS's Aviation and Fire Management departments in Washington, D.C., on July 16, 1979: "We are sufficiently concerned with the finding of dissimilar cylinder hold-down washers made of dissimilar metals that Mr. Steward wished to recommend that other R-1830-94 engines in the U.S. Forestry Service fleet be checked to verify that they did not share this condition." Pilots of the era did not think this precaution was carried out; most argued it would have been unforgettable because the task would have required removal of all the cylinders on in-service engines—no small undertaking. Instead, only two in-house directives were released from the USFS to its many aviation departments: June 14, 1979 and July 14, 1979. The directives required checks on fuel lines, hydraulic lines, pressure checks, and fire-extinguisher systems. At the very least, Region 4 should have determined if any other in-service engines had been overhauled by the companies involved with the engines on 148Z. No evidence of this was uncovered.

As mentioned, the management and oversight issues of maintenance were partially addressed by consolidating these matters in Ogden, but the general structure of the organization and the related job descriptions remained in place. Region 4 did do away with the canvas troop-style seats and had specialized removable bench seats built by Simula added to each side of the DC-3/C-47s. The new seats, however, were a continuation of the side-facing seating arrangement. When carrying non-crewmembers, Region 4 continued using the modified, hand-me-down Boeing airline seats at the discretion of the PIC. Based on interviews with pilots, forward-facing seats were rarely implemented except during the winter when the planes were used to transport management personnel to meetings. A very different approach was taken in Region 1. When Region 1 was given ownership of its DC-3-TP67 (while still undergoing the Basler conversion) it made an order change to the contract for removable rear-facing seats to be used when non-crewmembers were aboard—a change unquestionably influenced by the Selway accident.

The Selway tragedy forced the Region 4 Aviation Program to make some much needed changes to improve overall safety for its pilots, crews, and passengers, albeit at a plod. For many critics it was a case of "too little, too late." To other observers, the protracted evolution of the direct and indirect changes was like treating a symptom rather than its cause.

AIRCRAFT ON THE REGION 4 RAMP IN BOISE, SUMMER 1979. (*W. Williams*)

CHRIS HAYNE AT THE CONTROLS OF A REGION 4 DC-3/C-47 DURING A FERRY FLIGHT. (*S. McGrew*)

STAN MCGEW WITH 148Z, WEST YELLOWSTONE, 1978. (*S. McGrew*)

WHITEY HACHMEISTER AND STAN McGREW,
WEST YELLOWSTONE, 1978. *(S. McGrew)*

REGION 4'S DC-3-TP-67 (142Z). *(W. Williams)*

REGION 1'S DC-3-TP-67 (115Z). *(W. Williams)*

16

LEGAL TAILSPINS

I don't wish to speak ill of the gentleman,
but I believe, sir, he is a lawyer.
—DR. SAMUEL JOHNSON

In August 1979, with the release of the USFS's in-house accident report, it became evident to grieving families who had lost loved ones aboard 148Z that they had legitimate legal claims with the parties responsible for aspects of poor maintenance. Whitey Hachmeister's family hired Howard Humphery with the Boise firm of Clemons, Cosho & Humphrey. On December 24, 1979 it filed their lawsuit against Cooper Industries, Inc.; Trans-West Air Services, Inc.; Gary Aircraft Corporation, Morrison-Knudsen Company, Inc.; and five other John Does. Since Whitey had been a resident of Ada County at the time of his death, the lawsuit was filed in the Fourth Judicial District, Ada County, located in Boise. The Hachmeisters sued for $1,702,024 in damages derived from $1,000,000 in general damages, $700,000 in special damages for the loss of future earnings, and $2,024 for funeral and burial-related expenses. The lawsuit pursued a wrongful death action against these defendants related to mechanical work done or not done to the aircraft's engines.

Cooper, Inc. was represented by Alan Hull of Quane, Smith, Howard, & Hull. Trans-West was represented by Robert Koontz of Conklin & Alder, Ltd. and Elam, Burke, Evans, Boyd & Koontz. Gary Aircraft was represented by Perkins, Coie, Stone, Olsen & Williams of Seattle, and its local counsel was Don Farley of Moffatt, Thomas, Barrett & Blanton. Morrison-Knudsen was represented by Joseph Imhoff and Mike Moore of Imhoff & Lynch.

Coinciding with the suit filed by the Hachmeisters, several other families hired Gerald C. Sterns, one of the best-known aviation litigation lawyers in the West. Sterns's law partner, Thomas Smith, managed most of the casework, but he also hired Boise attorney Allen Derr of Derr, Derr & Schindle as local counsel. The Sterns team represented the families of Catherine Smith Hodgin, Don Easthouse, Ron Hagan, and John Slingerland. The Sterns team then approached Charlie and Bryant to join the suit in seeking damages, advising them that their inclusion and testimony would strengthen the overall lawsuit for the other families. Both were apprehensive.

Charlie and Julie wanted to focus on the future. The thought of a lawsuit had crossed Charlie's mind, but he did not go so far as to inquire with anyone regarding legal counsel. His only financial reprieve until now, covering lost wages and medical expenses, was provided through the Federal Employees' Compensation Act. It was a time of healing for the Dietzes. Charlie was spending his weeks enduring physical therapy and rehabilitation on his knee and leg in Spokane, living in the Moran's spare bedroom—the same home wherein he found refuge following discharge from the hospital. The situation was awkward, yet extremely generous of his hosts. Julie, meanwhile, was working solo from the Selway Falls Guard Station to complete the season. Then in November, before closing the Selway Falls cabin, Charlie joined her. A letter arrived with the following address: "Law Offices of Gerald C. Sterns: A Professional Corporation, 490 Pacific Avenue, San Francisco, California 94133." Charlie sliced the envelope open with a pocket knife and found a solicitation to join a lawsuit. His reaction was mixed. He wanted the party or parties who were responsible for the accident to be held accountable. After a sleepless night (and no telephone), he and Julie decided to drive the 20 miles to the nearest payphone at Three Rivers and listen to what the lawyers had to say. After a lengthy conversation, he reminded himself that he wanted to do what was right. So he agreed to join the case. Several days later, a contract arrived in the mail with standard industry terms: the plaintiff's attorney fees were 33.3 percent of the remaining net sum recovered in the event that the claim was settled before trial commenced, and 40 percent of such sum recovered by settlements or judgment after trial commenced. Charlie signed. Then, for more than three years, he found himself mired in depositions, updates from attorneys, and statements to review.

As for Bryant, his opinion of a lawsuit coincided with Charlie's. He was young and wanted to move on, and he was more concerned with life after high school—starting college, and preparing for his mission for the LDS Church. With the encouragement of his parents, however, at the last minute he too joined the lawsuit.

With Charlie and Bryant on board, the second lawsuit was filed in the Fourth Judicial District, Ada County, Boise, seeking damages for wrongful death and personal injuries. In the following months, the families of other victims secured their own individual legal counsel and filed separate lawsuits—these included the families of Taylor, Leber, TerKeurst, and McGreevey.

. . .

Simultaneously, the TerKeurst's wrongful death action was filed in Idaho, against the same, and the TerKeursts also sued the USFS (the US federal government) in the US District Court of the Western District of Michigan, where they were residents. The US government moved to dismiss the case, arguing, among other issues, that TerKeurst was a federal employee/volunteer at the time of his death, and therefore his exclusive remedy had already been addressed in accordance to the Federal Employees' Compensation Act, commonly referred to as "FECA." From a legal standpoint, "remedy" means redressing a wrong or anything a court can do for a litigant who has been wronged. The remedy took the form of compensation payments that had been paid on behalf of TerKeurst for funeral, burial, and termination of his employment (since he died). The government argued that TerKeurst had applied to be a volunteer for summer work projects; he boarded the USFS DC-3 after signing an agreement for individual voluntary services. TerKeurst's estate argued that he was not killed while in the performance of his job (duty), thus not covered by FECA; the Court disagreed. According to the Court, TerKeurst was under the direct and immediate supervision of USFS personnel from the date he reported until his death. He was on the USFS DC-3 in his capacity as a federal employee/volunteer en route to a federal job to fulfill the terms of his agreement. Even though he was traveling and not performing his job, he was still an employee within the "zone of special danger" created by the conditions of his employment/volunteer status when he died. The federal government was awarded summary judgment in its favor and the case dismissed. A summary judgment motion is what some attorneys call, "a halftime motion." It is filed before trial and presents an argument to the Court that judgment should be entered now as a matter of law because there are no facts in dispute. The Court ultimately found that the FECA procedures had been followed and they were the family's remedy.

Rightly or wrongly, based on available records, no other lawsuits are known to have been filed against the USFS or individual USFS employees as a result of the 148Z accident. As an entity of the federal government, the USFS as a whole cannot be sued under the doctrine of sovereign immunity, unless the government consents to participate in such lawsuit. One also can speculate that plaintiffs' lawyers recognized that the USFS did not make the airplane, did not manufacture parts for the airplane, and did not directly make any major repairs to the airplane resulting in the cause of the accident. Moreover, as was decided in the TerKeurst case, the remedy on behalf of the federal government had been addressed and complied with. Again, the accident investigation report concluded the cause of the accident was a result of poor maintenance stemming from four individual companies that the USFS either contracted with or obtained parts from.

Even though the USFS was unsuccessfully sued by the TerKeursts, it was likely the Agency would end up in court again if the lawsuits were tried by a jury. Under Idaho law, one or more of the defense lawyers would likely have brought the USFS into court through what is known as an "empty chair," essentially pointing at a party not included in the lawsuit as the party liable. Non-parties can even be used on a special verdict form in which a jury apportions the parties guilt compared with others. This could have been done because in Idaho negligence/fault of a nonparty may be considered, meaning even though an employer (USFS) who has paid for workmen's compensation (as per FECA) cannot be sued, it is common for defense lawyers to ask the Court that the employer be put on the special verdict form, with the argument that the employer did in fact bear a measure of fault causing the accident. Whether or not the facts support it, it exists as a defense tactic. In the case of the 148Z accident, there were people pointing at the USFS (Region 4 Aviation Program) for allegedly not doing proper maintenance and not keeping appropriate maintenance records. As such, it could be argued that the USFS was also at fault. The defendant's hope is that the jury would find some percentage of USFS fault, thereby reducing a percentage from a defendant or defendants' liability.

• • •

Once the lawsuits were filed in Idaho's Fourth Judicial District, the legal system crawled along. Early on, three of the defendants—Gary Aircraft, Morrison-Knudsen, and Trans-West—asserted the metallurgical tests could cause damage to the parts/components that in the end allegedly would prove that their maintenance work was satisfactory. US District Judge Raymond McNichols issued a temporary restraining order in February 1980 to the USFS to halt such tests on components of 148Z.

Two months later, Gary Aircraft challenged the right of the Idaho court to hear the case against it, claiming it did not have jurisdiction because Gary was a Texas corporation doing business only in Texas. This threatened the standing not only of a suit with Gary, but the lawsuits against Cooper (Texas) and Trans-West (Utah) as well, and if the plaintiffs lost this argument, it would have forced their lawyers to file lawsuits in each of the respective states.

Plaintiffs' attorneys took depositions from the president of Gary Aircraft, whereby the president had to answer questions under oath transcribed by a court reporter. The plaintiffs' attorneys believed the testimony clearly showed that Gary knowingly was doing business in Idaho. On June 23, 1980, arguments were presented to the Court, asserting the plaintiffs' claim that Gary was subject to the Court's jurisdiction. Gary argued to the contrary. Presiding Judge Gerald F. Schroeder took the matter under advisement and later ruled that Gary was in fact subject to the Court's jurisdiction. At the same hearing, Judge Schroeder consolidated the Hachmeister lawsuit with all the plaintiffs represented by Sterns. The other individual lawsuits were also eventually consolidated.

By mid-1981, defendants' attorneys had taken depositions, and it had become clear that all of the defendants were blaming each other. None of them admitted liability, and all of them delayed the case. It was abundantly clear from the depositions, however, that the plaintiffs had a strong case.

In early 1982, all parties were informed that the jury trial was scheduled to begin with Judge Schroeder in the Fourth Judicial District on January 10, 1983. With a deadline, attorneys began working more actively on their respective cases. Judge Schroeder granted summary judgement in favor of Cooper, dismissing the complaint and causes, but it is unclear, based on the available files, on what grounds the ruling was made. According to the Fourth Judicial District Court clerk, the court file is not intact.

On November 22, 1982, several plaintiffs were dismissed on the grounds that under Idaho law they had no cause of action for wrongful death. Again, while the court files are unclear on what grounds the ruling was made, it appears that these plaintiffs were family members who were too remote from the cause of action. Typically, personal representatives of estates sue on behalf of the deceased's spouse, children, or parent(s), who have rights to sue for wrongful death, but not necessarily a sister, brother, or some distant relative. The passengers on 148Z were mostly young individuals who presumably did not have written wills. Thus, the remaining plaintiffs in the lawsuit were verified personal representatives of an estate, such as spouses, children, and in some instances parents. Nearly a month following the dismissal (December 28, 1982), Morrison-Knudsen was also dismissed in a summary judgment; again, it is unclear from the surviving files on what grounds. The plaintiffs did not oppose the summary judgment, and the Court dismissed the claims, leaving Trans-West and Gary as the only defendants.

· · ·

As the wintry days of early January 1983 arrived, the Dietzes began preparing for the upcoming trial; their notice came by mail, indicating the trial date had been pushed to the end of March. Still, they expected their attorney, Tom Smith, to reach out regarding trial preparation. No such communications were forthcoming. They had met Tom just once during depositions in Boise. Then one evening in late March, Charlie and his family were at his in-law's house, about to sit down for dinner, when the telephone rang. Julie's mother answered. Tom asked to have a serious conversation with Charlie. Charlie sat down and was informed all plaintiffs in the lawsuit were ready to settle with the remaining two defendants, but in order to do so they needed him to also agree to the terms. He was informed that he was the last "holdout." To persuade Charlie, Tom disclosed that he had conversations with the presiding judge, and the judge forewarned him that juries in

Idaho were notorious for awarding low monetary compensation for damages. Therefore, there was substantial risk that if the case were tried, the payout would be far less than the existing settlement offer. To further tempt Charlie, the attorney offered to waive his 33.3-per-cent contingency—something he apparently did not offer any of the others. He told Charlie the amount of his individual settlement offer, ending with, "We need your decision right now." Charlie sat there dumbstruck. "First off, I was trying to process all of the information and sort out what was true…the settlement number was astonishing low. Astonishing low! I started to think about all the medical issues I'd already had, and then thought about the future issues I could likely have…I thought, are you kidding? Then I thought of all the other families…widows and the kids left behind…what are they supposed to do…how would this [assumedly low] amount of money even begin to rectify their lives moving forward? It was upsetting. But then I thought, what if the judge's [alleged] comment about Idaho juries was fact, then it could be less? And, here I'm supposedly the guy holding it all up. And I'm supposed to give an answer now? It was a lot to think about." Charlie asked more questions; more discussion followed. The conversation ended with Charlie agreeing to settle.

On March 28, 1983, a settlement was reached with the remaining plaintiffs, and with defendants Trans-West and Gary. Based on the documents available by request to the Court, and discussions with some of the parties involved, one assumes payments were paid by their respective insurance companies. As a reminder, Gary was responsible for overhauling the right engine, which failed owing to the random mixing of phosphor-bronze and steel washers placed under the number eight cylinder base hold-down nuts. Trans-West was accountable for mating the engine nose case to the bare power section on the left engine. The missing oil-transfer tube should have been installed when these two units were coupled. "The whole thing did not leave a good taste in our mouths," Charlie explained. "We don't waste our time thinking about it anymore, but at the time we did wonder if settlement was the plan all along. We don't know if I was offered an exclusive deal with the waiving of the contingency fee, and we don't even know if I really was the 'holdout.' We had a lot of suspicion...I wanted to see the case go to trial, not because of the chance of a better payment, but to see the responsible parties publically held accountable for what they had done. With the settlement, I felt they [defendants] were let off the hook. We were not to talk about it again, and all of it just did not sit well." For many years following the settlement, the Dietzes stayed in touch with Karen Easthouse and Sue Taylor. Settlement amounts and terms were never disclosed, but the general understanding was that justice was not administered. No court, no judge, no lawyer, no named defendant, and not even the federal government provided any of the plaintiffs the human restitution they really sought.

The plaintiffs who received settlements and who had collected federal workmen's compensation between the time of the accident and the settlement were legally required to reimburse the federal government for all workmen's compensation collected. This prevents what the Court terms "double recovery," meaning an individual cannot receive compensation from the government and a private company for the same event. The clients represented by Sterns tried unsuccessfully to fight the reimbursement. The Dietzes, however, did successfully challenge the federal government on Charlie's living expenses associated with medical recovery in Spokane. The Dietzes thought it was only right to give this reimbursement check to the Morans for their assistance and costs while Charlie lived with them.

With lawsuits dating to 45+ years ago, it is difficult to speculate litigation strategies. The available Court records pertaining to the lawsuits filed in Idaho were obtained from the Ada County Courthouse and reviewed. As with other lawsuits, those documents never reveal the story's complexities. Since settlements of this type are not public record, depositions, pretrial motions, and amounts paid are lost in a heavy fog. Court records thus provide an inadequate window on what was a complicated litigation.

17

THE OUTCOME

I have come to believe that there is an appointed time for all of us—
'a time to live and a time to die.' How else can one make sense
of tragedies such as this one. I thank God for the gift of faith.
—DOLLIE MCGREEVEY, LETTER TO CINDY SCHACHER (2009)

I n 1980, at the suggestion of Art Seamans, a bronze plaque affixed
to a granite boulder was placed at the Moose Creek Ranger Station
in memory of the people aboard 148Z on that June day in 1979. The
boulder and plaque placement was selected and set by the Kecks. It is
simple, tasteful, and in harmony with the surrounding wilderness and
the station's historic buildings.[16] In the fall of 1982, US Senator James
McClure of Idaho and US Senator John Warner of Virginia visited

---

16 In 1989, a second bronze plaque was affixed to the memorial to honor victims aboard
the Ford Tri-Motor that crashed on landing at Moose Creek in August 1959. The additional plaque used the existing 1980 memorial to reduce the overall impact of the site,
thus viewed as more in keeping with wilderness management goals.

the Moose Creek Ranger Station. One of their objectives was a flag presentation at the memorial. Warner had recently spent three days fly-fishing the waters of East Moose Creek with District Ranger Barry Hicks, Regional Forester Tom Coston, and Nez Perce NF Supervisor Tom Kovalicky. Upon his return to the station, McClure met the group, and a small ceremony ensued. He presented a flag that had been flown over the US Capitol in memory of those who perished in the accident.

Art Seamans and University of Idaho professor Dr. Jim Fazio established a Selway-Bitterroot Memorial Scholarship Fund commemorating the crash victims, as well as the memory of Kevin Leber. Leber was a third-year student at the University in the Department of Wildland Recreation Management and a student of Jim's, who was the chairman of the Department. Under the sponsorship of Art, the Moose Creek Ranger District employees pooled $4,000 to establish the scholarship. At Jim's urging, the 1980 yearbook for the Department was dedicated to Kevin with a special mention of his achievements and the scholarship. "This yearbook, too, will record the event for posterity and serve as a memorial for Kevin. More than all else, however, the most lasting memorial would be to help forward the work to which Kevin and the others on that plane were dedicated. Happily, the scholarship will be one way to achieve this. Each year, a student in Wildland Recreation Management will be selected to receive the scholarship. The selection will be made on the basis of his or her interest in wilderness management...In memory of Kevin and the others, let us learn and heed the message of wilderness stewardship. This will truly be a lasting memorial." Since its inception, nearly 50 students have applied and received the scholarship.

Steve Waterman, the Nez Perce NF public affairs officer, with author Judith King Norgaard, who also worked for the USFS, collaborated on a story about the accident. The article was published at the request of Bill Rooney, the editor of *American Forests* magazine, and appeared under the title "Wilderness Tragedy" in the June 1980 issue. It was the most complete account of the crash, using information gleaned from the official accident report. A heavily marked-up draft of the article found in Art's files indicates he was highly critical.

Owing to the hardship of the accident, Art transferred to another position in the Agency. In reference to the accident, Art's daughter, Cindy, said, "It was something that haunted my dad for his entire life. He somehow felt directly responsible. After he left the position in the spring of 1980, my father never returned to Moose Creek. It was just too painful for him."

Art did not stray far from his passion for wilderness management, taking a job as the area manager of the then newly established (1980) Hells Canyon National Recreation Area. It was a challenging job and one he performed with pride retiring in 1992. Retirement was difficult. Art applied his jet-boat pilot skills as a tour-and-fishing-guide for Snake River Adventures in Hells Canyon. He also became involved with a number of nonprofit and hobby groups, including the Northwest Professional Power Vessel Association, Northwest River Runners, River Access for Tomorrow, American Legion, Blue Ribbon Coalition, National Rifle Association, and the Selway-Bitterroot Frank Church Foundation. When not volunteering or running the river, he enjoyed photography and polished his artistic talents—painting acrylic landscapes and fashioning unique wooden pieces, as well as drawing in pen and ink. Many of his pieces focused on places and scenes from his former days on the Moose Creek District. He even sold some of his work from a business he called "Hells Canyon Arts." Art died on June 12, 2014, at age 77.

• • •

In the wake of the accident and Art leaving the Moose Creek District, the mission passed to Barry Hicks, who held the district ranger position from 1980 through 1985. Hicks was no stranger to the Moose District, having worked there from 1974 through 1977 as the fire management officer. He began his career in 1964 with the Agency as a Missoula smokejumper. Later, he jumped for three years based in Grangeville and then spent several years in the military deployed to Vietnam, where he was sent home early to resume smokejumping, and then worked his way up to base manager in West Yellowstone. Through his background in smokejumping, he developed an interest in aviation; retiring from the Agency as a regional aviation officer. As Moose Creek FMO in 1976, he initiated a risk-assessment analysis for aviation on the District. It analyzed the risk of using USFS DC-3s versus contracting with an approved 135 Air Taxi operator, such as Frank Hill's Grangeville Air Service, that used single-engine, piston aircraft. The assessment looked at a number of factors, such as exposure—the number of single-engine flights required compared to one DC-3 (multi-engine), and performance characteristics, chiefly the DC-3's single-engine capabilities in the event of an engine failure. The analysis concluded that a DC-3 was not only overall safer, but also more cost-efficient. Barry's analysis paved the way for the implementation of DC-3s for the major flights, such as at the early season Guard School. He therefore felt somewhat responsible for the 1979 crash; however, given his background, he reasoned that the DC-3 was an airworthy aircraft when proper maintenance procedures were followed. "The DC-3 is no doubt a safe airplane. The crash of 148Z was an isolated tragedy."

Although Barry believed statistically in the safety of the DC-3, as the Moose Creek District ranger, he and the other district managers gradually scrapped its use. In fact, Richard Hildner, the Moose Creek FMO from May 1980 through 1983, noted that the District really leaned on him to eliminate—other than for station resupplies—use of aircraft altogether. The exception to DC-3 use in the few years following the accident occurred in 1981, when a fire camp was set up at the airstrip to help supply firefighters near Meeker Creek and Wahoo Pass. Barry's directive transformed the Guard School travel into "a two-day, one-night camping meet-and-greet trip" where, beginning in 1980, people walked in from Selway Falls to Moose Creek and, led by Wilderness Rangers Warren Miller and Dick Kuhl, the 26-mile hike was mandatory, heavily emphasizing wilderness education and ethics. The curriculum on the hike was hands-on-in-the-field.

The hike at the beginning of the Guard School was embraced by new and old employees in the District's post-accident period. The trip proved to be tri-fold: it promoted wilderness values, brought new employees into the fold of the Moose Creek culture, and reinforced a dedication to the stewardship of a beloved place. Regarding this annual tradition, Betsey Kepes, a Moose Creeker from the era, wrote, "Our summer season began with a two-day training hike up the Selway River Trail, a spectacular twenty-six mile path to the Moose Creek Ranger Station. Along the way, we watched osprey dive for trout, and visited white sand beaches leading into the clear, icy water. At night, sitting around the campfire, we began intense friendships that lasted long beyond the summer season."

Beginning in 1986, Dennis Dailey followed Barry Hicks as the Moose Creek District Ranger. During the Dailey years, the use of aircraft was further reduced, not as a result of the 148Z accident, but rather as a reflection of his management style and interpretation of the Wilderness Act. Dennis, along with his superiors at the regional level, minimized the reliance on aircraft for personnel transportation and resupply by increasing the use of pack strings. Longtime Moose Creek employees, who understood what looked good in theory or on paper was not necessarily so when applied in the field, resented the change. Seasoned wilderness managers and workers know that the concept of wilderness cannot exist without some compromise. Implementation of aircraft in wilderness has the *potential* for negative impacts; so does heavy stock use. Responding to the change, Penny Keck commented, "He [Dennis] wanted to be back in the 1930s or 1940s and brought in 30 head of stock to help supply the station. But it's unrealistic in wilderness. The stock, the feed, and so on has a very high impact on the land." Penny, along with other Moose Creekers, tended to think a balance of stock and aircraft was best—both in moderation. An internal report from Moose Creek to the forest supervisor bragged about their efforts: "In order to conform more to the intent of the Wilderness Act, the District reduced its flights nearly 50 percent in 1986. Flights have now been reduced to about one-third of the number flown 6-7 years ago. In 1987, there were 93 administrative landings, 277 commercial and 598 private."

· · ·

The Kecks, who were the cornerstone of the District's mentorship and traditional-tool teaching were let go at the end of the 1987 field season. Emil, already retired, (officially from payroll in 1980) was less affected, but it left Penny jobless. Her reputation spoke for itself, and she was hired as an assistant fire management officer on the neighboring Selway Ranger District. She and Emil bought an unassuming house on the lower Selway River—a close commute to work at Fenn Ranger Station, but still largely in a remote, inconspicuous part of the country they loved. In January 1990, Emil suffered a stroke and died two months later at age 77. Penny remained with the Selway District until her retirement in 2002, finishing her career as an FMO. Her jurisdiction encompassed the west half of the District, or the non-designated wilderness area. Penny sold her home on the lower Selway and settled into a house along the Middle Fork of the Clearwater River near Kooskia, where she enjoyed many years of gardening. In retirement, she stayed active as an EMT for the upper Clearwater, and she participated in many events associated with the Selway-Bitterroot Frank Church Foundation. Since their benchmark years on the Moose Creek District, the Kecks have become as legendary as Bill Bell, Ed Mackay, and Bud Moore—all old school forest rangers of the Selway-Bitterroot.

. . .

Before and after the events of 1979, Frank Hill and his Grangeville Air Service were instrumental in the fixed-wing flight operations surrounding the Moose Creek District. Some District employees regarded Frank as their "life line to the outside world" as with his good friends the Kecks, the decade following the 148Z crash was one of change for him. Following the accident, he continued to do any kind of flying that came through the office. He flew on contracts for the USFS, performed work for local farmers, hauled supplies for ranchers, and taught dozens of others to fly. His flying skills were not his only competitive advantage, so was his location: the River of No Return Wilderness to the south, the Selway-Bitterroot Wilderness to the east, the remote Snake River to the west, and nearby croplands to spray. But, at age 54, Frank wanted to slow down. He brought his son Greg into the family business. Frank taught Greg to fly at age 16, and like Frank, he became a Navy pilot. After seven years with the Navy, Greg moved back to Grangeville and to his aviation roots. Greg, along with Frank and John Moberly, was heavily involved with the fixed-wing flights surrounding the events of the 148Z accident.

On November 20, 1986, seven years after locating the wreckage of 148Z near Wolf Creek Rapid, Frank found himself again tracking the ELT signal of a downed airplane in the Selway River canyon. As the signal intensified, he spotted the burning wreckage of one of his own Cessna 206s less than one mile downstream from the Moose Creek Airstrip and nine miles upriver from where he had found the DC-3 in June 1979. As he circled over the smoldering debris in the trees along the south shore of the river, he faced a parent's worst fear: the loss of their child.

Just hours earlier, Frank and Greg were working together with two airplanes, hauling loads of hay to the Moose Creek Ranger Station and then shuttling hunting gear and game meat back out to Grangeville. Squeezing in another trip before lunch, Frank departed Moose Creek fully loaded. Greg took off minutes behind him in a Cessna 206. Frank gained sufficient altitude, and since they were to be in proximity to each other, he tried to contact his son on the radio for a position report. Unable to reach him, Frank continued his flight until he heard the squeal of an ELT signal in his headset.

Frank notified authorities, and a medical rescue helicopter from Orofino was promptly dispatched. Meanwhile, Moose Creek District employees Bruce Farling and Ian Barlow saddled two horses and headed toward the site of the accident. The two rode south across the Tony Point Bridge over the Selway River and downstream to the Tony Point Campsite, where they paused. In the drizzle it was difficult to see smoke, but they could smell it, mixed with a chemical odor and burnt flesh—presumably from the burning wreckage and game meat aboard it. The trail on left side of the river ended at the campsite, but low water allowed them to rein their horses along the rocky shoreline, weaving in and out of boulders and trees. Fewer than 500 yards after leaving the campsite, they viewed a clearing—in its center flames wavered among burning shards of aluminum. In the background were shattered trees. Only the airplane's tail was recognizable. Stunned, they tried to absorb the scene. Then they heard a voice: "Over here. Over here!" They dismounted and ran toward it. It was Pete Schoo, whom they both knew. He was badly burned and had multiple compound fractures. The two aided him, then spotted Greg's body. Killed on impact. They covered him with a piece of canvas. With their handheld radio, they called the ranger station.

Pete, who was along for the ride, later told NTSB investigators that immediately after takeoff, he and Greg had heard a metallic clicking sound "like a valve tap" coming from the engine compartment. Attempting to return to Moose Creek, Greg executed a left 180-degree turn in the narrow gorge between the end of the runway and Halfway Creek. At the apex of the descending turn, the engine lost all power. The plane struck treetops.

The cause of the accident was never fully determined. An inspection of the engine and prop revealed everything in working order. Like the parents who lost children in the DC-3 accident, Frank never recovered from the loss of his son, age 33. For the rest of his life, he tried to reason what must have gone wrong. The next summer, Frank's son-in-law, Mike Hill, and Mike's son Jim, visited the site. To honor Greg, Jim crafted a memorial from a piece of the plane's aluminum. They nailed it to a tree.

Years following Greg's accident, Hill's son-in-law, Jay Cawley, began flying for the company and considered taking over the business, but in late 1992, Hill was offered a substantial sum for the company and decided to sell. The new owner, quickly troubled by a string of bad accidents, liquidated the business within five years. Frank resisted complete retirement, and years later quietly backed Greg's daughter, Jayce, and her husband, Chad Frie, on a venture to start an ag-flying business in Grangeville. Once it was successful, he stepped aside. Frank died in November 2006 and is buried in Grangeville's Prairie View Cemetery with his wife Joanne, who died two years later. More tragedy prevailed: Chad was killed in a car accident; his former son-in-law, Jay, was killed in a mid-air collision; and Jay's brother was killed in an aircraft accident.

• • •

The Selway Ranger District headquartered at Fenn Ranger Station (adjacent and west), was absorbed into the Moose Creek Ranger District in 1995 but retained the Moose Creek name. Referring to the merger, Penny Keck commented, "Integrity of wilderness took a back seat." Most of the longtime Moose Creekers concurred. The USFS as an agency and from a management standpoint diluted the only true wilderness ranger district in the United States. To some in the Agency, the unification was practical from logistical and staffing standpoints. Geographically, it pushed the Nez Perce NF's portion of the Selway drainage within one boundary and logistically enabled the corridor and surrounding area to be serviced from Fenn Ranger Station. The latter long-established administrative site was accessible year-round from a good road and was on the route to the end of the Selway River Road to supply the Moose Creek Ranger Station by pack string. The union further reduced the need for administrative flights to Moose Creek, and thus arguably reduced costs. Tom Kovalicky, who finished his career with the Agency in 1991 as the Nez Perce NF supervisor, was of the belief the merger represented a tremendous loss of a 'boots on the ground' district ranger, and was a financial misrepresentation. Superficially, it appeared to save money, but from a budgetary perspective maintaining the two districts as they existed before 1995 would have been more beneficial. Each district is allocated its own funding. It is not as though the spending was cut in half. Instead, one district's budget was spread thinly over a much larger management area. "If you asked the Agency at the time that Moose Creek was absorbed into the Selway District how much money it saved, they could not have published a response that made any sense." The focus of the newly formed District became everything, except wilderness: it concentrated on timber harvest in the frontcountry areas, which generated revenue. "The combining of the districts diluted the career professionalism necessary for managing wilderness as a resource, rather than as an activity. It cut short the original District's historical place as an imperfect-perfect landscape, largely 'untrammeled by man,' as defined by the Agency since its inception. The original boundaries represented a special place in the history of the Agency...It was one-of-a-kind." Cindy Schacher echoed Tom's opinion, adding, "It was also the end of the 'Moose Creeker.' To me the term or name is wilderness...people who work and live in wilderness. So to become a Moose Creeker and live up to the name, you have to be living and working in wilderness. The new Moose Creek was no longer all wilderness."

• • •

In June 1980, after high school graduation, Bryant returned to Moose Creek, this time working trail. The major assignment for his crew that summer was to constructed a new trail on Little Copper Butte. Its purpose was to reroute an old trail that went over the top of the summit. The new trail, which was laid out by Emil and Penny, contoured below the butte in an effort to prevent future erosion and provide improved access to an outfitter camp. Emil and Penny had a summer camp set up so that they could come and go on the project as supervisors while they juggled all of their other duties across the District. Below their living area was the crew's main base camp. Satellite camps also were set up to the east and west at each end of the new trail. Alan Carroll and Dolly Koons each ran a crew. Others on the team included Carol Holmes, Tom Van de Water, Alan Hobbs, Paul Mandeville, and Cheryl Warren. Among Bryant's regular crew was Tom Van De Water who described Bryant as, "A strong guy, quiet, and religious with a reverent personality. He had a subtle personality. For example, another trail crew member was very into organic foods. One morning at breakfast Bryant held up his processed Pop Tart and said, 'It's organic.' He only spoke of the accident if asked about it, and he was open about it…he attributed his survival to his faith."

The crew on Copper Butte became known as "The Little Copper Butte-ies" and they bonded with each other. Tom said, "Many of us formed lifelong friendships and have kept in touch ever since. It is a summer that I'm still reflecting on." Resupplies were brought in with a pack string by Emil and Penny; days off were spent hiking to nearby Indian Hill Lookout to visit with lookouts John and Judy Crawford. Indian Hill was accessible by motor vehicle; it felt like civilization to them. A small portion of the reroute extended outside of the designated wilderness boundary, and this section of trail was constructed with some mechanized tools, displaying Emil's wisdom, "You have to learn to tread this world with practical feet." The majority of the trail, however, was within wilderness and was built in keeping with the highest wilderness standards, using only traditional hand tools—an accomplishment of which Bryant and his fellow trail crew members are still proud.

For their efforts, they were recognized by the Northern Region of the USFS with the prestigious "Wilderness Primitive Skills Award." It was presented by Bill Worf from the Regional Office to the Little Copper Butte-ies the following year during the annual Guard School at the Moose Creek Ranger Station. To attend, Alan and Dolly floated down the Selway River from their caretaking job at Running Creek along with Selway River Ranger Barry Miller. At Selway Lodge, they picked up Everett and Freddie Peirce, and to allow room, Alan hiked the rest of the way. A few former Moose Creekers, such as Dick and Sarah Walker, were present, along with a few other folks from across the forest and region. The only other crew members in attendance were those who had returned to the District for the 1981 field season. Mostly symbolic, the award consisted of a highly polished, double-bitted ax head tailored to a hickory handle and affixed with a plaque. The award is still displayed along with a black and white group photograph of the crew in the ranger station's cookhouse.

. . .

In the fall of 1980, Bryant enrolled at Ricks College in Rexburg, Idaho. Upon completion of his first year, he served an LDS Church missionary assignment based in Coventry, England, and was later assigned to sites within the Midlands region of the United Kingdom. During his mission abroad, his faithful dog Beetle, who had survived the airplane crash with him, died at age eight.

Upon return from his mission, Bryant attended Lewis and Clark State College in Lewiston, Idaho, for a semester, and then in February 1983, enrolled in the Spokane Police Academy. He took his first law enforcement position in Clarkston, Washington, for the city of Clarkston. After seven years, he moved to the Walla Walla Police Department, where he retired in February 2023 after 39 years in law enforcement. While with the Walla Walla police, he served in a number of capacities from patrol, detective, SWAT team, and as a trained sniper.

Bryat met his future wife, Teresa, at Ricks College. They raised a family of four—two boys and two girls. He and his family became active community members in Walla Walla and in the local LDS Church. His children also were involved in youth groups and the Boy Scouts of America, as well as other outdoor experiences similar to his own: camping, fishing, and hunting. Many of their family outings were spent visiting places on the Selway River. When his two boys became physically strong enough to hike long distances, Bryant took them and their youth group on a backpacking trip from Selway Falls to the Moose Creek Ranger Station. As part of enjoying nature with his children and grandchildren, he has shared with them his passion for fishing. As a youngster, he grew up fishing with bait and spinners, but after his time at Moose Creek in high school, he turned to fly-fishing. To this day, his favorite fly is the Grey Wulff, introduced to him by Steve Wright during the summer of 1978.

· · ·

At the close of the 1979 season, Charlie was determined to continue his career in wilderness management. Over the winter, he applied for several more seasonal jobs with the USFS. He accepted one on the Gallatin NF near Livingston, Montana, as a wilderness ranger in the Absaroka-Beartooth Wilderness. At last minute, the position fell through; he pivoted to a job based at the Fenn Ranger Station, supervising YCC kids on fuel-reduction projects. The Dietzes liked Idaho and formed a number of close relationships with people they had met through the USFS. For the winter of 1980–1981, they continued to rent a duplex between Fenn and Lowell. Julie found full-time work as a resource clerk at the Fenn Ranger Station. In the spring, Charlie started a new job as the recreation guard at Fenn, charged with general maintenance of the administration site, as well taking care of area campgrounds. In 1981, the Dietzes welcomed their first child, Emily, who was born in Lewiston. Becoming a father pushed Charlie to consider steadier employment. He weighed positions on the Coeur d'Alene NF in northern Idaho, but Ronald Reagan's recent election and an altered environmental landscape resulted in a tightening of federal natural-resource jobs.

The Dietzes relocated their family to Julie's hometown of Republic, Kansas. They rented a house from her father; in fact, it was the house she had grown up in. Charlie drove a cement truck for a while and eventually went into farming with his father-in-law, mainly growing wheat, corn, and soybeans. In 1983, a second daughter, Briton, joined the family, and with the settlement money from the lawsuit, the Dietzes made a down payment on a house and farm. "We have never looked back. It has been a great place to raise a family, and each of my kids got to know their grandparents. Their children now each have two boys of their own. I still think about the accident, it's hard not to. I've been out in the field working and hear an airplane…it all comes back to me: the smells, the noise, and most of all the faces. It is just hard to forget. It could have been worse; Julie could have been on the plane, and at one point she was supposed to be. But I get through it all because I have her by my side. I consider myself a lucky man."

Julie and Charlie stay in touch with many of their Idaho friends from the bygone days. The Dietzes have also made several family trips to the area to camp and visit. In the early 1990s, Charlie hiked solo from the end of the Selway River Road to the accident site. He left early on an August morning and was back at the trailhead and his pickup before dark. "The river was low compared to the last time I'd seen the area around Wolf Creek Rapid, which made it completely unrecognizable and different. I looked at things. I found and saw pieces of aluminum from the airplane. I did it just to do it."

• • •

In 1972, Harvey Young, the lead river guide on the ARTA preseason training trip, began running the Selway River as a commercial guide. He built a career in the river business and guided commercial trips on the river through 1999. For the first few years after the DC-3 crash, Harvey found "monstrous amounts" of aluminum and debris in the river from Dry Bar on down, and even higher concentrations below Wolf Creek. By mid-summer in the early 1980s, the bottom would be flecked with speckles of glimmering aluminum. "It really caught your eye. The Selway is such a pristine, clean river. It was not like we were floating a river where trash was common and overlooked. The contrast of something unnatural was obvious."

Harvey was not the only routine river traveler reminded of the accident by the fragments. Pete Mills, who was integral to the USFS's salvage operation, was tasked the following year with gathering pieces of the wreckage on each trip. Once the water warmed up in mid-summer, Pete selected camps below Dry Bar where he snorkeled for hours gathering debris from the aircraft. He regularly floated out piles of aluminum on the frontend of his boat and disposed of them at a holding site near Grangeville, where other parts of the airplane were stored for years. "It was alarming, the amount of debris I'd find. The river shredded the airplane like a pop can. It was everywhere."

Beginning in 1981, Barry Miller followed Mills as the USFS Selway River ranger. He stretched the job into a year-round position in which he worked for nearly 30 years. For the first decade on the job, he spent significant time carrying out debris churned up by the high water. "It was always a mission to pick up plane parts as they resurfaced in different places after that particular year's high-water flow. Lots and lots of stuff. In the early years, I deposited them at a site at the jump center in Grangeville. I was told the pile was still part of an investigation. Afterwards, the trash diminished, but every once in a while something big or small would be exposed."

Coincidentally, Barry's inaugural float on the Selway was to be a private trip with his friend Douglas Butterwick. They launched post-accident on June 23, 1979. With each piece retrieved from the river in the ensuing years, Barry had memories of floating through the accident site and seeing major portions of the aircraft trapped in the river. His most obscure discovery occurred in the early 1990s on a late season patrol. As he was walking along a small beach on river right, just below Otter Creek, he spotted an incongruous, soggy object on the wave line of the shore. Puzzled, he walked closer and recognized a wallet. He picked it up, unfolded it, and inside found a faded, aged Oregon driver's license for a young woman. Given its issue date he suspected it was connected to the 1979 crash. He carefully slipped it into a dry bag and delivered it to the Fenn Ranger Station. Investigation confirmed it belonged to a victim of 148Z: Catherine Hodgin. It was returned to her family.

Marty Smith, an outfitter based at Three Rivers, also hauled out pieces of the wreckage. His family owned Three Rivers Resort. The popular tourist spot included a restaurant and bar where he displayed his collection of salvaged DC-3 parts.

For years, Harvey Young felt the unexplainable when he floated by Dry Bar. He would glance up the bank at the topped Douglas fir and be reminded of the unforgettable June day. Then one year, he drifted around the corner below the long, straight reach to find an osprey nest atop the fir. Tragedy transformed. For several seasons, the osprey pair hatched renewed life in the river canyon. "Just when you weren't thinking about it [the accident] anymore, and if you weren't too focused on what lay ahead on the river, I, or an astute guest, would notice the big nest. In the right light, and at the right time of year, it would dominate the horizon at that point in the river." When the nest or a piece of aluminum was spotted by a guest, Harvey often shared his experience of the events from June 1979.

With each passing season on the river, reminders grow fainter. In the early 1990s, during a winter storm, "the Osprey Tree," as it became known, snapped off several feet from its trunk. As of this writing, the major portion of the tree with its top severed by the DC-3 is lying above the riverbank, slowly returning to earth. With the loss of their roost, the osprey pair (they mate for life) built on a neighboring ponderosa pine, upslope and closer to the trail.

In Harvey Young's last decade on the river, as the signs of the accident faded, he often found himself bewildered by the memories, even without the old triggers. "It was a major event in my life that happened in the Selway River canyon. It was not uncommon to camp, on one of the last nights on the river, below Dry Bar. There are a few eddies near the camp we relied on to gather driftwood for the evening campfire. I often found myself humbled, standing in reverence gazing into the eddies...I knew them to be the places where several of the victims were found. It was always totally humbling."

While one cannot measure or compare the gravity of the impact the accident had on different persons, or their futures, Moose Creekers who came to the District in succeeding seasons knew their opportunity resulted from the crash. Tom Van de Water captured it this way, "Ever since I first walked up the Selway in 1980, I've been struck by the chance of my being there (and continuing to be there) due to an engine falling off a plane and trail crew deaths. For that reason, every time I pass the site of the tree that snagged the wing of the DC-3, and whenever passing the memorial plaque at Moose Creek, I bow to those who died. It's a bow of sorrow, and also of appreciation for lives like mine who loved this place, and of gratitude for the mountains and rivers of Moose Creek. Penny and Emil never mentioned our being there as 'replacement' crew. All of us who started work shortly thereafter—Laura Mae Jackson on Shissler, Charlie Mabbot, Dave McDonald, Carol Holmes, Barry Miller as river ranger—all still dear friends, were fully accepted as Moose Creekers, and no mention was made of the chance of our being there. In some ways, I think, tragedies remind us that all of us are here by deep chance."

RICHARD H. HOLM, JR.

MEMORIAL AT THE MOOSE CREEK RANGER
STATION, 1980. (*Seamans Collection*)

Dear Friend:

On July 24, 1980 employees of the Moose Creek Ranger District forwarded to the Univ. of Idaho, College of Forestry, a check for 4,000 dollars establishing the Selway-Bitterroot Wilderness Memorial Scholarship fund.

Your generous support has provided a permanent memorial to those Forest Service employees who died in the DC-3 crash on the Selway River June 11, 1979.

ART SEAMANS' PEN AND INK SELWAY-BITTERROOT MEMORIAL SCHOLARSHIP FUND CARD. (*Seamans Collection*)

FLAG PRESENTATION AT THE 148Z MEMORIAL, 1982. L TO R:
SENATOR JAMES MCCLURE, BARRY HICKS, MARTIN HICKS,
AND SENATOR JOHN WARNER. (*S. Waterman/USFS Collection*)

LITTLE COPPER BUTTE TRAIL CREW, 1980. BACK ROW (L
TO R): CAROL HOLMES, BRYANT STRINGHAM, TOM VAN DE
WATER, ALAN HOBBS, AND DOLLY KOONS. FRONT ROW (L
TO R): PAUL MANDEVILLE, ALAN CARROLL, AND CHERYL
WARREN. (*Paul Mandeville/T. Van de Water Collection*)

LITTLE COPPER BUTTE TRAIL CREW, 1980. BACK ROW (L TO R): DOLLY
KOONS, TOM VAN DE WATER, AND BRYANT STRINGHAM. FRONT
ROW (L TO R): ALAN HOBBS, CAROL HOLMES, ALAN CARROLL, PAUL
MANDEVILLE, AND CHERYL WARREN. *(Paul Mandeville/USFS Collection)*

EMIL AND PENNY KECK, TONY POINT BRIDGE, 1983.
(Glenn Cruickshank, Lewiston Tribune Archives)

BRYANT STRINGHAM, 1980. (*Dolly Koons Carroll*)

LITTLE COPPER BUTTE-IES' WILDERNESS PRIMITIVE SKILLS
AWARD, MOOSE CREEK RANGER STATION. (*R. Holm, Jr.*)

BARRY MILLER, SELWAY RIVER, 1981. (*B. Farling*)

BRYANT STRINGHAM (STANDING CENTER), 2013
MOOSE CREEK REUNION. *(C. Gindler)*

CHARLIE DIETZ WITH GRANDSON AT HIS
KANSAS FARM, 2018. *(Dietz Collection)*

Afterwords and Appreciations

B uilding on the photocopies collected from the Suzzallo Library, mentioned in the foreword, while researching the 148Z account for the book *Bound for the Backcountry*, I accumulated a number of primary documents and interviewed one of the eyewitnesses. At the time, I felt I had written one of the more accurate narratives of the event—albeit not riveting, it was factual. And although it was only one story among hundreds of others in the book, it was one that continued to captivate me.

Years later, *Bound for the Backcountry* was published, and I traveled, promoting it in communities throughout the state. Cindy Schacher, an archeologist and historian with the Nez Perce NF, became a friend because of my research, and in May 2013 invited me to Grangeville to give a presentation for Idaho Archeology Month. At the end of the program, she mentioned that she wanted to introduce me to her father, Art Seamans. He and I got along well, gabbing about backcountry places, people, and stories. In his career with the USFS, Art held many positions and it happened that he was the Moose Creek district ranger from 1975 to 1980. He told me that my "version" of the Selway DC-3 accident was "mostly" accurate. He pointed out a few details to alter, which I did before my next printing.

Following my introduction to Art, a friendship developed as I wrote a volume II of *Bound for the Backcountry*, detailing the history of remote runways in the Wallowa Mountains, Hells Canyon, and the lower main Salmon River. Art had retired from the Hells Canyon National Recreation Area and was a repository of the area's history. He and I corresponded until he passed away in June 2014. Obviously and unfortunately, he, never saw the finished book.

Two years and another book later (Christmas 2016), Cindy sent me an email with several photographs, wanting to know whether I could confirm if a six-inch-by-eleven-inch piece of aluminum, clearly from the wreckage of an airplane, was in fact part of DC-3 148Z. She had my full attention. As I read the email, I wondered how someone could determine with certainty one scrap of airplane wreckage from another. I opened the photograph attachments. It was not just any piece of aircraft skin. This fragment of aluminum held the serial number plate and an aircraft manufacturing tag.

A few weeks before her email, a stranger had called the Nez Perce-Clearwater NF, asking for someone familiar with the history of the forest. His inquiry was directed to the forest archeology department. In a brief conversation, the man explained that he was an antique dealer from Florida. Earlier in his life, in the fall of 1979, he had been on a float trip on the Selway River and had found this piece of aluminum in some rocks. He identified the scrap as belonging to the ill-fated DC-3 and wanted to "return it."

He agreed to mail it to the Supervisor's Office in Grangeville. Steve Armstrong, an archeologist on the Forest, thanked the man and then reached out to Cindy, knowing she had a personal interest in the accident. A few weeks later, the package arrived. Cindy was puzzled. Why, after nearly 40 years, would a person "return" a souvenir from a long ago river trip? Why here of all places? She began to study the artifact and noticed one of the tags was scripted "Douglas Aircraft" and the other "US Army Air Forces," both stamped with C-47A and not DC-3.

I responded to her email, explaining that during World War II the Selway DC-3 was technically built as a C-47. I later learned some converted C-47s had a conversion tag, but not all of them. The artifact certainly could be from a DC-3. And very few DC-3s/C-47s are associated with the Selway River. Likely a match? Yes. How could the artifact, however, be linked to the Selway by an "antique dealer from Florida." Still, why would someone concoct such fabrication? Again, the Internet was not the resource it is today, and verification took time, but in the end it proved to be a piece of DC-3 148Z—and a significant piece it was.

In the interim, Cindy and I exchanged many more emails and had phone conversations. From these discussions, I realized Cindy was far more closely connected to the accident than I knew, or at least had remembered, because just days before the flight, she and her father, mother, and sister were on the plane's flight manifest. She also shared with me a several-page recollection of the event written by Art, which revealed intimate personal details that he had not told me. She also reminded me that in the summer of 2013 the Moose Creek employees of the 1970s and 1980s had had a big reunion on the lower Selway. One evening, people told stories around the campfire as part of the group. When it was Barry Hicks' turn, he volunteered Bryant to tell his account of surviving the airplane crash. At first, people were a little shocked that Barry would ask Bryant to share something so private. No one else knew that earlier in the day Bryant had conveyed his story to Barry, and then agreed to repeat it to the group that evening. Cindy gave me a condensed overview of the story, and she said she followed up with Bryant, requesting that he put his story in writing for preservation in the Forest archives. With his permission, she then offered to share it with me, and off-handedly added that I ought to write a book. "It would be nice to see someone address the human element of the tragedy and I think you are the person to do it." After some thought, and after seeing Bryant's written version, I too thought it would be a worthy, compelling book. But I explained to her "we" were missing two key elements: first, Bryant's permission to publish his story, and second the official accident report.

Cindy connected me with Bryant and he consented. I explained to her the accident report was a major impediment and not all that easy to find, because 148Z operated as a Public Aircraft, and thus it would require locating the USFS's in-house report. Since years earlier I had found an incomplete copy at the University of Idaho Special Collections, I knew one likely existed, and based on the selections I had read, I knew the key to developing the story would be discovering a complete and *unaltered* copy.

She, too, had read portions of an incomplete report, and we began trading copies by email—they were not an identical match. I disclosed my source and she, hers. In the fall of 2012, Bob McCue walked into her office in Kooskia and introduced himself. He was hired by Art to be on a Moose Creek trail crew for the summer of 1979. Therefore, he was supposed to be on the June 11 flight. At the last minute, he decided to take a different summer job. The accident and the alternate path had affected his life. The two of them connected during this fortuitous meeting. In the course of their conversation, Bob revealed that with the help of a friend who worked in the USFS's Region 1 legal department, he had tracked down a copy of the in-house accident report. He read portions of it and took pictures with a digital camera of the pages that interested him, and passed them on to Cindy.

I began corresponding with Bob. He said the copy he had reviewed had been purged from Region 1's Missoula offices and sent to the National Archives branch in Seattle. I had frequented those archives while writing *Bound for the Backcountry*, and there became acquainted with Ken House, an archivist. Ken had explained to me that technically when a government agency donates documents to the archive, the agency of origin has rights or access to them, and an employee from the originating agency can often avoid the requisite in-person visit and copying fees. I connected Ken and Cindy. Together, they completed a digital copy. Throughout all of this research only one other complete physical copy surfaced. This was not some hint of government conspiracy. It illustrates the substantial heartache surrounding the June 11 tragedy. On multiple occasions during interviews, the report was touched upon. One retired forest supervisor said, "I'm surprised you found a copy. It was always closely guarded and rarely discussed. At the time, there was such a sense of loss and guilt." Another who retired from the Region 4 Aviation Program noted, "I am astonished that you were able to get your hands on a copy of the resulting accident report. That document seemed to be pretty 'close hold' back in the day, and I was never able to get to see more than a few pages."

With the second hurdle surmounted, the book evolved. The

872-page USFS report was a springboard to unlocking many unanswered questions. It is comprised of dozens of primary documents detailing key individuals involved with the accident, from pre-flight through the final days of the recovery. Such a collection of primary documents filled in gaps where memories could not—or it led me to sources that could. The accident report is cited in the Selected Bibliography, but the individual, primary documents, where quotes were extracted, are not in all cases given a single citation.

Throughout the writing, the book expanded into multiple stories, all interwoven by the events—among them are the airplane, its pilots, the Region 4 Aviation Program, the passengers and their families, the Moose Creek Ranger District and its employees, rescuers, first responders, smokejumpers, boatmen, hikers, and salvage crews. The USFS accident investigators interviewed several of these people, and its transcripts or summaries, or both, were integrated into the final report.

As is common with oral interviews, they often ask more questions than they answer. Consequently, an effort was made to establish a relationship with many of the original interviewees and conduct new interviews with them. Quotes from both the 1979 interviews and contemporary interviews are therefore entwined. Timing is critical, and perhaps enough years had passed that those involved were less guarded talking about the tragedy. Nearly every person interviewed was pensive about the accident. Most still think about it often. Many said they had obviously learned to live with the tragedy or at least had come to terms with it. Several people, however, declined an interview. One politely told me, "No, that accident should never have happened. It is best to leave such things in the past where they belong. Not that I wish you ill, but I will not contribute."

The gathering at the Moose Creek reunion in 2013 was pivotal, not only in the emergence of Bryant's remarkable story, but also from the connections that established a list of current contacts, easing my task of finding interviewees. Universally, the Moose Creekers proved to be a congenial group. Some were more connected to the accident than others, of course, but all were incredibly generous with their own accounts, memories, and knowledge, and each contributed in his or her different way. Some deserve special recognition. Gary Miller was an invaluable resource, answering questions by telephone and responding to a barrage of emails across the years. In addition to general and specific details of the 1979 field season at Moose Creek, he allowed me the use of his USFS daily work diaries. They disclosed activities on the District: participants and particulars about past Guard Schools. Alan Carroll and Tim Rich were two of the first Moose Creekers I interviewed, and their enthusiasm and willingness to reach out to others on my behalf were beyond helpful. When I was looking for an enigmatic answer to one of my countless questions, fellow writer, John McCarthy intuitively knew where to steer me. When I began, John was finishing his own Moose Creek book, and unlike many authors who warily protect their information, he willingly opened his files. Pete Mills, the river ranger who was intimately involved in the activities surrounding the wreckage, beginning with the day of the accident, had indispensable insights. He, too, dug through boxes of memorabilia and sent his daily USFS work diary from June and July 1979—many entries of which were inscribed in blue pen on cardboard. Tom Van de Water, a retired educator, who, since 1980, has worked in the Selway-Bitterroots each season on trails and fire lookouts, captured the post-1979 happenings on the Moose Creek District and their loss would have been incalculable.

Laura Mae Jackson, who staffed Shissler Peak Lookout from 1980 through 1991, also deserves special thanks for providing contacts for Moose Creekers and former employees of the Selway Ranger District. Through her connections, I reached Charlie and Julie Dietz.

Whether or not the Dietzes would participate in my undertaking was a consequential question. Many Moose Creekers were skeptical. You miss 100% of the shots you do not take, however. I also knew that I owed it to them and to the reader to at least offer them an opportunity to participate in the narrative. Through this growing mesh of interconnections, I was introduced to the Dietzes. My apprehensions were for naught: Charlie and Julie were welcoming, open, obliging, supportive. Charlie excavated what he calls his "archives," providing more primary documents. I am graciously indebted to both of them for their encouragement and contributions—most of all for entrusting me to tell their story of a profoundly difficult chapter in their lives.

As with the Dietzes, it was not always easy to reach out to family and friends of loved ones who lost someone in the accident. For the most part, the effort was well received. Without their willingness to share memories and photographs and revisit the singular lives aboard that airplane, this book would not have been possible. Motivation along the way from people like the Dietzes and Kevin Leber's older sister, Fig Dehlinger, helped: "Loss is hard to talk about…but it is such a treasure to have the opportunity to talk about him [Kevin] with someone. What you are doing is important. I'm sure other families feel the same way."

As a teen-ager, Cindy Seamans, née Schacher, grew up within the Moose Creek family while Art, her father, was district ranger. Her summer experiences at the remote ranger station, along with her father's other USFS assignments, impelled her to follow a career with the Agency. Working within the Nez Perce–Clearwater NF Archeology Department as an archeologist and historian, her life came full circle when she began to work on assignments associated with the long-gone Moose Creek Ranger District. In fact, during her career on the forest she came to be recognized as the authority on the District's history. The events surrounding the 1979 crash still linger. She has indelible memories of the news reaching Moose Creek, of greeting an exhausted Bryant Stringham after his hike and horseback ride to the ranger station, and later listening to her father talking about the search, recovery, and salvage. In her youth, she overheard Art discussing sightings of victims in eddies and how the bodies would surface and then submerge as the current carried them back under. "As a young girl, I had dreams about it, and that is the reason I never wanted to float the Selway River. In fact, I've never liked water much since. I had opportunities to float the Selway as a part of my work, but decided instead to travel by aircraft or by horseback on the trail."

Given her background and personal connection to the story, this book would not exist without her unfaltering assistance for years. From the forest archives, she provided me with primary documents, secondary sources, oral histories, transcripts, and scores of photographs. Moreover, she trusted me to use two profoundly personal files she discovered in 2017 while empting her parents' Lewiston house after her mother died. As mentioned earlier, the accident bedeviled Art and Joyce the rest of their lives. The folders Cindy found illustrate their endless emotional turmoil. One folder contained items Art likely kept when he left the Moose Creek District; the other was compiled by Joyce. Combined they were essential to this story. Within the folders were maps, internal memos, passenger release forms, a handwritten flight manifest, handwritten notes from rescue and recovery operations, photographs, 35mm slides, letters exchanged with victims' families, newspaper clippings, and funeral service programs.

Cindy also introduced me to members of her Moose Creek family, and she often proved to be just the right go-between to establish trust for this book. From the beginning, she urged me to collect Penny Keck's perspectives on Moose Creek during this era and about the accident. Penny was amenable. In May 2017, the first of many visits with her was arranged by Cindy and occurred at Penny's house along the Middle Fork of the Clearwater River. Penny greeted Cindy with a hug and me with a firm handshake, "I heard you were afraid to visit this old lady by yourself." Wry humor and laughter from all...I knew then we would easily engage. It was clear Penny had little interest in recounting memories of the crash—"Those were terrible times." But she did think I was preserving something significant for those families. Her insights into the Keck's activities at that time and about the accident were priceless. And when I asked others to participate, her endorsement was a platinum key.

Contributing greatly to the events, details, and the involvement of Region 1 smokejumpers were Wayne Williams, John Nichols, Jeff Kinderman, and Lowell Hanson—all exceptionable individuals.

Mike "Mickey" Hill, another Region 1 smokejumper, who was based in Grangeville in 1979 and linked more closely to the salvage operations, granted me the use of his USFS daily work diaries and photographs. They proved vital to sorting out the sequence of events.

Grateful acknowledgement is made to Harvey Young and Rick Byers for sharing their invaluable accounts of ARTA's link in the story and for loaning me their photographs. Additionally, they connected me with other ARTA boatmen who were on the trip.

Cort Conley, steadfast mentor (friend) and fellow backcountry historian, has to bear part of the responsibility for this book for his measureless assistance.

Stan McGrew was the "aviation equivalent" of Cindy. He was a mainstay for years. When my enthusiasm waned he would say, "You have to get it done! I want to see the final product and I'm not getting any younger." When confirming the authenticity of the 148Z data plates, I was introduced to Stan by a mutual friend, Scott Anderson, a retired McCall smokejumper. Stan and I exchanged emails and telephone calls, and in 2018 met in McCall while he was there for a smoke-jumper reunion. Our rapport budded. Known among his Region 4 aviation and smokejumper peers as "The Wizard" of DC-3s, he knows the aircraft thoroughly as both pilot and mechanic. Stan earned his commercial pilot license and flight instructor certificate in 1953. Two years later, he entered the Air Force, where he flew T-28s, T-33s, T-34s, B-25s, C-47s and C-124s (he even managed to log a few hours in B-29s). After retirement from the Air Force, he went back to school in 1975 and earned his A&P Mechanic's Certificate. Subsequently, he joined the Region 4 Aviation Program as a DC-3/C-47 pilot. His initial detail was to West Yellowstone, flying right seat with Whitey in 148Z.

With the departure of Chris Hayne in the fallout of the Selway crash, in 1981 Stan became the supervisory pilot for large airplanes. As a manager, he was central to the Agency's decision to convert two of the Region 4's DC-3/C-47 to the turbine-powered Basler BT-67. By the end of his career, Stan was recognized as a flight instructor for radial-powered DC-3/C-47s and for the Basler BT-67, and he trained pilots nationally and internationally on them. When the Agency moved to the BT-67, he developed a ground-school training course for USFS pilots. His course was adopted by Basler as the standard program for the aircraft. Over the course of his career, he logged more than 10,000 hours of flight time, of which approximately 3,000 hours were in the cockpit of Region 4-owned "Dougs." In 1992, after 14 years with Region 4, Stan retired. He continued to own a number of gliders and single-engine aircraft. Stan was the recipient of the FAA's Wright Brothers Master Pilot Award in 2004; in May 2024, he was awarded the Gail Halvorsen Lifetime Achievement Award for his contributions to the Utah aviation industry.

As the book's aviation-related chapters grew, Stan became my principal source for technical details regarding the DC-3/C-47— from airframe to power plant to flight characteristics. Being a fellow collector and history buff, Stan often rescued Region 4 primary documents, flight manuals, and general aviation paperwork from dumpsters. He generously shared these papers. Among them was a Region 4 DC-3/C-47 flight manual inscribed "Whitey Hachmeister" on the front cover. He had weight and balance documents for Region 4 Dougs, including one for 148Z as it was configured the day of the accident. He introduced me to other Region 4 personnel from the 1970s and 1980s, often calling them on my behalf. He also reviewed drafts of the aviation-related chapters. He suggested improvements and navigated me past misnomers. He parsed often complex aviation language into more readable terms. This book would have suffered without his dedication and critical feedback.

Dick Williams, another friend, mentor, and author, was a coach on aviation aspects of this story from take-off to landing. Dick has logged nearly 20,000 hours of flight time in private and commercial aviation. He has flown the Idaho backcountry for decades, ranging from single-engine Cessnas to Twin Otters, ending his working career flying corporate jets. He is a recipient of the FAA's Wright Brothers

Master Pilot Award, and a member of the Idaho Aviation Hall of Fame. His background and years as a pilot with the BLM and as an FAA-designated pilot examiner assisted my comprehension of federal regulations that applied or did not apply to 148Z. Like Stan, he reviewed and edited the aviation portions of my drafts and offered numerous thoughts and suggestions for greater clarity.

Penn Stohr, Jr., son of a legendary backcountry pilot, is an esteemed aviator in his own right. He was among the first professional aviators to encourage my interest in commercial flying and backcountry aviation history. For more than 20 years, Penn has introduced me to his numerous friends in order to preserve backcountry aviation history. In my early 20s, he invited me to ride along as a passenger on a Ford Tri-Motor that he piloted to and from a smokejumper reunion. That crystalized my curiosity. Penn contributed indispensably to this undertaking by providing historical context of DC-3/C-47 contract operations in the Idaho backcountry. Beginning in 1960, he worked at Johnson Flying Service, and in 1964 became a line pilot for the company. Two years later, he began flying its DC-2 and DC-3/C-47s, until the company sold to Evergreen Aviation in 1976. He had a lengthy career with Evergreen, piloting assorted aircraft in its museum and Boeing 747s, and in 2003 retired. In 2018, he was the recipient of the Wright Brothers Master Pilot Award.

I am ever indebted to Mike Dorris for his enduring friendship, mentorship in aviation, and in all of my backcountry historical pursuits. With more than 25,000 hours of flight time (most of it in the Idaho backcountry) and as a member of the Idaho Aviation Hall of Fame, Mike possibly holds more aviation knowledge and flight experience in the remote central part of the state than anyone else of his generation. He is always willing to extend himself to verify facts, participate in field research, and pass along his encompassing familiarity with the backcountry.

Individual thanks go to a number of impressive persons: William Acton, Cheshire (Peirce) Agusta, Ed Allen, Tor Andersen, Bob Anderson, Scott Anderson, Peter Armichardy, Richard "Skip" Atkinson, Dennis Baird, Ian Barlow, Bob Beckley, Anna Bengtson, Rusty Bentz, Bob J. Black, Charlie Blaine, Ian Bock, Jacob Bonessi, Ray Bosch, Alan Carroll, Dave Clarke, Laurie Clark, Cort Conley, Glenn Cruickshank, Neal Davis, Fig Dehlinger, Paul "Buster" Delmonte, Eleanor Dixon, Gayle Dixon, Earl Dodds, Regis Ertle, Rene Eustice, Don Farley, Bruce Farling, Mary Helen Ferguson-Pope, Ralph Fireoved, August Frank, Josh Frei, Jack Garnsey, Charles Gindler, Cheryl (Warren) Goodman, Mary (Cook) Goodson, Allan Greenleaf, Ron Hanks, Ken Harris, Ken Hatcher, Chris Hayne, Nick Hazelbaker, John Hibbs, Ruthanne Hibbs, Barry Hicks, Richard Hildner, Dan Hodgin, Dave Holley, Ellen Holm, Richard Holm, Sr., Jane Holman, Amy Hoover, Dick Hughes, Alan Hull, Jason Hull, Jim Huntley, Mary (Gramling) Hurst, Jane Johnson, Glenn Johnston, Larry Keown, Tom Kovalicky, Ray Kresek, Marge Kuehn-Tabor, Ken Kuther, Charlotte Larson, Randy Leber, Caryn Mason, Richard Mauer, Dave McDonald, Marc McDonald, Dollie McGreevey, Eddie McGreevey, Barry Miller, Gary Miller, Nancy Miller, Bobby Montoya, Mike Moore, Peter Morrill, Matt Mosman, Timothy Patrick, Dan Pearson, Chad Pickett, Gary Power, Carol (Mytron) Ratcliffe, Ray Reel, Allen Renshaw, Jim Renshaw, Rick Ripley, Merrill Saleen, Connie Saylor-Johnson, Cory Schuler, Art Seamans, Joyce Seamans, Dave Shallow, Jessie Shallow, Chuck Sheley, Marty Smith, Steve Smith, Rod Snider, Bob Solberg, Adam Sowards, Dave Stack, Penn Stohr, Jr., Eva Strand, John Stright, Larry Swan, Dale Swee, Mark Tabor, Jim TerKeurst, Doug Tims,

Doug Walberg, Dick Walker, Neil Walstad, Linda Walters, Catherine Wardwell, Marlee Wilcomb, Terry Williamson, Gale Wilson, and Steve Wright.

No history endeavor of mine would ever be possible or completed without the continuous support of my family—especially my perceptive and patient wife, Amy.

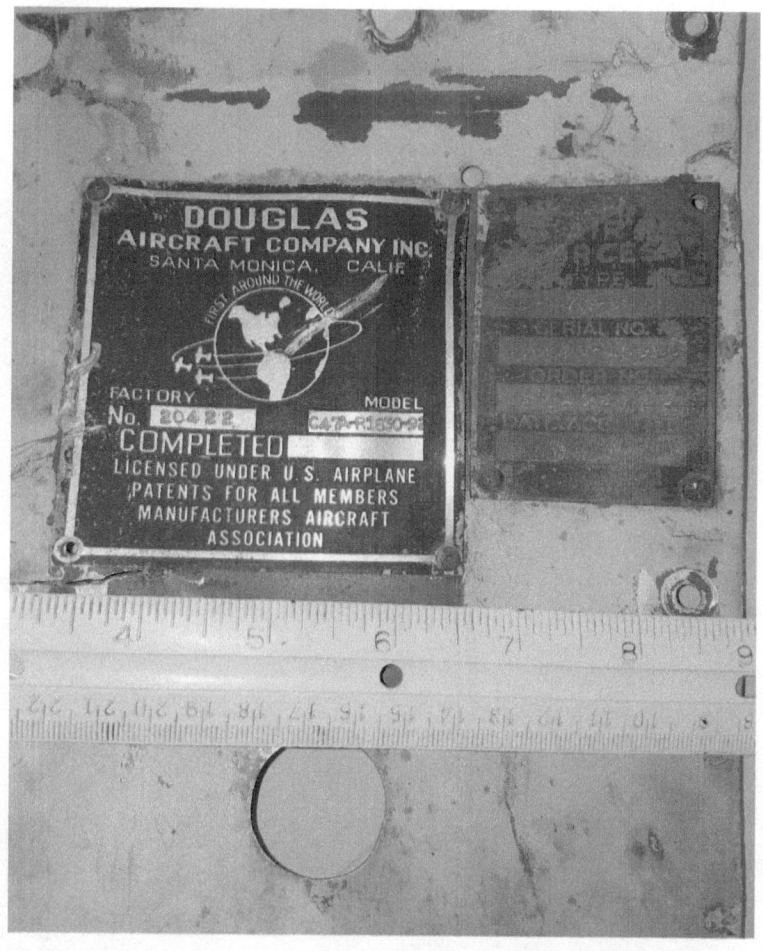

148Z DATA PLATES, 2016. (*C. Schacher/USFS Collection*)

Selected Bibliography

Agusta (Peirce), Cheshire. Personal Communication. 7 March 2024.

Anderson, Bob. Personal Communication. 2 July 2019.

Anderson, Marc (Andy). Personal Communication. 16 May 2024.

Anderson, Marc (Andy). "End of an Era." Unpublished essay, 2005.

Armichardy, Peter. Personal Communication. 16 February 2024.

Arno, Stephen F. and Sneck, Kathy M. *A Method for Determining Fire History in Coniferous Forests of the Mountain West* (General Technical Report INT-42). Ogden, UT: Intermountain Forest and Range Experiment Station, Forest Service, US Department of Agriculture, November 1977.

Associated Press. "Forest Service told to stop plane crash tests." *Lewiston Morning Tribune.* 9 February 1980.

Bankey, Viki, Brickey, Mike, & Kleinkopf, M.D. *Principal Facts for Gravity Stations in the Selway-Bitterroot Wilderness, Montana—Idaho* (Open File Report 82-708). US Department of the Interior, Geological Survey, 1982.

Barlow, Ian. Interview by Bob Beckley, November 2003, Smithsonian Folklife Interview, Smithsonian Institution.

Barlow, Ian. Personal Communication. 12 April 2017.

Beckman, Diane. (edited and compiled by) *Camp Mouse Creek Newsletter 2*. Moose Creek Ranger District, Nez Perce NF: USDA Forest Service, 1978. Mills Collection.

Becoming a Moose Creeker, Moose Creek Ranger District, Nez Perce NF: USDA Forest Service, 1979. Schacher Collection.

Biddison, Donald and Smolinski, Carole Simon. *Moose Creek Ranger District Historical Information Inventory and Review*. Clarkston, WA: Northwest Historical Consultants/USDA, 1988.

Black, Bob J. Personal Communication. 30 March 2017 (And extensive other dates).

Blackbird, Mike. *One Flaming Hour: A Memoir of Jerry Blackbird*. Carlton, OR: Ridenbaugh Press, 2014.

Blegen, Hal. Personal Communication. 29 March 2010.

Bower, Jerry D. Letter to Art Seamans, "Wilderness Ranger Training—Warren Miller and Dale Swee." 7 August 1979. Seamans Collection.

Bradley, Jim. The 1977 Moose Creek Safety Plan. Nez Perce NF, USDA Forest Service, Grangeville, Idaho. Seamans Collection.

Bradley, Jim. (Illustrated by Bob Svec). *Selway-Wilderness Primer: A Handbook with Drawings, Checklists, Field Guides, Stories, Manuals, Glossaries, and Other Handy Information*. US Department of Agriculture, Forest Service, Northern Region, Publication Number R1-78-23. 1st and 2nd editions.

Bradley, Jim. (Illustrated by Bob Svec and revised by Sarah Walker and Shelly Dumas). *Selway-Wilderness Primer 3rd Edition: A Handbook with Drawings, Checklists, Field Guides, Stores, Manuals, Glossaries, and Other Handy Information.* US Department of Agriculture, Forest Service Northern Region, Publication Number R1-92-47, Revised 1992.

Bradley, Jim. (Illustrated by Bob Svec and revised by Cindy Schacher). *Selway-Wilderness Primer 4th Edition: A Handbook with Drawings, Checklists, Field Guides, Stores, Manuals, Glossaries, and Other Handy Information.* US Department of Agriculture, Forest Service Northern Region, Publication Number R1-21-42, Revised October 2021.

Bradley, Jim. Letter to Art Seamans, "DC-3 Accident." 11 June 1979. Seamans Collection.

Butters, MaryJane. *MaryJane's Ideabook, Cookbook, Lifebook.* New York, NY: Clarkson Potter/Publishers, 2005.

Byars, Rick. Personal Communication. 17 November 2023.

Carroll, Alan. Personal Communication. 7 May 2019 (And extensive other dates).

Cheyney, Winston. Personal Communication. 10 October 2019.

Cheyney, Winston. Personal Communication. 21 November 2023.

Christopherson, Edmund. *The Night the Mountain Fell: The Story of the Montana-Yellowstone Earthquake.* Missoula, MT: Lawton Printing, Inc., 1962.

Clarke, Dave and Laurie. Personal Communication. 26 April 2017.

Cohen, Stan. *A Pictorial History of Smokejumping.* Missoula, MT: Pictorial Histories Publishing Company, 1983.

Cook, Stephen and Dorothy. Letter to Don Biddison. 26 August 1980. Goodson Collection.

Cook, Stephen and Dorothy. Letter to Art and Joyce Seamans (news clippings and a copy of a letter written by Bob Cook to his girlfriend Jenny on June 10, 1979 are attached). 26 June 1979. Seamans Collection.

Cook, Stephen and Dorothy. Letter to Joyce Seamans. 16 July 1979. Seamans Collection.

Cutright, Steven. "The Selway Passage," pages 45–56. Linford, Dick and Volpert, Bob (written and compiled by), *Halfway to Halfway: And Other River Stories*. Bend, OR: Halfway Publishing, 2012.

Davis, Neal. Personal Communication. 19 December 2023.

DC-3 Manual R1830-94—A.D. Notes and Service Bulletins N143Z, undated, Whitey Hachmeister Copy, Region 4 Aviation. McGrew Collection.

Dehilnger (Leber), Fig. Personal Communication. 9 December 2024.

Dietz, Charlie. Personal Communication. 7 June 2023 (And extensive other dates).

Dietz, Julie. Personal Communication. 7 June 2023 (And extensive other dates).

Dotson, Bob. "Choices in the Autumn of Life: The Kecks," *The American Story*. NBC. 5 June 1986. 2.57 minute video clip.

Douglas DC-3 Cargo Airplane Flight Manual/Handbook US Forest Service SV. N100Z, N146Z & N148Z, undated, Dale Major Copy, Region 4 Aviation. McGrew Collection.

Dumas, Shelly. (edited and compiled by) *A 'Moving' Experience: Moose Creek Recollections of By-Gone Days By Those That Have Been There*, Moose Creek Ranger District, Nez Perce NF: USDA Forest Service, 1995. Schacher Collection.

Easthouse, Don. *Don Easthouse Book of Poetry 1973-79*. Privately published by Karen Easthouse in 1983 for family and friends. McCarthy Collection.

Easthouse, Karen. Letter to Moose Creek Ranger District [Friends]. 25 June 1979. Seamans Collection.

Eller, Zelda. "White Bird Mourns Death of Andy Taylor; Large Turnout Celebrates Special Day." Undated newspaper clipping. Seamans Collection.

Esden, Jim. "A Tribute to Steve Wright." *Common Voice: A Journal For the Sterling Community*. Undated. Seamans Collection.

Farley, Don. Personal Communication. 1 June 2019.

Farley, Don. Personal Communication. 29 February 2024.

Farling, Bruce. (edited and compiled by) *Brusher's World*. Moose Creek Ranger District, Nez Perce NF: USDA Forest Service, 1982. Kepes/ Van de Water Collection.

Farling, Bruce. (edited and compiled by) *Brusher's World*. Moose Creek Ranger District, Nez Perce NF: USDA Forest Service, 1983. Kepes/ Van de Water Collection.

Farling, Bruce. "Irascible, Immovable, Unforgettable Emil Keck." *Missoulian*. Undated newspaper clipping. Schacher Collection.

Farling, Bruce. Personal Communication. 12 February 2024.

Fasken, Scott. Personal Communication. 29 September 2019.

Fazio, James R. "A Lasting Memorial—Care of the Wilderness." *Trailhead* Vol 7. No.4 August 1980. Seamans Collection.

Federal Aviation Administration, Aircraft Registration Number N148Z Documents. Retrieved from FAA Aircraft Registry AFB-710 on 12 May 2022.

Federal Aviation Administration, Aircraft Serial Number 20422 (also as: 43-15956) Airworthiness Documents. Retrieved from FAA Aircraft Registry AFB-710 on 12 May 2022.

Federal Aviation Administration Type II DC-3 Pilot Standardization Course: Student Study Guide 21102. Department of Transportation Federal Aviation Administration Aeronautical Center, FAA Academy, April 1971 (Region 4 Aviation). McGrew Collection.

Ferguson-Pope, Mary Helen. Personal Communication. 7 May 2024.

Fireoved, Ralph. Personal Communication. 18 June 2019.

Fireoved, Ralph. Personal Communication. 3 January 2023.

Floating the Wild Selway. West Fork Ranger District, Bitterroot NF: USDA Forest Service Northern Region, Publication Number R1-78-10. 1978. Mills Collection.

Franklin, Rod. "Bitterroot's First National Recreation Trail Named for Don Easthouse." Undated newspaper clipping. McCarthy Collection.

Gann, Ernest K. *Fate is the Hunter*. New York, NY: Simon and Schuster, 1961.

Garnsey, Jack. Personal Communication. 22 November 2023.

Gilbert, Barrie K. *One of Us: A Biologist's Walk Among Bears*. Victoria, B.C.: Friesen Press, 2019.

Gindler, Charles. Personal Communication. 19 June 2019.

Glines, Carroll G. and Moseley, Wendell F., *Grand Old Lady: Story of the DC-3*. Cleveland, OH: Pennington Press, Inc., 1959.

Goodman (Warren), Cheryl. Personal Communication. 6 June 2019.

Goodson (Cook), Mary. Personal Communication. 16 September 2024.

Gormley, Donald W. Letter to Mr. Art Seamans, District Ranger, Moose Creek, Idaho, "Subject—Hal Blegen's DC-3 Picture." The Spokesman Review Managing Editor. 21 June 1979. Seamans Collection.

Greenleaf, Allan. Personal Communication. 25 March 2017.

Greenleaf, Allan. Personal Communication. 30 March 2017.

Grubb, Peter. Personal Communication. 14 December 2023.

Grunsey, Patricia, et al. v. Morrison-Knudsen, et al. Fourth District Court, State of Idaho, Ada County. Case No. 70539.

Gue, Forrest. Personal Communication. 7 May 2019.

Gzowski, Peter. *The Sacrament: The Incredible Story of Brent Dyer and Donna Johnson.* Toronto, Ontario: McClelland & Steward Limited, 1980.

Habeck, James R., Mutch, Robert W. "Fire-dependent Forests in the Northern Rocky Mountains," pages 408–424. *Quaternary Research 3.* 1973.

Habeck, James R. "Forests, Fuels and Fire in the Selway-Bitterroot Wilderness, Idaho," pages 305–353. *Proceedings, 14th Tall Timbers fire ecology conference and Intermountain Fire Research Council fire and land management symposium.* Missoula, MT. Tallahassee, FL: Tall Timbers Research Station. 1974.

Hachmeister, Leona G., et al. v. Cooper Industries, Inc. et al. Fourth District Court, State of Idaho, Ada County. Case No. 70082. 24 December 1979.

Hage, P.A. Letter to Don Easthouse, "Thank You—Wilderness Training Program." 6 June 1979. Seamans Collection.

Haney, Glenn P. *Accident Report DC-3 Aircrash Nez Perce National Forest, Idaho—June 11, 1979.* Aircraft Accident Investigation Report, US Department of Agriculture, Forest Service, Northern Region. National Archives, Seattle, WA, RG#95, Box 80, Region 1, Historical Collection.

Hanson, Lowell. Personal Communication. 30 March 2017.

Hartig, Louis. *A Summer at Moe Peak: As Remembered by the Lookout Sixty-three Years Later.* Self-published. 1986. Seamans Collection.

Hazelbaker, Nick. Personal Communication. 8 May 2024.

Hedberg, Kathy. "Forest Tragedies Haunt Survivors." *The Lewiston Tribune.* 14 June 2009.

Hibbs, John and Ruthanne. Personal Communication. 14 December 2023.

Hicks, Barry. Personal Communication. 19 December 2023.

Hildner, Richard. Personal Communication. 12 December 2023.

Hill, Mike. *USFS Daily Diary,* June 16–22, 1979. M. Hill Collection.

Hill, Mike. Personal Communication. 15 May 2019.

Holley, Dave. Personal Communication. 22 July 2022.

Holm, Richard H., Jr. *Bound for the Backcountry: A History of Idaho's Remote Airstrips.* McCall, ID: Cold Mountain Press, 2013.

Holm, Richard H., Jr. *Bound for the Backcountry: A History of Airstrips in the Wallowas, Hells Canyon, and the Lower Salmon River.* McCall, ID: Cold Mountain Press, 2015.

Holman, Bill. Letter to Forest Supervisor, "Wilderness Administration Techniques." 14 January 1970. Seamans Collection.

Holman, Jane. Personal Communication. 9 June 2019.

Hull, Allan. Personal Communication. 24 May 2019.

Hulla, Richard. Personal Communication. 13 March 2024 (And extensive other dates).

Huntley, Jim. Personal Communication. 24 July 2019.

Hurst (Gramling), Mary. Personal Communication. 22 June 2019.

Jackson, Laura Mae. Personal Communication. 21 June 2019 (And extensive other dates).

Keck, Emil. Interview by Don Biddison, 4 November 1988, Nez Perce-Clearwater NF, USDA Forest Service, Grangeville, Idaho.

Keck, Penny. Interview by Cindy Schacher and Richard H. Holm, Jr., 19 May 2017, Nez Perce–Clearwater NF Oral History Project, Kooskia, Idaho (Penny Keck's home on Highway 12).

Keck, Penny. *Moose Creek Airfield Management Plan*. Moose Creek Ranger District, Nez Perce NF: USDA Forest Service, ca. 1980–85.

Keck, Penny. Personal Communication. 25 May 2017 (And extensive other dates).

Kenops, Darrel L. "Search & Rescue Plan DC-3 Crash June to July 1979." Cover letter and large packet of primary documents sent to Nez Perce NF Supervisor on August 13, 1979. Seamans Collection.

Keown, Larry D. Personal Communication. 27 April 2017.

Keown, Larry D. *Fire Management In The Selway-Bitterroot Wilderness, Moose Creek Ranger District*, Nez Perce NF: USDA Forest Service, 1978.

Keown, Larry D. (Revised by Richard Hildner, Terry Williamson, and Jim Saveland) *Fire Management In The Selway-Bitterroot Wilderness, Moose Creek Ranger District*, Nez Perce NF: USDA Forest Service, Revised 1984.

Kepes, Betsey. "The Adventure Family," pages 201–13. Jennifer Bove' (edited and compiled by), *A Mile in Her Boots: Women Who Work in the Wild*. Palo Alto, CA: Travelers' Tales, Inc., 2006.

Kiilsgaard, Carl C. Letter to Mr. Arthur Seamans, "University of Idaho Foundation—Selway-Bitterroot Wilderness Memorial Scholarship Fund." 12 September 1980. Seamans Collection.

Kincaid, Terry. Personal Communication. 21 November 2023.

Kinderman, Jeff. Personal Communication. 7 June 2023.

Kinderman, Jeff. Personal Communication. 8 June 2023.

Koehler, Gary M. and Hornocker, Maurice G., "Fire Effects on Marten Habitat in the Selway-Bitterroot Wilderness," pages 500–05. *The Journal of Wildlife Management.* Vol. 41, No. 3. July 1977.

Kovalicky, Tom. "High Drama Higgins Ridge," pages 227–29. Gilbert W. Davies and Florice M. Frank (edited and compiled by), *Memorable Forest Fires: Stories by US Forest Service Retirees.* Hat Creek, CA: History Ink Books, 2001 (Fourth Printing—revised).

Kovalicky, Tom. Letter to Art Seamans, "DC-3 Accident." 15 June 1979.

Kovalicky, Tom. Personal Communication. 17 March 2017 (And extensive other dates).

Kresek, Ray. *Fire Lookouts of the Northwest.* Spokane, WA: Historic Lookout Project, 1998.

Larkin, Jim. *A History of Forest Service Air Operations.* Region 4: USDA Forest Service, Date Unknown (circa 1970). McGrew Collection.

Larkin, Jim. *Development of Transport Operations in Region Four.* Region 4: USDA Forest Service, Date Unknown (circa 1970). McGrew Collection.

Leber, Bernice. Letter to Mrs. Seamans & Family with Kevin Leber eulogy and clippings. 10 August 1979. Seamans Collection.

Leber, Randy. Personal Communication. 30 April 2024.

Leber, Walter Philip, et al. v. Morrison-Knudsen, et al. Fourth District Court, State of Idaho, Ada County. Case No. 74065.

Lee, Debbie. "Listening to the Land: The Selway-Bitterroot Wilderness as Oral History," pages 235–48. *The Oral History Review.* Vol. 37, No.2. Summer/Fall 2010.

Leopold, Aldo. *A Sand County Almanac and Sketches Here and There.* New York, NY: Oxford University Press, 1949.

Loftus, Bill. "A Love For the Wild Places." *Lewiston Morning Tribune.* Undated newspaper clipping. Seamans Collection.

Maclean, Norman. *A River Runs Through It And Other Stories.* Chicago, IL: The University of Chicago Press, 1976.

Maclean, Norman. *Young Men and Fire: A True Story of the Mann Gulch Fire.* Chicago, IL: The University of Chicago Press, 1992.

Macy, John. (edited and compiled by) *The Moose Creek Newsletter: Filled with Humor, Thoughts, and News.* Moose Creek Ranger District, Nez Perce NF: USDA Forest Service, 1977. Schacher Collection.

Mason, Caryn. Letter to Cindy Schacher, "My Sister Catherine 'Tykie' Hodgin." Clippings and photographs attached. 19 June 2017.

Mauer, Richard. "DC-3 Crash Gives Grim Name to Selway: Permanent Impression Left on Area." *The Idaho Statesman.* 19 June 1979.

Mauer, Richard. Personal Communication. 23 July 2019.

McCall Smokejumper Training Jump Records—June 6, 1979 through June 8, 1979. On file at the McCall Smokejumper Base, McCall, ID.

McCarthy, John. "Backcountry Pilot: Grangeville Flyer Always Brings Them Back Alive." *Lewiston Morning Tribune.* 25 September 1983.

McCarthy, John. "Brain Trust's Goal: Managing People's Needs in a Wilderness Setting." *Lewiston Morning Tribune.* 1 July 1985.

McCarthy, John. "Emil & Penny: Voices in the Wilderness." *Lewiston Morning Tribune.* 16 October 1983.

McCarthy, John. "The Selway-Bitterroot Wilderness: Wilderness Ranger." *Lewiston Morning Tribune.* 1 July 1985.

McCarthy, John. "Wilderness Couple Given Three Options: None Very Good." *Lewiston Morning Tribune*. 18 December 1987.

McCarthy, John. Personal Communication. 15 February 2019 (And extensive other dates).

McCarthy, John. *Working the Wilderness: Early Leaders for Wild Lands.* Caldwell, ID: Caxton Press, 2019.

McCombs, Don. *Trails and Tales of North-Central Idaho.* Western Printing, 1982.

McCue, Bob. Letter to Steve Smith, "Moose Creek Air Disaster—June 11, 1979." Includes various attached documents. 7 September 2011. Holm Collection.

McCue, Bob. Personal Communication. 7 February 2017 (And extensive other dates).

McGreevey, Dollie. Letter to Cindy Schacher. 9 September 2009. Schacher Collection.

McGreevey, Eddie. Personal Communication. 29 April 2024.

McGreevey, Eddie. Personal Communication. 14 May 2024.

McGreevey, Mary Ann v. Cooper Industries, Inc. et al. Fourth District Court, State of Idaho, Ada County. Case No. 75530.

McGrew, Stanley E. *A Brief History of the Cargo Net Installations in the Two Remaining Forest Service DC-3s.* Self-published, 1994. McGrew Collection.

McGrew, Stanley E. *Metamorphosis: An Attempt to Capture the "Real and Whole Story" Surrounding the Conversion of the USDA Forest Service's Last Two DC-3/C-47 Type Airplanes to Turboprop Power.* Self-published, 2017. McGrew Collection.

McGrew, Stanley E. *On the Adequacy of Current Maintenance and Inspection Programs for USDA Forest Service Owned/Operated DC3-TP67s, as Specifically Related to Safe Operational Service Life Considerations.* Self-published, 2005. McGrew Collection.

McGrew, Stanley E. *DC3-TP67 Pilots Ground School—Version Foxtrot.* January 2004.

McGrew, Stanley E. "The Aviation Thread." *McGrew's Memoirs.* Unpublished manuscript, 2023.

McGrew, Stanley E. "U.S. Forest Service Years." *McGrew's Memoirs.* Unpublished manuscript, 2023.

Medel, Dave. "Moose Ck. Airplane Crash Claims Life of Local Pilot." *Idaho County Free Press.* 26 November 1986.

Michels, Bob. Personal Communication. 21 November 2023.

Miller, Barry. Personal Communication. 24 June 2019 (And extensive other dates).

Miller, Gary. Personal Communication. 18 April 2018 (And extensive other dates).

Miller, Gary. *USFS Daily Diary*, June 9—September 11, 1975. G. Miller Collection.

Miller, Gary. *USFS Daily Diary*, June 10—October 9, 1977. G. Miller Collection.

Miller, Gary. *USFS Daily Diary*, June 11—October 5, 1978. G. Miller Collection.

Miller, Gary. *USFS Daily Diary*, June 11—September 6, 1979. G. Miller Collection.

Miller, Gary. *USFS Daily Diary*, July 7—July 21, 1983 [Incomplete]. G. Miller Collection.

Miller, Gary. *USFS Daily Diary*, June 1—November 30, 1984. G. Miller Collection.

Miller, Warren. *Crosscut Saw Manual*. Missoula, MT: USDA Forest Service Technology and Development Program, 1977.

Miller, Warren. *Suggestions for Wilderness Ranger Inventory Materials and Techniques*. Nez Perce NF: USDA Forest Service, Undated. Schacher Collection.

Miller, Warren. *Wilderness Ranger Handbook: Some of the Ins and Outs of Being a Moose Creek Banana*. Nez Perce NF: USDA Forest Service, Undated. Schacher Collection.

Miller, Warren Q. Interview by Debbie Lee and Jane Holman, May 6, 2011, The Selway-Bitterroot Wilderness History Project, University of Idaho Library Special Collections and Archives, Moscow, Idaho.

Montoya, Bobby. Personal Communication. 10 October 2019.

Moore, Al. Personal Communication. 26 May 2019.

Moore, Mike. Personal Communication. 29 February 2024.

Moose Creek Ranger District—Nez Perce National Forest. Map 1972 (Base 1971 Forest Series). G. Miller Collection.

"Moose Creek Ranger Spends Winters in Grangeville, Preparing for Wilderness." *Idaho County Free Press*. 14 January 1981.

Moosenews [Newsletter of the Moose Creek Ranger District]. Nez Perce NF: USDA Forest Service, 1987. Schacher Collection.

Moosenews [Newsletter of the Moose Creek Ranger District]. Nez Perce NF: USDA Forest Service, 1995. Schacher Collection.

Moser, Don. "Changing Life-styles: Man and Wife Team Up as Forest Rangers," pages 30, 32, 38, and 40. *Family Circle*. August 1974.

Moser, Don. "Fire in the Big Woods," pages 74–91. *The Snake River Country: The American Wilderness*. Alexandria, VA: Time-Life Books Inc., 1974.

Murphy, Brian. *81 Days Below Zero*. Boston, MA: Da Capo Press, 2015.

Nash, Roderick. *Wilderness and the American Mind.* New Haven, CT: Yale University Press, 1967.

Nichols, John. Personal Communication. 8 June 2023.

Nichols, John. Personal Communication. 13 June 2023.

Northern Region (Region 1) 1979 Jump Records. Digitally archived and available on the National Smokejumper Association Database (originals are housed at the Missoula Smokejumper Base, Missoula, MT).

Oliver, Mike. Personal Communication. 13 March 2024 (And extensive other dates).

Parsell, Neal. *Major Fenn's County: A history of the lower Lochsa, the lower Selway, the upper Middlefork of the Clearwater, and surrounding lands.* Privately published. 1990.

Patrick, Timothy. Personal Communication. 30 May 2019

Peirce, Everett and Frederica. "Annual Letter to Friends & Guests of Selway Lodge." Fall 1979. McCarthy Collection.

Peirce, Everett and Frederica. Letter to Art Seamans, "Thank You— Re: Independence Fire." 19 October 1979.

Pope, Clem. Personal Communication. 24 March 2017.

Power, Gary. Personal Communication. 14 May 2019.

Public Service Announcements—Moose Creek Ranger District. Summer/ Fall 1978 and Fall 1979. Audio Recordings. Schacher Collection.

Ratcliffe (Mytron), Carol. Personal Communication. 18 March 2024.

Reel, Ray. Personal Communication. 21 May 2019.

Renshaw, Jim. Personal Communication. 13 March 2017.

Rhodes, Pat. "Trail Dedicated to Easthouse." Undated newspaper clipping. McCarthy Collection.

Rich, Tim. Personal Communication. 12 April 2017.

Riggers, Steve. Personal Communication. 13 August 2021.

Riggleman, Clyde "Chub." "Crash of Region 4's DC-3 on June 11, 1979," pages 7–8. *Smokejumper and Static Line Magazine*. National Smokejumper Association, April 1995.

Rock Fitzpatrick, Candy S. *United States Department of Agriculture Forest Service Fatal Aviation Accident History*. USDA. 2002.

Russell, Jerry and Renny. *On the Loose*. San Francisco, CA: Sierra Club, 1967.

Rust, Damon. "Crash of a DC-3: Tragedy in Idaho." *International Association of Dive Rescue Specialists Journal*. January 1980. (Seamans Collection).

Schacher, Cindy. *A Comprehensive History of the Moose Creek Ranger Station, Moose Creek RD, Selway-Bitterroot Wilderness*. Kooskia, ID: USDA Nez Perce-Clearwater NF. 2022.

Schacher, Cindy. *A Comprehensive History of the Selway Falls Guard Station, Moose Creek RD*. Kooskia, ID: USDA Nez Perce-Clearwater NF. 2019.

Schacher, Cindy. *A Little Piece of Forest Service History—Selway Falls Cabin*. Grangeville, ID: USDA, Nez Perce–Clearwater NF, undated.

Schacher, Cindy. *Faces of the Selway-Bitterroot Wilderness*. Grangeville, ID: USDA, Nez Perce–Clearwater NF, R1-21-18, May 2021.

Schacher, Cindy. "Remembering the Moose Creek Crash 1979," pages 41–42. *History Line: A Newsletter of the Forest Service History Program*. Summer 2004.

Seamans, Art. *Flight Manifests and Schedules Draft—June 8-16, 1979—Moose Creek Ranger District, Nez Perce NF*. 1979. Seamans Collection.

Seamans, Art. *Flight Manifests—June 11-13, 1979—Moose Creek Ranger District, Nez Perce NF*. 1979. Seamans Collection.

Seamans, Art. Interview by Cindy Schacher, 17 March 2008, Nez Perce NF Centennial, Nez Perce-Clearwater NF, Fenn Ranger Station, Idaho.

Seamans, Art. Interview by Debbie Lee, 28 April 2013, The Selway-Bitterroot Wilderness History Project, University of Idaho Library Special Collections and Archives, Moscow, Idaho.

Seamans, Art. Newspaper Clippings Folder—extensive clippings from 1979 local and regional newspapers along with an extensive collection of Nez Perce NF press releases. Seamans Collection.

Seamans, Art. Letter to Bob McCue and other documents regarding employment on the Moose Creek Ranger District. 30 May 1979. McCue Collection.

Seamans, Art. Letter to Steve Gabrielson—Society of American Foresters, "Wilderness Management Presentation." 13 January 1977. Seamans Collection.

Seamans, Art. Letter to Thomas J. TerKeurst along with other documents regarding volunteer program on Moose Creek Ranger District. 30 May 1979. Seamans Collection.

Seamans, Art. *Personal Pocket Calendar—1979.* Seamans Collection.

Seamans, Art. *Remembering DC-3 Crash June 11, 1979.* Unpublished paper. 22 January 2013. Schacher Collection.

Seamans, Art. "The Interagency Whitewater Committee," pages 18–22. *Naturalist: Conservation Through Education (River Recreation edition).* Summer 1982.

Seamans, Art. *The Moose Creek Wilderness School [Agenda] 1978—Moose Creek Ranger District, Nez Perce NF.* 1978. Seamans Collection.

Seamans, Art. *Training Program & Agenda for the 1979 Moose Creek Crew—Moose Creek Ranger District, Nez Perce NF*. 1979. Seamans Collection.

Seamans, Art. *Wilderness Speech—Moose Creek Ranger District, Nez Perce NF*. 1977. Seamans Collection.

Seamans, Art. "Affidavit of Arthur L. Seamans Regarding June 11, 1979 Aircraft Accident & Complaint Against the US by the Representatives of the Estate of Thomas J. TerKeurst to Jeff Ross, USDA Office of General Council." 9 March 1982. Seamans Collection.

Seamans, Joyce. *Moose Creek Guard School Orientation List of Attendees and Food Menu for June 14, 1979—Moose Creek Ranger District, Nez Perce NF*. 1979. Seamans Collection.

Seamans, Joyce. *Seamans Family Christmas Letter*. 1975. Seamans Collection.

Seamans, Joyce. *Seamans Family Christmas Letter*. 1977. Seamans Collection.

Selway-Bitterroot Wilderness Management Plan. Nez Perce, Clearwater, Bitterroot, and Lolo National Forests, Northern Region, Forest Service, US Department of Agriculture. Revised 1976.

Selway-Bitterroot Wilderness Management Plan and General Management Direction. Nez Perce, Clearwater, Bitterroot, and Lolo National Forests, Northern Region, Forest Service, US Department of Agriculture. Revised 1982.

Selway-Bitterroot Primitive Area. (Map) US Department of Agriculture, Forest Service, Region 1, Bitterroot, Nez Perce, Lolo and Clearwater National Forests, Idaho and Montana. 1937. Holm Collection.

Selway DC-3 Newspaper Article Scrapbook—Fenn Ranger Station. 65 pages of local and regional newspaper clippings from June through August 1979. Assembled by Fenn Ranger Station Administration in 1979. On file Nez Perce-Clearwater NF Archives, Fenn Ranger Station.

Selway River Hydrograph at Paradise Launch Site Report 1973–1978. West Fork Ranger District, Bitterroot NF.

Selway River -Launch Schedule—Complete 1979 Season—Revised May 21, 1979. West Fork Ranger District, Bitterroot NF. Mills Collection.

Selway River—Paradise Launch Site at White Cap Creek River Water Levels 1978–1979. West Fork Ranger District, Bitterroot NF.

Selway River Whitewater Management Plan. Bitterroot And Nez Perce National Forests, Northern Region, Forest Service, US Department of Agriculture. Revised March 1976.

Singels, Catherine E. Letter to Mr. Charles H. Dietz, "Re: Grangeville DC-3 Crash." 10 March 1981. Dietz Collection.

Singels, Catherine E. (for Thomas Smith). Letter to Clients, "Re: Grangeville DC-3 Crash." 4 March 1982. Dietz Collection.

Smith, Diane. "From Research to Policy: The White Cap Wilderness Fire Study," pages 4–12. *Forest History Today.* Spring/Fall 2014.

Smith, Steve. *Fly the Biggest Piece Back: Tough pilots. Tough planes. Tough flying in America's Mountain West.* Missoula, MT: Pictorial Histories Publishing Company, 1994 (Fourth Printing—revised).

Smith, Steve. *Sons of the Western Sky: Kenny Roth and the Mountain Pilots of Johnson Flying Service.* Missoula, MT: Unpublished manuscript, 2002.

Smith, Steve. *Stevedore Smith's Fly the Biggest Piece Back: The Johnson Flying Service Story Start to Finish.* Missoula, MT: Unpublished manuscript, 2017.

Smith, Thomas G. Letter to Mr. Charles H. Dietz, "Re: Grangeville Crash." 10 April 1980. Dietz Collection.

Smith, Thomas G. Letter to Mr. Charles H. Dietz, "Re: Grangeville Crash." 10 July 1980. Dietz Collection.

Smith, Thomas G. Letter to Mr. Charles H. Dietz, "Re: Grangeville DC-3 Crash." 2 February 1982. Dietz Collection.

Spotleson, Bruce. "Without Whitey, behind controls we'd rather walk." *Lewiston Morning Tribune.* 13 June 1979.

Stawkey, George. Letter to Art Seamans, "DC-3 Accident." 14 June 1979.

Sterns, Gerald C. Letter to Mr. Charles H. Dietz, "Re: DC-3 Crash at Grangeville, Idaho." 23 November 1979. Dietz Collection.

Sterns, Gerald C. Letter to Mr. Charles H. Dietz, "Re: Grangeville DC-3 Crash." 17 January 1980. Dietz Collection.

Stright, John. Personal Communication. 20 May 2024.

Stringham, Bryant. Personal Communication. 17 February 2017 (And extensive other dates).

Stringham, Bryant. Recollections of the June 11, 1979 DC-3 Crash in the Selway River. Written to and for Cindy Schacher, Archaeologist Nez Perce-Clearwater NF. 23 September 2013. On file Nez Perce-Clearwater NF Archives, Supervisor's Office, Grangeville, ID.

Taylor, Susie G. v. Cooper Industries, Inc. et al. Fourth District Court, State of Idaho, Ada County. Case No. 75289.

Technical Manual Maintenance Instructions USAF Series: C-47, C-47A, C-47B, C-47C, C-117A, C-117B And C-117C Aircraft (T.O. 1C-47-2), USAF, August 1967 (Region 4 Aviation). Holm Collection.

TerKeurst, Jim. Personal Communication. 22 December 2023.

TerKeurst, Marilyn and John, et al. v. Morrison-Knudsen, et al. Fourth District Court, State of Idaho, Ada County. Case No. 74452.

TerKeurst, Marilyn, Temporary Personal Representative of the Estate of Thomas J. TerKeurst, Deceased, Plaintiff. v. United States of America, Defendant. United States District Court, W.D. Michigan, S.D. February 16, 1982. On motion for reconsideration July 7, 1982. Case No. G80-853 CA-1.

Tinker, Frank A. "Smoothing the Rough Chukar Road," pages 66–67, 98, & 100–02. *Field & Stream*. November 1969.

USDA Forest Service Equipment Development Center. "Backpack Trail Maintenance." Moose Creek Ranger District, Nez Perce NF, 1971. 13 minute video. On file at The National Museum of Forest Service History, Missoula, MT. Catalog Number 2018.005.055.

Van de Water, Tom. "Lightning Scar." Unpublished essay, December 2023.

Walker, Richard. Personal Communication. 26 May 2019.

Walker, Richard. Personal Communication. 29 March 2024.

Walters, Linda. Personal Communication. 10 October 2019.

Walstad, Neil. Personal Communication. 3 July 2019.

Waterman, Steve. "Flag Presented to Moose Creek Ranger District." *Northern Region News: For Forest Service Employees*. 26 October 1982.

Waterman, Steve and Norgaard, Judith King. "Wilderness Tragedy." *American Forests*. June 1980.

"Wildlands Scholarship Fund Established As Memorial to 10 Killed in Wilderness Crash," *News from the Forest Service*, Nez Perce NF: USDA Forest Service, 17 April 1980. Seamans Collection.

Wilhelm, Doug. "Steve Wright Leaves a Legacy of Passionate Devotion." *Common Voice: A Journal For the Sterling Community.* December 1992. Seamans Collection.

Williams, Wayne. Personal Communication. 8 June 2023.

Williams, Wayne. Personal Communication. 17 June 2023.

Williams, Wayne. Personal Communication. 26 June 2023.

Williamson, Terry. Personal Communication. 27 June 2023.

Worf, William A. Letter to Forest Supervisors, "Subject—Wilderness Management—Orientation for Seasonal Wilderness Rangers." USDA, Forest Service, Region 1. 6 June 1979. Seamans Collection.

Wright, Steve. Personal Communication. 27 March 2017.

Wright, Steve. Personal Communication. 21 June 2021.

Wright, Steve. Letter to Art Seamans, "Tom TerKeurst." 25 June 1979. Seamans Collection.

Wright, Steve E. Letter to Tom Coston, "Two Year IPA Assignment on the Moose Creek Ranger District." 12 January 1982. Seamans Collection.

Wuerthner, George. *Idaho Mountain Ranges: Idaho Geographic Series.* Helena, MT: American Geographic Publishing, 1986.

Young, Harvey. Personal Communication. 7 July 2023.

Young, Harvey. Personal Communication. 7 December 2023.

INDEX

I

Idaho Aeronautics Department, 85

Idaho Archeology Month, 367

Idaho Aviation Hall of Fame, 379

Idaho Batholith, 4, 19

Idaho City, Idaho, 273–74

Idaho County Sheriff's Department, 83, 86–88, 90, 204

Idaho County, 50, 86, 177

Idaho Department of Fish and Game, 68, 162

Idaho Primitive Area, 19

Idaho Statesman, 195–96, 282

Imhoff & Lynch, 330

Imhoff, Joseph, 330

Imlay, Gene, 182

Immigration and Naturalization Services, 277

Independence Fire, 241–52

Indian Creek (Middle Fork of the Salmon River), 273

Indian Creek Chronicles: A Winter Alone in the Wilderness, 68

Indian Creek, 68

Indian Hill Lookout, 353

Intermountain Aviation, 274, 280

Irwin Seating, 179

J

Jackson, Laura Mae, 56, 75, 80, 359, 374

Jaseca, Ken, 155

Jensen, Nels, 182, 197

Jim Bridger Ranger District, 49

Johnson Flying Service, 22, 116, 270, 272–75, 279, 379

Johnson, Bob, 253, 267

Johnson, Jane, 179, 213

Johnson, Laurie, 184

Johnson, Samuel, 329

Johnson, Shep, 200, 202

Jones, Jay, 86

Judd, Paul, 73

Jughandle Mountain, 23

O

O'Hara Bridge, 177, 199

Oakley, Kansas, 97

Ogden, Utah, 6, 253, 274, 276–77, 291, 309, 321, 323

Ohio River Basin, 156

Oklahoma City, Oklahoma, 191

Oliver, Mike, 50–52, 55–56, 68–70, 74

Olsen, Milt, 299–300, 320

Olympia, Washington, 61–62

Operation Market Garden, 121

Operation Neptune, 121

Orofino, Idaho, 31, 119, 125, 175, 176, 183, 195, 348

Oshkosh, Wisconsin, 322

Otter Creek, 144, 358

Outward Bound, 223

Oye, Gary, 65

P

P-47 Thunderbolt, 23

Pacific Avenue, 331

Pacific Coast Trail, 193

Pacific Ocean, 5

Paczesniak, Mary, 57, 73

Panama Canal Zone, 156

Pancake House, 24

Paradise Guard Station, 138, 142–43, 145–46, 198, 200–01, 203

Parrotts Ferry Road, 140

Parsell, Jack, 47

Patrick, Timothy, 231

Paulson, Vern, 162

Payette Lake, 19, 23, 24

Payette National Forest, 13, 20, 280–81

Payette, Idaho, 256

Peirce, Cheshire, 163–64, 170, 229–30

Peirce, Everett, 163–64, 170, 246–47, 353

Peirce, Freddie, 163–64, 170, 246–47, 353

Pennell, Mary Lane, 80

Perkins, Coie, Stone, Olsen & Williams, 330

Peterson, Gene, 188

Peterson, Max, 163

U

ABOUT THE AUTHOR

Richard Holm is a fourth-generation Idahoan who holds a commercial pilot license with a multi-engine instrument rating and many hours of backcountry flying. He is an outdoorsman with an abiding interest in Idaho history. He has written other books about fire lookouts and backcountry flying. Holm lives in McCall, Idaho, with his wife Amy and their two children.

AUTHOR—MOOSE CREEK. (*Holm Collection*)